FOCUS on MEAP

Supporting On-Grade Level GLCEs

Mathematics

GRADE

Focus on MEAP, Supporting On-Grade Level GLCEs, Mathematics, Grade 6
53MI
1-59823-315-7

EVP, Publisher: Bill Scroggie
VP, Editorial Director: Marie Spano
VP, Creative Director: Rosanne Guararra
VP of Production: Dina Goren
Art Director: Farzana Razak

Senior Development Editor: Andie Liao
Author: Keith Grober
Senior Designer: Hyun Kounne
Cover Design: Farzana Razak
Cover Photo: John Jinks/Images.com

Triumph Learning® 136 Madison Avenue, 7th Floor, New York, NY 10016

Printed in the United States of America.

10 9 8 7 6 5 4 3 2 1

Table of Contents

Letter to the Student

Dear Student,

Welcome to the ***Focus on MEAP, Supporting On-Grade Level GLCEs, Mathematics, Grade 6***. This book will help you as you prepare to strengthen your math skills this year. It also provides practice with the kinds of questions you will have to answer on tests, including the state test.

This book is divided into **chapters** and **lessons**. Before you begin the first chapter, you may want to take the **Pretest** at the beginning of the book. The Pretest will show you your strengths and weaknesses in the skills and strategies you need to know this year. This way, you will be aware of what you need to concentrate on to be successful. At the end of the book is a **Posttest** that will allow you and your teacher to evaluate how much you have learned. We have tried to match the style of the state test in the Posttest for better test practice.

The lessons in this book will help you review and practice your skills and get you ready to take tests. Some of the practice will be in the style of the state test. In general, you will be answering multiple-choice and open-ended or extended-response questions. Questions like these may appear on your state test. Practicing with these types of questions will give you a good idea of what you need to review to triumph.

Here are some **tips** that will help you as you work through this book. Remembering these tips will also help you do well on the state test.

- Listen closely to your teacher's directions.
- When answering multiple-choice questions, read each choice carefully before choosing the BEST answer.
- When answering open-ended, or extended-response questions, think about how you will answer the question before you begin to write.
- Time yourself so that you have the time at the end of a test to check your answers.

We hope you will enjoy using this book and that you will have a fun and rewarding year!

Letter to the Family

Dear Parents and Families,

The *Focus on MEAP* series of workbooks is designed to prepare your child to master grade-appropriate skills in mathematics and to take the Grade 7 MEAP Mathematics Test. The test is administered in the fall each year in the state of Michigan. In your state, the grade-appropriate skills are called Grade Level Content Expectations. These are the skills the state has chosen as the building blocks of your child's education in mathematics, and these are the skills that will be tested on the MEAP. Your child's success will be measured by how well he or she masters these skills.

You are an important factor in your child's ability to learn and succeed. Get involved! We want to be your partner in making learning a priority in your child's life. To help ensure success, we suggest that you review the lessons in this book with your child. While teachers will guide your child through the book in class, your support at home is also vital to your child's comprehension.

Please encourage your child to read and study this book at home, and take the time to go over the sample questions and homework together. The more students practice, the better they do on the actual exam and on all the tests they will take in school. Try talking about what your child has learned in school. Perhaps you can show your children real-life applications of what they have learned. For example, you could discuss how math skills apply to everyday situations.

We ask you to work with us this year to help your child triumph. Together, we can make a difference!

The Parent Involvement Pledge

As an involved parent, I pledge to:

- promote the value of education to my child
- inspire my child to read
- discuss the skills my child needs with his/her teachers and principal
- expect my child to successfully fulfill school and homework assignments
- join in school activities and decisions

I hereby pledge my involvement in my child's educational success!

Parent Signature: ____________________

Student Signature: ____________________

Grade Level Content Expectations, Grade 6

Code	Expectation	Lessons
NUMBER AND OPERATIONS		
Multiply and divide fractions:		
N.MR.06.01	Understand division of fractions as the inverse of multiplication, e.g. if $\frac{4}{5} \div \frac{2}{3} = \square$, then $\frac{2}{3} \times \square = \frac{4}{5}$, so $\square = \frac{4}{5} \cdot \frac{3}{2} = \frac{12}{10}$.	7
N.FL.06.02	Given an applied situation involving dividing fractions, write a mathematical statement to represent the situation.	7
N.FL.06.04	Multiply and divide any two fractions, including mixed numbers, fluently.	7
Represent rational numbers as fractions, or decimals:		
N.ME.06.05	Order rational numbers and place them on the number line.	13
N.ME.06.06	Represent rational numbers as fractions or terminating decimals when possible, and translate between these representations.	13
Add and subtract integers and rational numbers:		
***N.MR.06.08**	Understand integer subtraction as the inverse of integer addition. Understand integer division as the inverse of integer multiplication.	14–15
N.FL.06.09	Add and multiply integers between −10 and 10; subtract and divide integers using the related facts. Use the number line and chip models for addition and subtraction.	14–15
N.FL.06.10	Add, subtract, multiply and divide positive rational numbers fluently.	1–7
Find equivalent ratios:		
N.ME.06.11	Find equivalent ratios by scaling up or scaling down.	22
Solve decimal, percentage and rational number problems:		
N.FL.06.12	Calculate part of a number given the percentage and the number.	11
N.FL.06.13	Solve word problems involving percentages in such contexts as sales taxes and tips.	11
N.FL.06.14	For applied situations, estimate the answers to calculations involving operations with rational numbers.	8–10
N.FL.06.15	Solve applied problems that use the four operations with appropriate decimal numbers.	1–3

* Not assessed on the Pretest or Posttest

Code	Expectation	Lessons
Understand rational numbers and their location on the number line:		
N.ME.06.17	Locate negative rational numbers (including integers) on the number line; know that numbers and their negatives add to 0, and are on opposite sides and at equal distance from 0 on a number line.	12
N.ME.06.18	Understand that rational numbers are quotients of integers (non-zero denominators), e.g., a rational number is either a fraction or a negative fraction.	12
N.ME.06.19	Understand that 0 is an integer that is neither negative nor positive.	12
N.ME.06.20	Know that the absolute value of a number is the value of the number, ignoring the sign; or is the distance of the number from 0.	12
	ALGEBRA	
Calculate rates:		
A.PA.06.01	Solve applied problems involving rates, including speed, e.g., if a car is going 50 mph, how far will it go in $3\frac{1}{2}$ hours?	22
Understand the coordinate plane:		
A.RP.06.02	Plot ordered pairs of integers and use ordered pairs of integers to identify points in all four quadrants of the coordinate plane.	18
Use variables, write expressions and equations, and combine like terms:		
A.FO.06.03	Use letters, with units, to represent quantities in a variety of contexts, e.g., *y* lbs., *k* minutes, *x* cookies.	17
A.FO.06.04	Distinguish between an algebraic expression and an equation.	17
***A.FO.06.05**	Use standard conventions for writing algebraic expressions, e.g., $2x + 1$ means "two times *x*, plus 1" and $2(x + 1)$ means "two times the quantity $(x + 1)$."	17
A.FO.06.06	Represent information given in words using algebraic expressions and equations.	17
***A.FO.06.07**	Simplify expressions of the first degree by combining like terms, and evaluate using specific values.	17

* Not assessed on the Pretest or Posttest

Code	Expectation	Lessons
Represent linear functions using tables, equations, and graphs:		
A.RP.06.08	Understand that relationships between quantities can be suggested by graphs and tables.	19
***A.PA.06.09**	Solve problems involving linear functions whose input values are integers; write the equation; graph the resulting ordered pairs of integers, e.g., given c chairs, the "leg function" is $4c$; if you have 5 chairs, how many legs?; if you have 12 legs, how many chairs?	19
***A.RP.06.10**	Represent simple relationships between quantities using verbal descriptions, formulas or equations, tables, and graphs, e.g., perimeter-side relationship for a square, distance-time graphs, and conversions such as feet to inches.	19
Solve equations:		
A.FO.06.11	Relate simple linear equations with integer coefficients, e.g., $3x = 8$ or $x + 5 = 10$, to particular contexts and solve.	20
A.FO.06.12	Understand that adding or subtracting the same number to both sides of an equation creates a new equation that has the same solution.	20
A.FO.06.13	Understand that multiplying or dividing both sides of an equation by the same non-zero number creates a new equation that has the same solution.	20
A.FO.06.14	Solve equations of the form $ax + b = c$, e.g., $3x + 8 = 15$, by hand for positive integer coefficients less than 20, using calculators otherwise, and interpret the results.	21
MEASUREMENT		
Convert within measurement systems:		
M.UN.06.01	Convert between basic units of measurement within a single measurement system, e.g., square inches to square feet.	23
***M.TE.06.03**	Compute the volume and surface area of cubes and rectangular prisms given the lengths of their sides, using formulas.	24–25

* Not assessed on the Pretest or Posttest

Code	Expectation	Lessons
	GEOMETRY	
Understand the concept of congruence and basic transformations:		
G.GS.06.01	Understand and apply basic properties of lines, angles, and triangles, including: • triangle inequality • relationships of vertical angles, complementary angles, supplementary angles • congruence of corresponding and alternate interior angles when parallel lines are cut by a transversal, and that such congruencies imply parallel lines • locate interior and exterior angles of any triangle, and use the property that an exterior angle of a triangle is equal to the sum of the remote (opposite) interior angles • know that the sum of the exterior angles of a convex polygon is 360°.	26–27
G.GS.06.02	Understand that for polygons, congruence means corresponding sides and angles have equal measures.	28
G.TR.06.03	Understand the basic rigid motions in the plane (reflections, rotations, translations), relate these to congruence, and apply them to solve problems.	29
G.TR.06.04	Understand and use simple compositions of basic rigid transformations, e.g., a translation followed by a reflection.	29
	DATA AND PROBABILITY	
Understand the concept of probability and solve problems:		
D.PR.06.01	Express probabilities as fractions, decimals or percentages between 0 and 1; know that 0 probability means an event will not occur, and that probability 1 means an event will occur.	30
D.PR.06.02	Compute probabilities of events from simple experiments with equally likely outcomes, e.g., tossing dice, flipping coins, spinning spinners, by listing all possibilities and finding the fraction that meets given conditions.	30–31

* Not assessed on the Pretest or Posttest

Remove Pretest Here

Focus on MEAP
Supporting On-Grade Level GLCEs,
Mathematics, Grade 6

PRETEST

Name:

PART 1

DIRECTIONS

This test has four parts. You may **NOT** use a calculator on this part. You may use open space in this practice test for scratch paper.

There is one type of item on this test: multiple choice.

1. Multiple-choice items will require you to choose the best answer from among four answer choices. For these items, use only a No. 2 pencil to mark your answer on your **Answer Sheet**. If you erase an answer, be sure to erase it completely. If you skip an item, be sure to mark the answer to the next item in the correct place on your **Answer Sheet**.

Sample Multiple-Choice Item:

Eddy's family rented a boat for 5 hours. They paid $225 for the 5-hour rental. At the same rate, how much would an 8-hour rental cost?

A $360

B $390

C $400

D $450

For this sample item, the correct answer is **A**.

GO ON TO THE NEXT PAGE

Remove Pretest Here

PRETEST

You will be timed to finish Part 1 of this test.

1. Once you have reached the word **STOP** in the practice test, do **NOT** go on to the next page.
2. If you finish early, you may check your work in Part 1 of the test **ONLY**. Do **NOT** look at items in other parts of the test.

WAIT. DO NOT GO ON UNTIL TOLD TO DO SO.

PRETEST

1 What is the solution to this equation?

$$\frac{7}{12} \times \frac{5}{9} = \square$$

A $\frac{17}{54}$

B $\frac{35}{108}$

C $\frac{1}{3}$

D $\frac{4}{7}$

2 Maya walked $2\frac{3}{4}$ miles from her home to the park. Then she jogged $4\frac{1}{2}$ miles. Her mother drove her home. How many miles did Maya walk or run altogether?

A $6\frac{1}{4}$ miles

B $6\frac{2}{3}$ miles

C $7\frac{1}{4}$ miles

D $7\frac{1}{2}$ miles

3 At the deli, Mr. Queensbury bought $4\frac{1}{8}$ pounds of cheese and $1\frac{3}{4}$ pounds of whitefish. How many *more* pounds of cheese than whitefish did Mr. Queensbury buy?

A $2\frac{3}{8}$ pounds

B $2\frac{1}{2}$ pounds

C $2\frac{3}{4}$ pounds

D $3\frac{1}{4}$ pounds

4 What is the missing number in this number sentence?

$$2\frac{3}{8} \div 1\frac{2}{3} = \square$$

A $1\frac{2}{5}$

B $1\frac{17}{40}$

C $1\frac{9}{20}$

D $1\frac{1}{2}$

5 The Movieplex has a total of 675 seats. Each day, they have four showings. If each movie is sold out, how many people can attend in a week?

A 2,700

B 4,050

C 4,725

D 18,900

6 What is the product?

$$2\frac{2}{5} \times 3\frac{1}{4} = \square$$

A $6\frac{1}{10}$

B $7\frac{1}{5}$

C $7\frac{4}{5}$

D $8\frac{1}{10}$

STOP. DO NOT GO ON UNTIL TOLD TO DO SO.

Remove Pretest Here

PART 2

DIRECTIONS

You will now begin Part 2 of this test. You may use a calculator on this part of the test, and you may use open space in this practice test for scratch paper.

If you finish early, you may check your work for Part 2 **ONLY**.

Do **NOT** look at items in other parts of this test.

You will be timed to finish Part 2 of this test.

WAIT. DO NOT GO ON UNTIL TOLD TO DO SO.

PRETEST

7 Cody was supposed to bring 4 gallons of bottled water to a barbecue. He brought the water in quart containers. How many containers did Cody bring?

A 1

B 2

C 8

D 16

8 A train is traveling 45 miles per hour. How far will the train travel in $2\frac{3}{4}$ hours?

A 101.25 miles

B 112.5 miles

C 123.75 miles

D 135 miles

9 In 1980, $1 was worth 4.9381 Norwegian krone. In 2004, $1 was worth 1.8018 more krone. How many krone could you get for $1 in 2004?

A 6.7399

B 6.7409

C 6.7499

D 6.7561

10 What is the rule of this function table?

x	*y*
5	10
7	12
13	18
18	23

A $y = x - 5$

B $y = x + 5$

C $y = 2x$

D $y = 3x - 3$

11 Population density is measured by dividing a population by the area of a place. Branch County has a population of 46,444 people and an area of 507 square miles. Which is the *best* estimate for the population density of Branch County?

A 90 people per square mile

B 100 people per square mile

C 900 people per square mile

D 1,000 people per square mile

GO ON TO THE NEXT PAGE

Remove Pretest Here

Remove Pretest Here

PRETEST

12 Jed is going to spin both spinners. What is the probability that both spinners will land on 3?

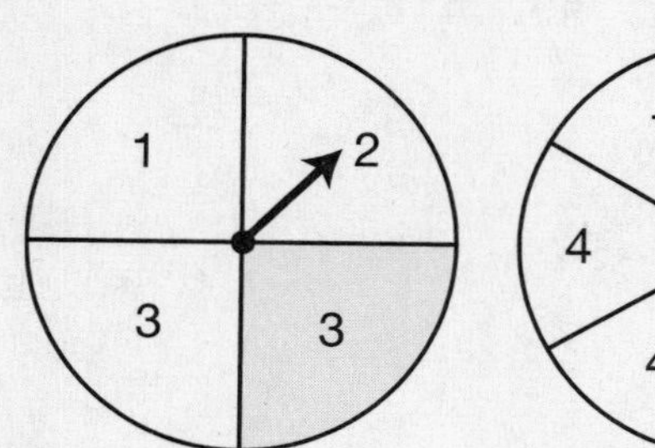

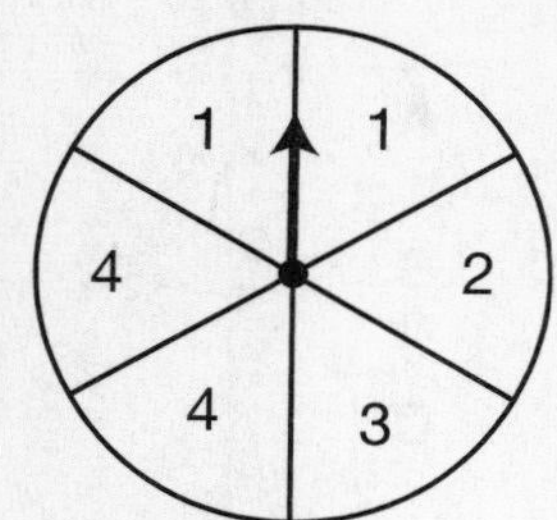

A $\frac{1}{12}$

B $\frac{1}{6}$

C $\frac{1}{4}$

D $\frac{2}{3}$

13 A carpenter works 8 hours each day. The variable h represents the number of hours that he works, and the equation $8h = \$360$ represents the amount he earns each day. How much money does the carpenter earn per hour?

A \$40

B \$42.50

C \$45

D \$47.50

14 The ratio of sixth-grade students to fifth-grade students in the Science Club is 5:3. If there are 15 fifth-grade students in the Science Club, how many sixth-grade students are there?

A 9

B 18

C 20

D 25

15 What is the location of point *A* on this coordinate grid?

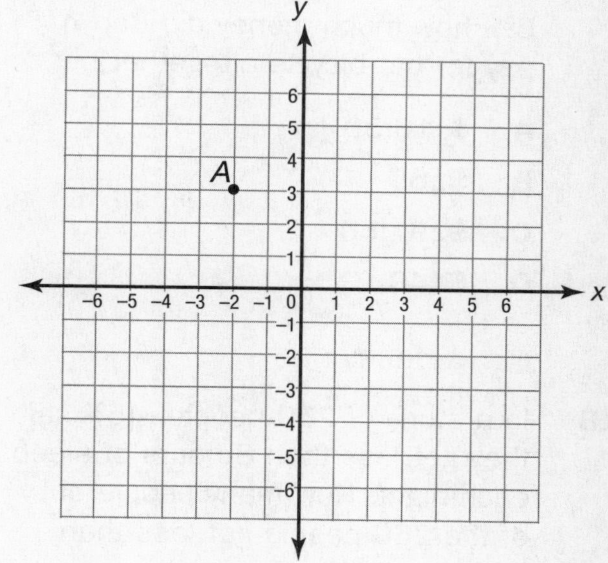

A (−2, −3)

B (−2, 3)

C (−3, 2)

D (−3, −2)

GO ON TO THE NEXT PAGE

PRETEST

Remove Pretest Here

16 What transformation can be used on the left figure to produce the right figure?

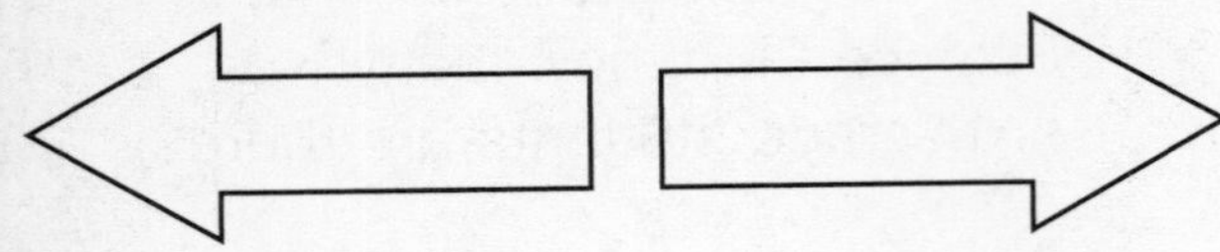

A translation

B rotation of 90° clockwise

C rotation of 180°

D reflection

17 Robyn bought a bicycle for $275. If the sales tax on the bicycle was 6%, how much money did Robyn pay for the bicycle altogether?

A $ 16.50

B $165

C $291.50

D $440

18 In a study of 260 people, 45% said they get less than 8 hours of sleep each night. How many people out of the 260 people get less than 8 hours of sleep?

A 117

B 125

C 135

D 143

19 Which number makes this sentence true?

$$\frac{3}{4} \div \frac{2}{3} = \frac{3}{4} \times \square$$

A $\frac{1}{2}$

B $\frac{2}{3}$

C 1

D $\frac{3}{2}$

20 Which *best* describes the transformations of rectangle *CDEF* to rectangle *C′D′E′F′*?

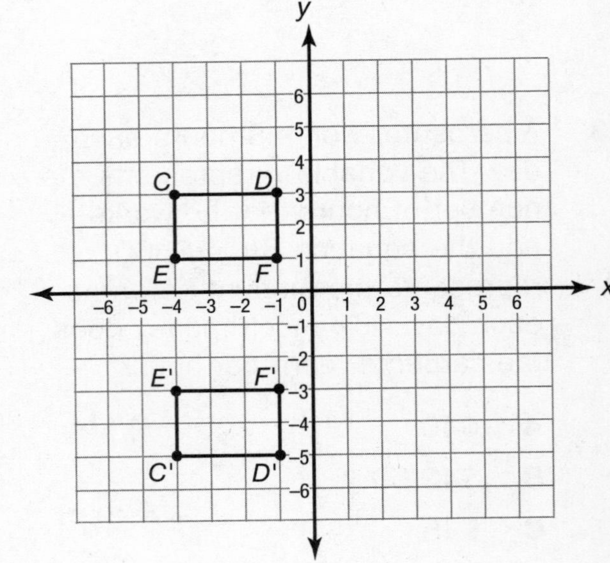

A reflection across the *x*-axis and rotation 90° about the origin

B reflection across the *x*-axis and translation

C rotation 180° about the origin and translation

D translation and reflection 90° about the origin

GO ON TO THE NEXT PAGE

"Remove Pretest Here" and "PRETEST" are printed in the margins.

21 Which equation has the same solution as $3z + 5 = 14$?

A $3z = 9$

B $3z = 19$

C $5z + 5 = 16$

D $z + 5 = 12$

22 Rodrigo is *y* years old. Esteban is 4 years older than Rodrigo. Which of the following expresses Esteban's age?

A $y - 4$ years old

B $y \div 4$ years old

C $4y$ years old

D $y + 4$ years old

23 Which position on the number line is represented by -7?

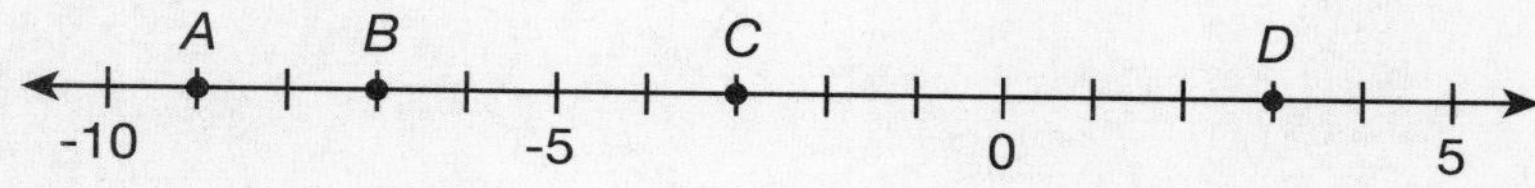

A *A*

B *B*

C *C*

D *D*

24 The exchange rate between a British pound (£) and dollar is £1 = \$1.83. At a pub, Ron's dinner cost £17.43. How much money would Ron's dinner cost in dollars? Round your answer to the nearest penny.

A \$30.90

B \$31.00

C \$31.90

D \$32.00

25 The distance between the school building and the playground is 78 meters. What is the equivalent measure in kilometers?

A 0.078 kilometers

B 0.78 kilometers

C 7,800 kilometers

D 78,000 kilometers

STOP. DO NOT GO ON UNTIL TOLD TO DO SO.

Remove Pretest Here

PART 3

DIRECTIONS

You will now begin Part 3 of this test. You may use a calculator on this part of the test, and you may use open space in this practice test for scratch paper.

If you finish early, you may check your work for Part 3 **ONLY**.

Do **NOT** look at items in other parts of this test.

You will be timed to finish Part 3 of this test.

WAIT. DO NOT GO ON UNTIL TOLD TO DO SO.

26 Mr. Richert bought dinner for his family, which cost $76.60 before the tip was applied. Mr. Richert left a 15% tip. How much was the tip?

A $11.40

B $11.49

C $88.00

D $88.09

27 Toni drew this triangle.

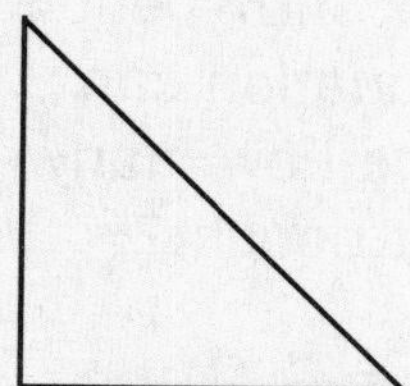

Sonya drew a congruent triangle. Which attribute of Sonya's triangle can be different from Toni's triangle?

A Its size

B Its shape

C Its area

D Its position

28 Eddie is going to toss these two number cubes, with faces numbered 1–6. What is the probability that the sum of the number cubes will be 3?

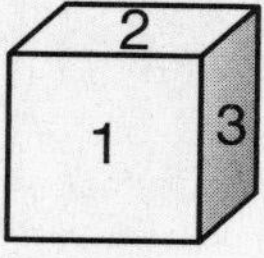

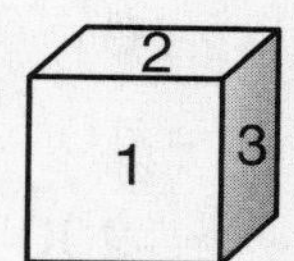

A $\frac{1}{36}$

B $\frac{1}{24}$

C $\frac{1}{18}$

D $\frac{1}{12}$

29 The metropolitan area with the highest average annual pay is San Jose, California, at $63,056. The metropolitan area with the lowest average annual pay is Jacksonville, North Carolina, at $22,362. Which is the *best* estimate of the difference between the highest and lowest average pay?

A $40,000

B $41,000

C $42,000

D $50,000

GO ON TO THE NEXT PAGE

PRETEST

Remove Pretest Here

30 What is the value of x in this equation?

$$5x = 40$$

A $x = 8$

B $x = 9$

C $x = 10$

D $x = 200$

31 Ms. Campbell bought 6 packs of printing paper for $27.36. Last week she bought 4 packs at the same unit price. How much did Ms. Campbell spend last week for printing paper?

A $ 4.56

B $13.68

C $18.24

D $20.52

32 The municipal center is sponsoring a 10-kilometer run. There will be volunteers with water standing every 0.5 kilometer. How many water stations will there be?

A 2

B 4

C 20

D 40

33 Which lists the numbers from *least* to *greatest*?

A $0.3, \frac{1}{2}, 0.7, \frac{2}{3}$

B $\frac{1}{2}, \frac{2}{3}, 0.3, 0.7$

C $\frac{1}{2}, 0.3, 0.7, \frac{2}{3}$

D $0.3, \frac{1}{2}, \frac{2}{3}, 0.7$

34 Margaret bought m magazines for $3 each. She spent $15 in all. Which equation can you write to determine how many magazines Margaret bought?

A $15m = 3$

B $3m = 15$

C $\frac{m}{15} = 3$

D $15 - m = 3$

GO ON TO THE NEXT PAGE

35 Kyle is going to toss a number cube, with faces numbered 1–6. Which event is certain?

A Tossing a prime number or an even number

B Tossing a number greater than 1 or less than 6

C Tossing a prime number or a composite number

D Tossing an odd or an even number

36 Which is equivalent to $\frac{1}{16}$?

A 0.0625

B 0.0875

C 0.125

D 0.16

37 Which expression is equal to $-\frac{15}{6}$?

A -15×6

B -15×-6

C $-15 \div -6$

D $-15 \div 6$

38 The graph shows the mileage that Mr. Campos drove each hour for 4 hours.

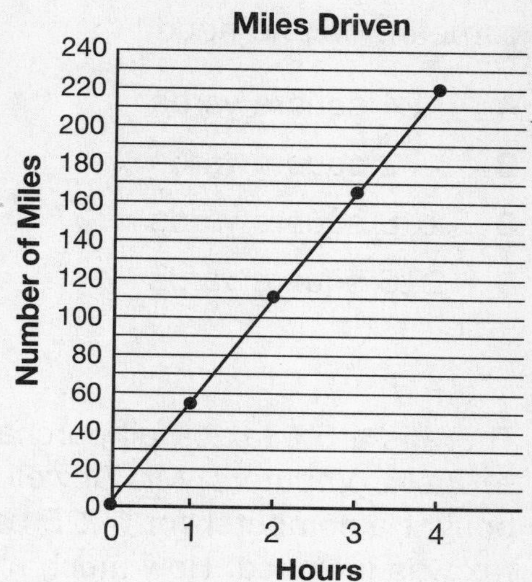

If Mr. Campos continues to drive at this speed, how many miles will he drive after 6 hours?

A 300 miles

B 330 miles

C 360 miles

D 390 miles

GO ON TO THE NEXT PAGE

PRETEST

39 Robbie's bedroom is 18 feet long and 12 feet wide. He wants to put wall-to-wall carpeting in his room. How many square yards of carpeting will he need?

A 24 square yards

B 72 square yards

C 108 square yards

D 216 square yards

40 There is a 5% tax on all purchases at Just Computers. Mr. Zipwell bought a computer for $725 before tax was included. How much money did Mr. Zipwell pay in tax?

A $ 3.63

B $ 36.25

C $362.50

D $758.25

41 There was $\frac{3}{4}$ of a pizza remaining when Carol, Annie, and Tara decided to split it evenly. Which equation can you write to find how much pizza each person received?

A $3 \times \frac{3}{4}$

B $3 \div \frac{3}{4}$

C $\frac{3}{4} \div 3$

D $\frac{3}{4} \div \frac{1}{3}$

42 Which describes this transformation?

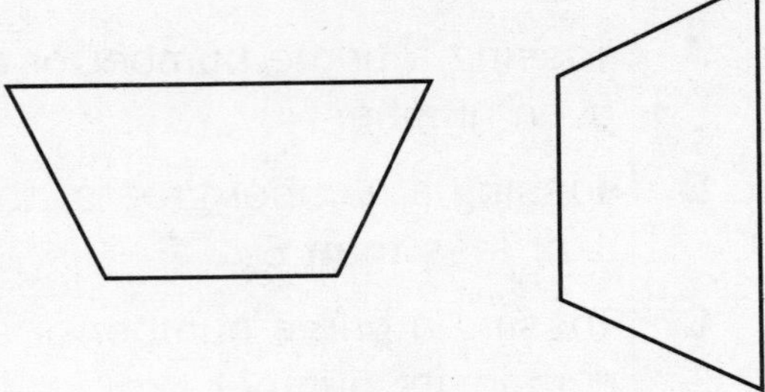

A translation

B rotation of 90°

C rotation of 180°

D reflection

43 This sweater is on sale for 70% of the price on the tag.

How much money does the sweater cost on sale?

A $24

B $26.50

C $28

D $30

STOP. DO NOT GO ON UNTIL TOLD TO DO SO.

Remove Pretest Here

PART 4

DIRECTIONS

You will now begin Part 4 of this test. You may use a calculator on this part of the test, and you may use open space in this practice test for scratch paper.

If you finish early, you may check your work for Part 4 **ONLY**.

Do **NOT** look at items in other parts of this test.

You will be timed to finish Part 4 of this test.

WAIT. DO NOT GO ON UNTIL TOLD TO DO SO.

44 Mr. Santoro earns $39,884 per year. He receives 52 paychecks in a year. How much money is in his paycheck before taxes are taken out?

A $708

B $711

C $761

D $767

45 Miles and Madison are playing a game. They will play three games. What is the probability that Madison will win all three games?

A $\frac{1}{8}$

B $\frac{1}{6}$

C $\frac{1}{4}$

D $\frac{1}{3}$

46 Which is an example of an equation?

A $3 + 2y + 5 + 4y$

B $18(12 + x) - 3x$

C $\frac{6}{x} + 7$

D $x + 3 = 5$

47 Which *best* describes 0?

A It is a positive integer.

B It is a negative integer.

C It is neither a positive integer nor a negative integer.

D It is not an integer.

48 Joel has cycled 6 miles in 20 minutes. At that rate, how many miles will he cycle in 2 hours?

A 18 miles

B 24 miles

C 36 miles

D 48 miles

GO ON TO THE NEXT PAGE

49 The auditorium has 48 rows of seats. Each row can seat 32 people. Which is the *best* estimate for the number of people who can sit in the auditorium at one time?

A 1,200

B 1,500

C 1,800

D 2,000

50 Which number makes this statement true?

$$\frac{15}{18} = \frac{10}{\underline{\quad}}$$

A 10

B 12

C 13

D 15

51 Which of the following pairs of equations have the same solution?

A $6x = 2$ and $12x = 4$

B $3x = 9$ and $6x = 12$

C $4x = 10$ and $8x = 5$

D $5x = 2$ and $10x = 7$

52 What is the probability of this spinner landing on 2 or 3?

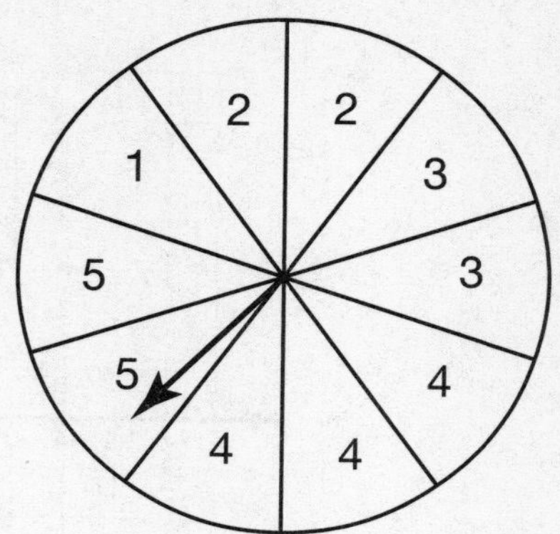

A 20%

B 30%

C 40%

D 50%

53 Which is an equivalent measure for 250 kilograms?

A 2.5 grams

B 25 grams

C 25,000 grams

D 250,000 grams

GO ON TO THE NEXT PAGE

PRETEST

Remove Pretest Here

54 Which point is located at (3, −4)?

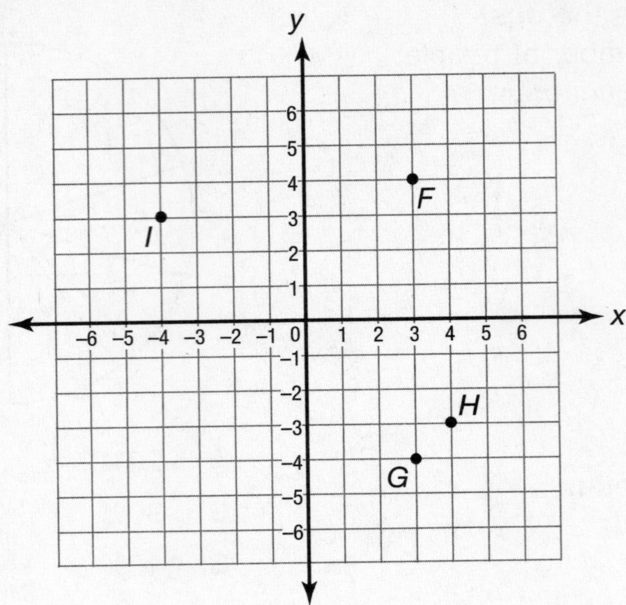

A *F*

B *G*

C *H*

D *I*

55 What is $|-2.5|$?

A −2.5

B −0.4

C 0.4

D 2.5

56 Among the 250 students at Grissom Middle School, 36% walk to school. How many students walk to Grissom Middle School?

A 72

B 80

C 90

D 96

GO ON TO THE NEXT PAGE

Remove Pretest Here

57 What is $3\frac{2}{5} + 4\frac{3}{8}$?

A $7\frac{7}{10}$

B $7\frac{29}{40}$

C $7\frac{3}{4}$

D $7\frac{31}{40}$

58 Which number completes the sentence?

$$\frac{3}{5} + \square = 0$$

A $-\frac{3}{5}$

B 0

C $\frac{3}{5}$

D $1\frac{2}{3}$

59 What is the missing number in this function table?

x	*y*
12	3
20	5
32	8
44	?

A $y = 11$

B $y = 20$

C $y = 29$

D $y = 35$

60 Millie is typing a paper. She typed her paper in 8 minutes. Her paper had 600 words. How many words did she type per minute?

A 70

B 75

C 80

D 85

PRETEST

GO ON TO THE NEXT PAGE

Remove Pretest Here

61 Which number makes this sentence true?

3 yd 2 ft = ______ in.

A 96
B 121
C 132
D 144

62 What changes when a figure is rotated?

A Its position
B Its size
C Its shape
D Its perimeter

63 Look at the number line. Between which two points would −0.15 fall?

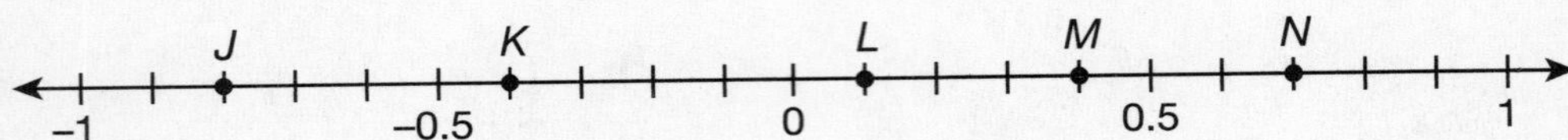

A *J* and *K*
B *K* and *L*
C *L* and *M*
D *M* and *N*

GO ON TO THE NEXT PAGE

64 Which two figures appear to be congruent to each other?

A

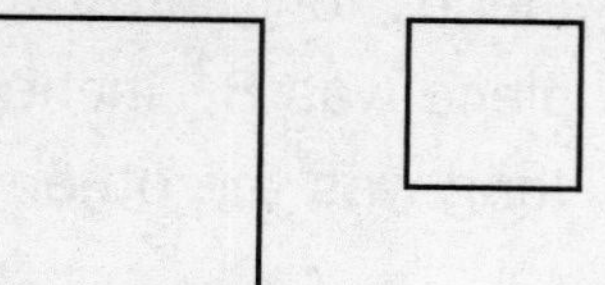

B

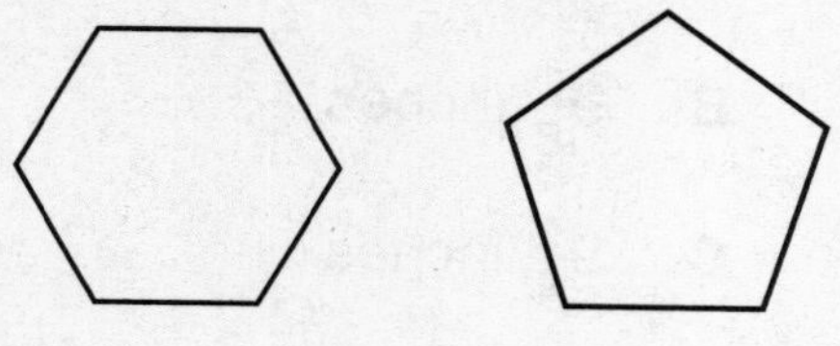

C

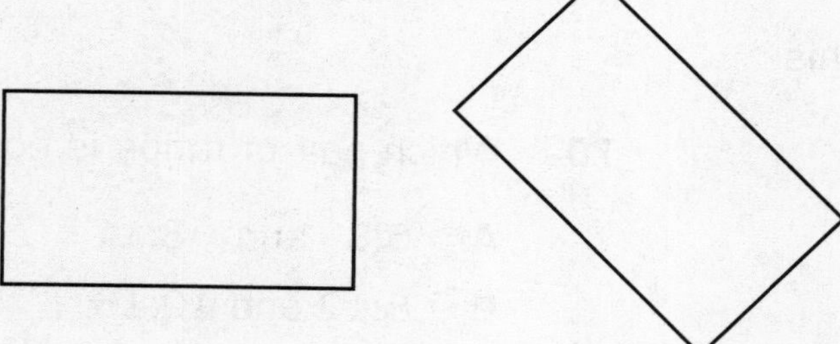

D

65 Which represents six less than two times a number?

A $2x - 6$ **C** $6x + 2$

B $2x + 6$ **D** $6x - 2$

66 Ms. Torres receives a 12% commission on everything she sells. Last month, she sold \$34,000 worth of goods. How much money did Ms. Torres receive in commission?

A \$ 408

B \$ 4,080

C \$ 4,800

D \$40,800

GO ON TO THE NEXT PAGE

PRETEST

67 A hotel room at Sweet Suites costs \$519 for 3 nights. At that rate, how much would it cost to spend a week in the same room at Sweet Suites?

A \$ 692

B \$1,038

C \$1,211

D \$1,557

68 Where is point *O* located on this coordinate grid?

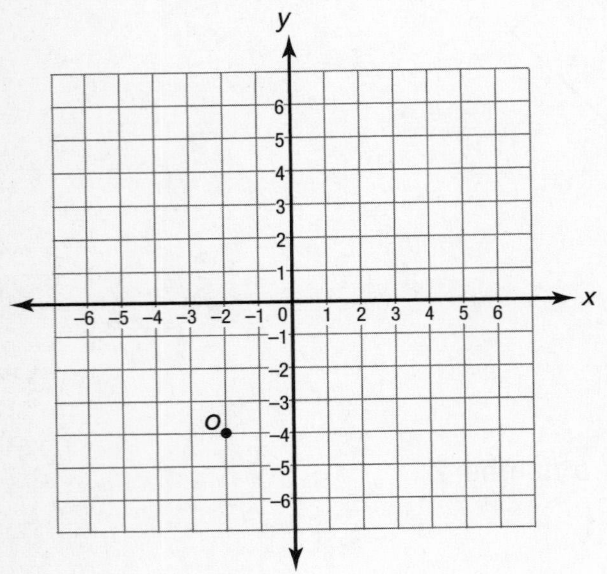

A (−4, −2)

B (−4, 2)

C (−2, 4)

D (−2, −4)

69 Mr. Griffin cut a board that was $17\frac{3}{8}$ inches long into two pieces. One piece was $8\frac{1}{2}$ inches long. How long was the other piece?

A $8\frac{7}{8}$ inches

B $9\frac{1}{8}$ inches

C $9\frac{1}{4}$ inches

D $9\frac{3}{4}$ inches

70 Which pair of ratios is equivalent?

A 5:8 and 8:11

B 8:12 and 10:16

C 9:15 and 16:25

D 9:12 and 15:20

71 Roscoe is going to toss two number cubes, each with faces numbered 1–6. He will subtract the lesser number from the greater number. What is the probability that Roscoe will toss a difference of 0?

A $\frac{1}{12}$

B $\frac{1}{9}$

C $\frac{1}{6}$

D $\frac{1}{4}$

GO ON TO THE NEXT PAGE

Remove Pretest Here

PRETEST

72 Which relationship could this graph display?

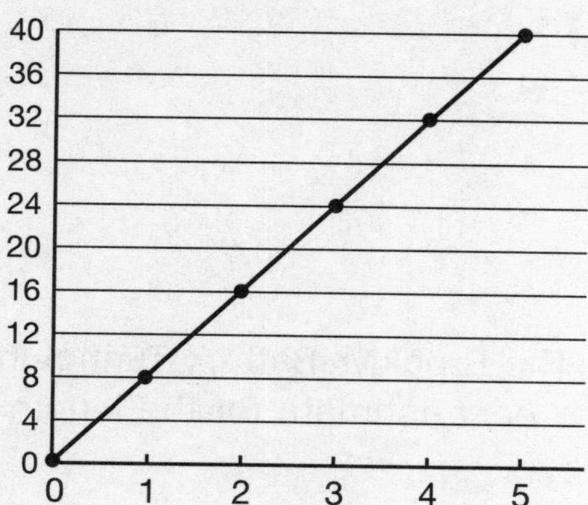

A The relationship between the length of the sides of a regular octagon and its perimeter

B The relationship between the length of the sides of a cube and its volume

C The relationship between pints and fluid ounces

D The relationship between days and weeks

73 Through 2005, the all-time high for the Dow Jones was 11,722.98 in 2000. The low since then was 7,286.27 in 2002. By how many points did the Dow Jones fall?

A 4,436.71

B 4,446.71

C 4,536.71

D 4,546.71

74 What is 84% of 75?

A 56

B 60

C 63

D 69

75 A playground has an area of 375 m^2. What is the area of the playground in square centimeters?

A 3,750 cm^2

B 37,500 cm^2

C 375,000 cm^2

D 3,750,000 cm^2

GO ON TO THE NEXT PAGE

Remove Pretest Here

76 Which is $\frac{9}{16}$ written as a decimal?

A 0.55

B 0.5625

C 0.575

D 0.625

77 The Detroit-Windsor Tunnel is 5,160 feet long. The Brooklyn-Battery Tunnel in New York City is 3,957 feet longer. Which is the *best* estimate for the length of the Brooklyn-Battery Tunnel?

A 7,000 feet

B 8,000 feet

C 9,000 feet

D 10,000 feet

78 What is the value of y in this equation?

$$y - 13 = 18$$

A $y = 5$

B $y = 15$

C $y = 21$

D $y = 31$

79 Of the customers at a bookstore, $\frac{2}{5}$ are senior citizens. Of the senior citizens, $\frac{3}{8}$ are women. What fraction of the customers at the bookstore are senior citizens who are women?

A $\frac{3}{20}$

B $\frac{1}{5}$

C $\frac{3}{10}$

D $\frac{5}{13}$

STOP.

CHAPTER

Number and Operations

1 Add and Subtract Whole Numbers and Decimals

GLCEs: N.FL.06.10, N.FL.06.15

Getting the Idea

In addition, the numbers you add are **addends**, and the answer is the **sum**. Add the digits from right to left. If a sum of a column is 10 or greater, you will have to **regroup**.

EXAMPLE 1

Texas has 3,359 miles of shoreline. Florida has 5,095 miles of shoreline. How many miles of shoreline do the two states have together?

STRATEGY **Add from right to left.**

STEP 1 Align the digits on the ones place. Add the ones. Write the 4 in the ones column. Regroup the 1 ten.

$$\begin{array}{r} {\scriptstyle 1} \\ 3{,}35\mathbf{9} \\ +\ 5{,}09\mathbf{5} \\ \hline \mathbf{4} \end{array}$$

STEP 2 Add the tens. Write the 5 in the tens column. Regroup the 1 hundred.

$$\begin{array}{r} {\scriptstyle 1\,1} \\ 3{,}3\mathbf{5}9 \\ +\ 5{,}0\mathbf{9}5 \\ \hline \mathbf{5}4 \end{array}$$

STEP 3 Add the hundreds. Write the 4 in the hundreds column.

$$\begin{array}{r} {\scriptstyle 1\,1} \\ 3{,}\mathbf{3}59 \\ +\ 5{,}\mathbf{0}95 \\ \hline \mathbf{4}54 \end{array}$$

STEP 4 Add the thousands. Write the 8 in the thousands column. The sum is 8,454.

$$\begin{array}{r} {\scriptstyle 1\,1} \\ \mathbf{3}{,}359 \\ +\ \mathbf{5}{,}095 \\ \hline \mathbf{8}{,}454 \end{array}$$

SOLUTION **Texas and Florida together have 8,454 miles of shoreline.**

In subtraction, the answer is the **difference**. The number you subtract from is the **minuend.** The number you subtract is the **subtrahend.**

EXAMPLE 2

What is the difference?

7,236 − 4,758 =

STRATEGY **Subtract from right to left. Regroup when necessary.**

STEP 1 Align the digits on the ones place. There are not enough ones to subtract. Regroup 1 ten as 10 ones. Subtract the ones.

```
      2 16
  7,2 3 6
− 4,7 5 8
        8
```

STEP 2 There are not enough tens to subtract. Regroup 1 hundred as 10 tens. Subtract the tens.

```
      12
    1  2 16
  7,2  3  6
− 4,7  5  8
       7  8
```

STEP 3 There are not enough hundreds to subtract. Regroup 1 thousand as 10 hundreds. Subtract the hundreds.

```
    11 12
  6  1  2 16
  7, 2  3  6
− 4, 7  5  8
     4  7  8
```

STEP 4 Subtract the thousands.

```
    11 12
  6  1  2 16
  7, 2  3  6
− 4, 7  5  8
  2, 4  7  8
```

SOLUTION **7,236 − 4,758 = 2,478.**

You can check the answer to a subtraction problem by adding the difference plus the subtrahend: 4,758 + 2,478 = 7,236.

Adding and subtracting decimals is like adding and subtracting whole numbers. As with whole numbers, compute from right to left. The difference is that when adding and subtracting decimals, the numbers are aligned on the decimal point.

It may be necessary to write an equivalent decimal before computing.

EXAMPLE 3

Katia worked 37.5 hours one week and 29.25 hours the next. How many more hours did she work the first week than the second week?

STRATEGY **Subtract from right to left, regrouping when necessary.**

STEP 1 Align the decimal points. Place the decimal point in the difference.

```
   37.5
 − 29.25
 -------
     .
```

STEP 2 Insert a 0 after the 5 in 37.5. Regroup 1 tenth as 10 hundredths. Subtract the hundredths.

```
     4 10
   37.5 0
 − 29.2 5
 --------
      . 5
```

STEP 3 Subtract the tenths.

```
     4 10
   37.5 0
 − 29.2 5
 --------
     .2 5
```

STEP 4 Regroup 1 ten as 10 ones. Then subtract the ones.

```
  2 17 4 10
  3 7 .5 0
− 2 9 .2 5
----------
    8 .2 5
```

STEP 5 Subtract the tens. The product does not have a tens place.

SOLUTION **Katia worked 8.25 hours more the first week than the second week.**

COACHED EXAMPLE

Lanie had a budget of $225.00 for costumes for the school play. She spent $86.56 on fabric. How much does she have left?

THINKING IT THROUGH

Compute from ____________ to ____________.

Subtract the hundredths. ____________

Do you need to regroup? ____________

Subtract the tenths. ____________

Do you need to regroup? ____________

Subtract the ones. ____________

Do you need to regroup? ____________

Subtract the tens. ____________

Do you need to regroup? ____________

Subtract the hundreds. ____________

Lanie has ____________ left after buying fabric.

Lesson Practice

Choose the correct answer.

1. What is 92,378 + 54,594?

A 146,962
B 146,972
C 147,962
D 147,972

2. In the 2004 presidential election, John Kerry received 44,282 votes in Muskegon County, and George W. Bush received 35,302 votes. How many more votes did John Kerry receive than George W. Bush in Muskegon County?

A 8,980
B 9,980
C 18,980
D 19,980

3. Calvin earned $158.75 mowing lawns over the summer and $95.38 working in his mother's office. How much money did he earn altogether?

A $143.03
B $244.13
C $253.03
D $254.13

4. What is 248.56 − 88.9?

A 159.66
B 160.47
C 239.67
D 260.66

5. The two longest roller coasters are both in Japan. The Steel Dragon 2000 is 8,133 feet long. The Daidarasaurus is 7,677 feet long. How much longer is the Steel Dragon 2000 than the Daidarasaurus?

A 456 feet
B 556 feet
C 1,446 feet
D 1,566 feet

6. In 2003, 10,526 people from Mexico visited the United States. The same year, 1,180 people visited from Germany and 409 visited from Italy. How many more people visited the U.S. from Mexico than from Germany and Italy combined?

A 8,927
B 8,936
C 8,937
D 9,047

7. Mr. Palmer had $5,675.68 in his saving account at the end of last year. Since then, he has saved $2,168.79. How much money does he have in his savings account now?

A $7,733.37

B $7,734.47

C $7,843.37

D $7,844.47

8. A greyhound can run 39.35 miles per hour. A quarterhorse can run 47.5 miles per hour. How much faster can a quarterhorse run than a greyhound?

A 7.2 mph

B 8.15 mph

C 9.45 mph

D 9.85 mph

OPEN-ENDED ITEM

9. Claire's family drove 129.75 miles on the first day of their vacation. The next day they drove 43.75 miles, and the third day they drove 37.75 miles.

How many more miles did they drive on the first day than the second and third days combined? Show your work.

Explain how you determined your answer.

2 Multiply Whole Numbers and Decimals

GLCEs: N.FL.06.10, N.FL.06.15

Getting the Idea

To find the **product** of a multi-digit whole number and a 2-digit **factor**, multiply by the ones and then the tens to find partial products. Then add the partial products to find the product.

EXAMPLE 1

What is 265 × 28?

STRATEGY **Multiply by each place value, regrouping as necessary.**

STEP 1 Multiply by the ones: 265 × 8.

```
   5 4
   265
 ×  28
 2,120
```

STEP 2 Write a 0 in the ones place. Multiply by the tens: 265 × 2.

```
   1 1
   5 4
   265
 ×  28
 2,120
 5,300
```

STEP 3 Add the partial products.

```
   1 1
   5 4
   265
 ×  28
 2,120
+5,300
 7,420
```

SOLUTION **So, 265 × 28 = 7,420.**

You can also use the **distributive property of multiplication** to find products. The distributive property states that to multiply a sum by a number, you can multiply each addend by the number and add the products.

EXAMPLE 2

What is 315×34?

STRATEGY **Use the distributive property to solve two simpler problems.**

STEP 1 Decompose one of the factors.

It does not matter which factor you decompose.

$315 \times 34 = (315 \times 30) + (315 \times 4)$

STEP 2 Find the partial products.

$315 \times 30 = 9{,}450$

$315 \times 4 = 1{,}260$

STEP 3 Add the partial products.

$$\begin{array}{r} 9{,}450 \\ +\ 1{,}260 \\ \hline 10{,}710 \end{array}$$

SOLUTION **$315 \times 34 = 10{,}710$**

Multiplying decimals is like multiplying whole numbers. The difference is that you have to place a decimal point in the product. To find how many decimal places the product of two decimals has, add the number of places in the factors.

EXAMPLE 3

What is 17.48 × 5.6?

STRATEGY **Multiply as you would whole numbers. Then place the decimal point.**

STEP 1 Write the problem this way and then multiply by the 6 ones.

$$\begin{array}{r} \mathbf{17.48} \\ \underline{\times \quad 5.\mathbf{6}} \\ \mathbf{10488} \end{array}$$

STEP 2 Put a 0 in the ones place. Multiply by the 5 tens.

$$\begin{array}{r} \mathbf{17.48} \\ \underline{\times \quad \mathbf{5}.6} \\ 10488 \\ \mathbf{87400} \end{array}$$

STEP 3 Add the partial products and insert the decimal point. The decimal factors have a total of 3 decimal places, so the product will have 3 decimal places.

$$\begin{array}{r} 17.48 \\ \underline{\times \quad 5.6} \\ \mathbf{10488} \\ \underline{+\ \mathbf{87400}} \\ \mathbf{97.888} \end{array}$$

SOLUTION **So, 17.48 × 5.6 = 97.888.**

COACHED EXAMPLE

The sixth-grade class and their parents are going to an amusement park. Tickets are \$44.99 for adults and \$29.99 for students. There are 18 students and 32 adults. How much will it cost altogether?

THINKING IT THROUGH

This problem has three parts. First, find out how much the adults' tickets cost:

$$\begin{array}{r} \$44.99 \\ \times \quad 32 \\ \hline \end{array}$$

Place the decimal point.

The product will have ______ decimal places.

Next, find out how much the ______ tickets cost:

$$\begin{array}{r} \$29.99 \\ \times \quad 18 \\ \hline \end{array}$$

Place the decimal point.

The product will have ______ decimal places.

Add the two products.

So, it will cost ______ for the adults and the students to go to the amusement park.

Lesson Practice

Choose the correct answer.

1. What is 347 × 72?

A 2,868
B 3,123
C 22,524
D 24,984

2. An artist sold his paintings for $485 each. If he sells 23 paintings, how much money will he make?

A $ 2,425
B $ 9,845
C $11,155
D $12,155

3. Ruben earns $285.47 a month at his part-time job. How much money does he earn in 2 years?

A $1,712.82
B $6,851.28
C $6,852.28
D $7,851.28

4. What is 0.385 × 0.026?

A 0.01001
B 0.308
C 0.1001
D 0.308

5. What is the product of this problem?

$$\begin{array}{r} 53.25 \\ \times\ 0.052 \\ \hline \end{array}$$

A 2.769
B 27.609
C 27.69
D 276.9

6. Kristina rode her bicycle 13.78 miles total going to and from swimming class. She went to that class for 29 weeks. How many miles did she ride altogether?

A 398.62 miles
B 398.75 miles
C 399.62 miles
D 399.75 miles

7. Jesse is planning a vacation to Sweden. He knows that 7.348 krona equals $1. How many krona will he have if he exchanges $96?

A 70.5408
B 705.408
C 7,054.8
D 7,540.8

8. The cheerleading uniforms that the coach has picked out cost $43.35 each. She needs to order 48 uniforms. How much will the uniforms cost?

A $ 486.60

B $ 520.20

C $1,946.40

D $2,080.80

OPEN-ENDED ITEM

9. Mrs. Ward earns $28.36 per hour. Last week she worked 37.5 hours.

How much money did she earn last week? Show your work.

How did you know where to place the decimal point in the product?

3 Divide Whole Numbers and Decimals

GLCEs: N.FL.06.10, N.FL.06.15

Getting the Idea

The number that is being divided is the **dividend**. The number that the dividend is divided by is the **divisor**. The answer is the **quotient**. Sometimes a number will remain when division has been completed. That number is called a **remainder**.

EXAMPLE 1

What is 6)790?

STRATEGY **Divide the dividend by the divisor by each place from left to right.**

STEP 1 Divide the hundreds by 6. Subtract.

```
  1
6)790
  6 → Multiply 6 × 1 = 6
  1 → Subtract 7 − 6 = 1
```

STEP 2 Bring down the 9 tens and divide the tens.

```
  13
6)790
 − 6
  19
 − 18 → Multiply 6 × 3 = 18
    1 → Subtract 19 − 18 = 1
```

STEP 3 Bring down the 0 ones and divide.

```
  131
6)790
 − 6
  19
 − 18
   10
  − 6
    4
```

STEP 4 Write the remainder.

```
  131 R4
6)790
 − 6
  19
 − 18
   10
  − 6
    4
```

SOLUTION **790 ÷ 6 = 131 R4.**

Dividing by 2-digit divisors is similar to dividing by 1-digit divisors. The steps are the same. The difference is that you may need to **estimate** to help determine the quotient. To estimate, round a 2-digit divisor to the nearest ten and use a basic multiplication fact. If the product of the multiplication fact is greater than the dividend, you many need to adjust your number by trying 1 less.

EXAMPLE 2

What is 6,406 ÷ 74?

STRATEGY **Divide the dividend by the divisor by each place from left to right.**

STEP 1 Decide where to place the first digit in the quotient.

74)6,406

There are not enough thousands or hundreds to divide, so the first digit will be in the tens place.

STEP 2 Divide the tens.

You know that 70 × 9 = 630, but that looks like it will be too much, so try 8.

```
   8
74)6,406
 − 5 92 → Multiply 74 × 8 = 592
     48 → Subtract 640 − 592 = 48
```

STEP 3 Bring down the 6 ones and divide the ones.

You know that 70 × 6 = 420, so try 6.

```
   86 R42
74)6,406
 − 5 92
    486
  − 444 → Multiply 74 × 6 = 444
     42 → Subtract 486 − 444 = 42
```

SOLUTION **6,406 ÷ 74 = 86 R42**

You can check the quotient by multiplying the quotient by the divisor and then adding the remainder. Since 86 × 74 = 6,364 and 6,364 + 42 = 6,406, the quotient is correct.

Dividing decimals is like dividing whole numbers. When dividing a decimal by a whole number, place the decimal point in the quotient above the decimal point in the dividend. Then divide just as you would with whole numbers.

EXAMPLE 3

What is 29.84 ÷ 4?

STRATEGY **Divide the dividend by the divisor by each place from left to right.**

STEP 1 Write the decimal point in the quotient. Divide the tens.

```
   7.
 4)29.84
 - 28 → Multiply 4 × 7 = 28
    1 → Subtract 29 − 28 = 1
```

STEP 2 Bring down the 8 tenths. Divide the tenths.

```
   7.4
 4)29.84
 - 28
    18
  - 16 → Multiply 4 × 4 = 16
     2 → Subtract 18 − 16 = 2
```

STEP 3 Bring down the 4 hundredths. Divide the hundredths.

```
   7.46
 4)29.84
 - 28
    18
  -16
     24 → Multiply 4 × 6 = 24
   - 24 → Subtract 24 − 24 = 0
      0
```

SOLUTION **29.84 ÷ 4 = 7.46**

To divide with decimal divisors, multiply the divisor by a power of 10 to ensure a whole-number divisor. Multiply the dividend by the same power of 10. Place the decimal point in the quotient. Then divide as you would with whole numbers.

EXAMPLE 4

What is 94.575 ÷ 3.9?

STRATEGY **Multiply by a power of 10 to ensure a whole-number divisor, then divide.**

STEP 1 Multiply the dividend and the divisor by a power of 10.

$$3.9\overline{)94.575}$$

$$3.9 \times 10 = 39$$

$$94.575 \times 10 = 945.75$$

STEP 2 Write the problem with the new dividend and divisor. Write the decimal point in the quotient.

$$\begin{array}{r} . \\ 39\overline{)945.75} \end{array}$$

STEP 3 Divide as you would with whole numbers.

$$\begin{array}{r} 24.25 \\ 39\overline{)945.75} \\ \underline{-\ 78} \\ 165 \\ \underline{-\ 156} \\ 97 \\ \underline{-\ 78} \\ 195 \\ \underline{-\ 195} \\ 0 \end{array}$$

SOLUTION **94.575 ÷ 3.9 = 24.25**

You may need to add zeros to the dividend in order to keep dividing.

EXAMPLE 5

What is 1.86 ÷ 0.8?

STRATEGY **Multiply by a power of 10 to ensure a whole-number divisor, then divide.**

STEP 1 Multiply the dividend and the divisor by a power of 10.

$0.8 \times 10 = 8$

$1.86 \times 10 = 18.6$

STEP 2 Write the problem with the new dividend and divisor. Write the decimal point in the quotient.

$$8\overline{)18.6}$$

STEP 3 Divide as you would with whole numbers. Add zeros as needed.

```
    2.325
  8)18.600
  - 16
     26
   - 24
      20
    - 16
       40
     - 40
        0
```

SOLUTION **1.86 ÷ 0.8 = 2.325**

COACHED EXAMPLE

Mr. Giametta's class sold raffle tickets for $1.50 each. They made $142.50. How many tickets did they sell?

THINKING IT THROUGH

Write the problem this way:

$1.5\overline{)142.5}$

Multiply the divisor and the dividend by _______ to get a whole number divisor.

The first digit in the quotient will go in the _______ place.

Divide the tens: 142 ÷ 15 = _______

Subtract 142 − ☐ = ☐.

Bring down the _______ ones.

Divide the ones: ☐ ÷ 15 = _______

Subtract. _______

Is there a remainder? _______

Check your answer.

So, the class sold _______ raffle tickets.

Lesson Practice

Choose the correct answer.

1. What is 6,528 ÷ 8?

A 793 R4

B 816

C 816 R1

D 826

2. Sixteen students held a fundraiser. They raised $890.88 and divided it equally so that each student could donate to his or her favorite charity. How much was each student able to donate?

A $41.61

B $54.16

C $55.68

D $55.69

3. The area of Detroit is 138.8 square miles. If the city were divided into 25 equal sections, what would be the area of each section?

A 5.552 sq mi

B 5.56 sq mi

C 55.52 sq mi

D 55.6 sq mi

4. What is 282.336 ÷ 6.8?

A 4.152

B 31.1

C 41.52

D 58.57

5. Jake had a pizza party for 28 people, including himself. He ordered 7 pizzas. How much of one pizza can each person have?

A 0.025

B 0.25

C 0.285

D 4

6. In 2002, the average annual salary in San Francisco, California, was $56,602. How much is this per week?

A $ 108.85

B $1,026.90

C $1,088.00

D $1,088.50

7. Victoria has $93.60 to spend on meals on her vacation. She figures out that she can spend $7.80 for each meal. How many meals will Victoria eat on vacation?

A 12

B 13

C 15

D 20

8. What is 2.375 ÷ 0.05?

A 4.75

B 5.55

C 44.35

D 47.5

OPEN-ENDED ITEM

9. Michael rode his bike around a park. The distance around the park is 6.4 miles. He rode a total of 134.4 miles. How many times did Michael go around the park?

What number sentence can you write to find out how many times he rode around the park?

____

What do you need to do first before you can divide?

____

How many times did Michael go around the park? Show your work.

____

4 Add Fractions and Mixed Numbers

GLCEs: N.FL.06.10

Getting the Idea

To find the sum of fractions that have like denominators, add the numerators. The denominator remains the same. Write the sum in simplest form.

EXAMPLE 1

What is $\frac{5}{16} + \frac{13}{16}$?

STRATEGY **Add the numerators. Then write the sum in simplest form.**

STEP 1 Add the numerators. The denominator stays the same.

$$\frac{5}{16} + \frac{13}{16} = \frac{5 + 13}{16} = \frac{18}{16}$$

STEP 2 Convert the improper fraction to a mixed number by dividing the numerator by the denominator.

$18 \div 16 = 1 \text{ R}2$ $\qquad \frac{18}{16} = 1\frac{2}{16}$

STEP 3 Write the mixed number in simplest form.

$$1\frac{2}{16} = 1\frac{1}{8}$$

SOLUTION $\mathbf{\frac{5}{16} + \frac{13}{16} = 1\frac{1}{8}}$

To add fractions with unlike denominators, rename one or both fractions so that they have like denominators. You can do this by finding the **least common denominator (LCD)**. The least common denominator is the **least common multiple (LCM)** of the denominators.

EXAMPLE 2

What is $\frac{3}{4} + \frac{5}{6}$?

STRATEGY **Use the LCD to write equivalent fractions. Then add the numerators.**

STEP 1 Find the LCD of $\frac{3}{4}$ and $\frac{5}{6}$.

The multiples of 4 are 4, 8, 12 . . .

The multiples of 6 are 6, 12 . . .

The LCD is 12.

STEP 2 Rename both fractions so they have 12 in the denominator.

$\frac{3}{4} \times \frac{3}{3} = \frac{9}{12}$

$\frac{5}{6} \times \frac{2}{2} = \frac{10}{12}$

STEP 3 Add.

$\frac{9}{12} + \frac{10}{12} = \frac{19}{12}$

STEP 4 Write the sum as a mixed number in simplest form.

$19 \div 12 = 1 \text{ R}7$

$\frac{19}{12} = 1\frac{7}{12}$

SOLUTION $\mathbf{\frac{3}{4} + \frac{5}{6} = 1\frac{7}{12}}$

Mixed numbers are part whole number and part fraction. You use a mixed number when you say your age is $10\frac{1}{2}$ or a recipe takes $2\frac{1}{2}$ cups of water. To add mixed numbers, first add the fraction parts and then add the whole number parts. Simplify the answer if possible.

EXAMPLE 3

What is $5\frac{7}{10} + 8\frac{2}{3}$?

STRATEGY **Use the LCD to write equivalent mixed numbers.**

STEP 1 Find the LCD of $\frac{7}{10}$ and $\frac{2}{3}$.

The LCD is 30.

STEP 2 Write equivalent fractions for the fraction parts.

$\frac{7}{10} \times \frac{3}{3} = \frac{21}{30}$, so $5\frac{7}{10} = 5\frac{21}{30}$

$\frac{2}{3} \times \frac{10}{10} = \frac{20}{30}$, so $8\frac{2}{3} = 8\frac{20}{30}$

STEP 3 Add the fraction parts.

$\frac{21}{30} + \frac{20}{30} = \frac{41}{30} = 1\frac{11}{30}$

STEP 4 Add the whole number parts.

$5 + 8 = 13$

STEP 5 Add the sums.

$1\frac{11}{30} + 13 = 14\frac{11}{30}$

SOLUTION $\mathbf{5\frac{7}{10} + 8\frac{2}{3} = 14\frac{11}{30}}$

COACHED EXAMPLE

Bianca is baking with two different recipes. One calls for $2\frac{1}{3}$ cups of flour, and the other calls for $3\frac{3}{4}$ cups. How much flour does she need altogether?

THINKING IT THROUGH

Find the LCD of $2\frac{1}{3}$ and $3\frac{3}{4}$, which is ______.

Rename $2\frac{1}{3}$ as ______.

Rename $3\frac{3}{4}$ as ______.

Add the fraction parts. ____________

Add the whole number parts. ____________

Add the sums. ____________

So, Bianca used ______ cups of flour altogether.

Lesson Practice

Choose the correct answer.

1. What is $\frac{5}{9} + \frac{7}{15}$?

A $\frac{4}{7}$

B $\frac{4}{5}$

C $1\frac{1}{45}$

D $1\frac{2}{45}$

2. Nathan ordered a sandwich tray for a party. $\frac{5}{8}$ of the sandwiches are turkey, and $\frac{1}{4}$ are ham. What fraction of the sandwiches is turkey or ham?

A $\frac{1}{4}$

B $\frac{3}{8}$

C $\frac{1}{2}$

D $\frac{7}{8}$

3. Charlie and Fred hiked $4\frac{5}{12}$ miles, then stopped for lunch. After lunch, they hiked $6\frac{2}{3}$ miles. How far did they hike that day?

A $6\frac{1}{12}$ miles

B $11\frac{1}{12}$ miles

C $11\frac{1}{6}$ miles

D $11\frac{1}{3}$ miles

4. Mr. Becker baked a lemon pie and a blueberry pie. After dinner, $\frac{7}{8}$ of the lemon pie was eaten and $\frac{5}{6}$ of the blueberry pie was eaten. How much pie was eaten altogether?

A $\frac{6}{7}$

B $1\frac{1}{2}$

C $1\frac{15}{24}$

D $1\frac{17}{24}$

5. What is $12\frac{3}{5} + 7\frac{5}{6}$?

A $3\frac{2}{3}$

B $19\frac{6}{15}$

C $20\frac{13}{30}$

D $21\frac{1}{6}$

6. Janine worked $5\frac{1}{2}$ hours on Saturday and $7\frac{3}{4}$ hours on Sunday. How many hours did she work over the weekend?

A $13\frac{1}{4}$

B $13\frac{3}{4}$

C 14

D $14\frac{1}{4}$

7. By the time school started, Brandon had read $5\frac{3}{4}$ of the books on his summer reading list. Garret had read $10\frac{1}{3}$ of the books on his list. How many books did they read altogether?

A $16\frac{1}{12}$

B $16\frac{1}{4}$

C $16\frac{1}{2}$

D $16\frac{2}{3}$

8. Carmella is making a quilt with 100 squares. She finished 53 squares in December. She finished another $\frac{3}{10}$ of the quilt in January. How many squares had Carmella completed by the end of January?

A 80

B 83

C 84

D 85

OPEN-ENDED ITEM

9. It is $4\frac{5}{10}$ miles from Leslie's house to the library. It is $5\frac{1}{4}$ miles from the library to the school. How far is it from Leslie's house to the library to the school?

___

Explain how you determined your answer.

___

___

___

___

Lesson

5 Subtract Fractions and Mixed Numbers

GLCEs: N.FL.06.10

Getting the Idea

To subtract fractions that have like denominators, subtract the numerators. The denominator remains the same. Write the difference in simplest form.

EXAMPLE 1

What is $\frac{11}{16} - \frac{5}{16}$?

STRATEGY **Subtract the numerators. Then write the difference in simplest form.**

STEP 1 Subtract the numerators. The denominator stays the same.

$$\frac{11}{16} - \frac{5}{16} = \frac{11 - 5}{16} = \frac{6}{16}$$

STEP 2 Write the difference in simplest form.

$$\frac{6}{16} = \frac{3}{8}$$

SOLUTION $\mathbf{\frac{11}{16} - \frac{5}{16} = \frac{3}{8}}$

To subtract fractions with unlike denominators, rename one or both fractions so that they have like denominators. You can do this by finding the least common denominator **(LCD)**.

EXAMPLE 2

What is $\frac{1}{2} - \frac{3}{8}$?

STRATEGY **Use the LCD to write an equivalent fraction. Then subtract the numerators.**

STEP 1 Find the LCD of $\frac{1}{2}$ and $\frac{3}{8}$.

The LCD is 8.

STEP 2 Rename $\frac{1}{2}$ so that it has 8 in the denominator.

$$\frac{1}{2} \times \frac{4}{4} = \frac{4}{8}$$

STEP 3 Subtract.

$$\frac{4}{8} - \frac{3}{8} = \frac{1}{8}$$

SOLUTION $\mathbf{\frac{1}{2} - \frac{3}{8} = \frac{1}{8}}$

EXAMPLE 3

What is $\frac{5}{9} - \frac{5}{12}$?

STRATEGY **Use the LCD to write equivalent fractions. Then subtract the numerators.**

STEP 1 Find the LCD of $\frac{5}{9}$ and $\frac{5}{12}$.

The LCD is 36.

STEP 2 Rename $\frac{5}{9}$ so that is has 36 in the denominator.

$$\frac{5}{9} \times \frac{4}{4} = \frac{20}{36}$$

STEP 3 Rename $\frac{5}{12}$ so that is has 36 in the denominator.

$$\frac{5}{12} \times \frac{3}{3} = \frac{15}{36}$$

STEP 3 Subtract.

$$\frac{20}{36} - \frac{15}{36} = \frac{5}{36}$$

SOLUTION $\mathbf{\frac{5}{9} - \frac{5}{12} = \frac{5}{36}}$

To subtract mixed numbers, it may be necessary to rename the minuend a second time after finding the LCD.

EXAMPLE 4

What is $10\frac{5}{9} - 6\frac{3}{5}$?

STRATEGY **Find the LCD, write equivalent fractions, and subtract.**

STEP 1 Find the LCD of $\frac{5}{9}$ and $\frac{3}{5}$.

The LCD is 45.

STEP 2 Write equivalent fractions for the fraction parts.

$\frac{5}{9} \times \frac{5}{5} = \frac{25}{45}$, so $10\frac{5}{9} = 10\frac{25}{45}$

$\frac{3}{5} \times \frac{9}{9} = \frac{27}{45}$, so $6\frac{3}{5} = 6\frac{27}{45}$

STEP 3 There are not enough forty-fifths to subtract, so rename $10\frac{25}{45}$.

$10\frac{25}{45} = 9\frac{70}{45}$

STEP 4 Subtract.

$9\frac{70}{45} - 6\frac{27}{45} = 3\frac{43}{45}$

SOLUTION $\mathbf{10\frac{5}{9} - 6\frac{3}{5} = 3\frac{43}{45}}$

COACHED EXAMPLE

Yuri lives $12\frac{1}{4}$ miles from the beach. Rupert lives $8\frac{2}{5}$ miles from the beach. How much closer to the beach does Rupert live than Yuri?

THINKING IT THROUGH

Find the LCD of the fraction parts. The LCD is ______.

$12\frac{1}{4}$ can be renamed as ______.

$8\frac{2}{5}$ can be renamed as ______.

There are not enough ______ to subtract so rename the minuend as ______.

Subtract. ____________________

Rupert lives ______ miles closer to the beach than Yuri.

Lesson Practice

Choose the correct answer.

1. What is $\frac{5}{12} - \frac{3}{8}$?

A $\frac{1}{24}$

B $\frac{1}{12}$

C $\frac{7}{24}$

D $\frac{1}{2}$

2. Geena and her brother Doyle each planted a tree in their yard. When they measured the trees, Geena's tree was $\frac{7}{12}$ foot tall and Doyle's was $\frac{1}{2}$ foot tall. How much taller was Geena's tree than Doyle's?

A $\frac{1}{16}$ foot

B $\frac{1}{12}$ foot

C $\frac{1}{4}$ foot

D $\frac{3}{5}$ foot

3. Peggy spent $\frac{1}{4}$ of her violin practice time doing scales. She spent $\frac{5}{12}$ of the time working on a piece for a concert. How much more of her practice time did Peggy spend on the concert piece than on her scales?

A $\frac{1}{6}$

B $\frac{3}{8}$

C $\frac{1}{2}$

D $\frac{2}{3}$

4. What is $5\frac{2}{3} - \frac{5}{9}$?

A 2

B $2\frac{2}{9}$

C $5\frac{1}{9}$

D $5\frac{2}{9}$

5. What is $9\frac{2}{3} - 6\frac{3}{5}$?

A 3

B $3\frac{1}{15}$

C $3\frac{2}{15}$

D $3\frac{1}{5}$

6. Mr. and Mrs. Baldwin were painting their fence. After an hour, Mr. Baldwin had painted $2\frac{1}{3}$ sections of the fence. Mrs. Baldwin stopped to answer the phone, so she only painted $\frac{5}{6}$ of a section. How much more of the fence had Mr. Baldwin painted than Mrs. Baldwin?

A $1\frac{1}{8}$

B $1\frac{1}{6}$

C $1\frac{1}{4}$

D $1\frac{1}{2}$

7. Richard jogged $\frac{1}{3}$ of his normal route on Monday. On Tuesday, he jogged $\frac{3}{5}$ of his route. How much more of his normal route did Richard jog on Tuesday than on Monday?

A $\frac{4}{15}$

B $\frac{2}{5}$

C $\frac{2}{3}$

D $\frac{4}{5}$

8. The Pumpkinhead Bakery used $12\frac{1}{2}$ cups of raisins on Friday. They used $10\frac{3}{4}$ cups of raisins on Saturday. How many more cups of raisins did they use on Friday than on Saturday?

A $1\frac{1}{4}$ cups

B $1\frac{1}{2}$ cups

C $1\frac{3}{4}$ cups

D $2\frac{3}{4}$ cups

OPEN-ENDED ITEM

9. Carla and Joy are having a race to see who can finish a 100-page book first. After a week, Carla had read 88 pages. Joy had read $\frac{7}{10}$ of the book. How many more pages had Carla read than Joy?

____

Explain how you determined your answer.

____

____

____

____

6 Multiply Fractions and Mixed Numbers

GLCEs: N.FL.06.04, N.FL.06.10

Getting the Idea

To multiply fractions, multiply the numerators. Then multiply the denominators.

EXAMPLE 1

What is $5 \times \frac{2}{3}$?

STRATEGY **Convert the whole number to a fraction, then multiply the fractions.**

STEP 1 A whole number can be written as a fraction with 1 as the denominator.

$5 = \frac{5}{1}$

STEP 2 Multiply the numerators.

$5 \times 2 = 10$

STEP 3 Multiply the denominators.

$3 \times 1 = 3$

STEP 4 Convert the improper fraction to a mixed number.

$\frac{10}{3} = 1\frac{1}{3}$

SOLUTION $\mathbf{5 \times \frac{2}{3} = 1\frac{1}{3}}$

Sometimes you can simplify the fractions before multiplying.

EXAMPLE 2

What is $\frac{5}{8} \times \frac{2}{15}$?

STRATEGY **Simplify the fractions, then multiply.**

STEP 1 Divide by the common factor of 5.

$$\frac{\overset{1}{\cancel{5}}}{8} \times \frac{2}{\underset{3}{\cancel{15}}}$$

STEP 2 Divide by the common factor of 2.

$$\frac{\overset{1}{\cancel{5}}}{\underset{4}{\cancel{8}}} \times \frac{\overset{1}{\cancel{2}}}{\underset{3}{\cancel{15}}}$$

STEP 3 Multiply.

$$\frac{1}{4} \times \frac{1}{3} = \frac{1}{12}$$

SOLUTION $\mathbf{\frac{5}{8} \times \frac{2}{15} = \frac{1}{12}}$

To multiply mixed numbers, first convert each mixed number to an **improper fraction.**

EXAMPLE 3

What is $6\frac{5}{9} \times 4\frac{2}{3}$?

STRATEGY **Convert the mixed numbers to improper fractions.**

STEP 1 Convert $6\frac{5}{9}$ to an improper fraction.

$6 \times 9 = 54$

$54 + 5 = 59$

$6\frac{5}{9} = \frac{59}{9}$

STEP 2 Convert $4\frac{2}{3}$ to an improper fraction.

$4 \times 3 = 12$

$12 + 2 = 14$

$4\frac{2}{3} = \frac{14}{3}$

STEP 3 Multiply.

$$\frac{59}{9} \times \frac{14}{3} = \frac{826}{27}$$

STEP 4 Convert the improper fraction to a mixed number.

$826 \div 27 = 30 \text{ R}16$

SOLUTION $\mathbf{6\frac{5}{9} \times 4\frac{2}{3} = 30\frac{16}{27}}$

COACHED EXAMPLE

Mary Ann is making jam to give as gifts. So far, she has filled $2\frac{2}{3}$ boxes. Of the jars in boxes, $\frac{1}{2}$ contain raspberry jam. How many boxes of raspberry jam are there?

THINKING IT THROUGH

First convert the ____________ to an ____________.

Simplify the fractions by dividing ______ and ______ by 2.

Multiply the numerators. ____________

Multiply the denominators. ____________

Convert the improper fraction to a mixed number.

So, ______ boxes contain jars of raspberry jam.

Lesson Practice

Choose the correct answer.

1. What is $\frac{5}{12} \times \frac{3}{8}$?

A $\frac{15}{90}$

B $\frac{5}{32}$

C $\frac{2}{3}$

D $\frac{5}{6}$

2. When you multiply a fraction less than one by a whole number, which is true?

A The product will always be a mixed number.

B The product will always be a fraction.

C The product will always be greater than the whole number.

D The product will always be less than the whole number.

3. Poppy learned that $\frac{2}{3}$ of her classmates have pets. Of those who have pets, $\frac{3}{8}$ have cats. What fraction of her classmates has cats?

A $\frac{1}{8}$

B $\frac{1}{4}$

C $\frac{1}{3}$

D $\frac{1}{2}$

4. Luciana is going to spin both spinners and then multiply the fractions. Which is **NOT** one of the products she can make?

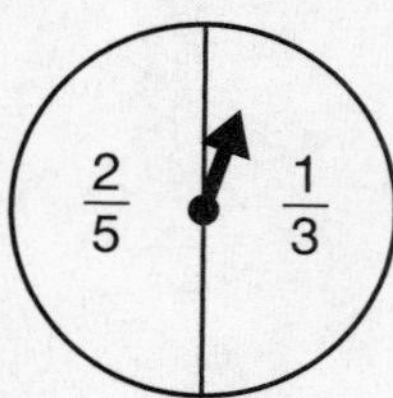

A $\frac{1}{10}$

B $\frac{1}{6}$

C $\frac{1}{5}$

D $\frac{3}{5}$

5. What is $8\frac{3}{4} \times 7\frac{2}{5}$?

A $64\frac{1}{4}$

B $64\frac{1}{2}$

C $64\frac{3}{4}$

D 65

6. Two-fifths of Martin's CD collection is made up of Irish music. Of the Irish music CDs, $\frac{1}{4}$ are instrumental. What fraction of Martin's CD collection is instrumental Irish music?

A $\frac{1}{10}$

B $\frac{1}{5}$

C $\frac{3}{10}$

D $\frac{3}{4}$

7. The outdoor club planned to hike $5\frac{7}{10}$ miles to their campsite. After they had hiked $\frac{1}{3}$ of that distance, they stopped to take cover from the rain. How far did they hike before stopping?

A $1\frac{2}{5}$

B $1\frac{2}{3}$

C $1\frac{7}{10}$

D $1\frac{9}{10}$

8. Mr. Farley drives $12\frac{2}{3}$ miles to work. After he drove $\frac{3}{5}$ of the way, he got a flat tire. How far did he drive before getting the flat tire?

A $7\frac{2}{5}$ miles

B $7\frac{3}{5}$ miles

C 8 miles

D $8\frac{1}{10}$ miles

OPEN-ENDED ITEM

9. Of the dolls in Karenna's collection, $\frac{5}{6}$ are antiques. Of the antique dolls, $\frac{2}{3}$ have brown hair.

What fraction of Karenna's dolls is antique with brown hair? Write your answer in simplest form.

____

Explain how you determined your answer.

____

____

____

____

Lesson

7 Divide Fractions and Mixed Numbers

GLCEs: N.MR.6.01, N.FL.06.02, N.FL.06.04, N.FL.06.10

Getting the Idea

Dividing fractions is the same as multiplying by the **reciprocal** of the divisor. To find the reciprocal of a divisor, switch the numerator and denominator.

EXAMPLE 1

What is $\frac{7}{12} \div \frac{4}{9}$?

STRATEGY **Write the reciprocal of the divisor and multiply.**

STEP 1 Write the reciprocal of $\frac{4}{9}$.

Switch the numerator and denominator of $\frac{4}{9}$ to get $\frac{9}{4}$.

STEP 2 Multiply by the reciprocal.

$$\frac{7}{\cancel{12}_{4}} \times \frac{\cancel{9}^{3}}{4} = \frac{21}{16}$$

STEP 3 Convert the improper fraction to a mixed number.

$21 \div 16 = 1 \text{ R}5$

$\frac{21}{16} = 1\frac{5}{16}$

SOLUTION $\mathbf{\frac{7}{12} \div \frac{4}{9} = 1\frac{5}{16}}$

In a **unit fraction**, a fraction with a numerator of 1, the reciprocal will be a whole number.

EXAMPLE 2

What is $6 \div \frac{1}{8}$?

STRATEGY **Write the reciprocal of the divisor and multiply.**

STEP 1 Write the reciprocal of $\frac{1}{8}$.

Switch the numerator and denominator of $\frac{1}{8}$, which is $\frac{8}{1}$ or 8.

STEP 2 Multiply by the reciprocal.

$6 \times 8 = 48$

SOLUTION $\mathbf{6 \div \frac{1}{8} = 48}$

You can also divide a fraction by a whole number. If the divisor is a whole number, the reciprocal is a unit fraction.

EXAMPLE 3

What is $\frac{7}{10} \div 7$?

STRATEGY **Write the reciprocal of the divisor and multiply.**

STEP 1 Write the reciprocal of 7.

Switch the numerator and denominator of 7 or $\frac{7}{1}$, which is $\frac{1}{7}$.

STEP 2 Multiply by the reciprocal.

$$\frac{\overset{1}{\cancel{7}}}{10} \times \frac{1}{\underset{1}{\cancel{7}}} = \frac{1}{10}$$

SOLUTION $\mathbf{\frac{7}{10} \div 7 = \frac{1}{10}}$

When you divide mixed numbers, first convert the mixed numbers to improper fractions and then multiply by the reciprocal of the divisor.

EXAMPLE 4

What is $3\frac{1}{3} \div 6\frac{1}{4}$?

STRATEGY **Convert the mixed numbers to improper fractions. Write the reciprocal of the divisor and multiply.**

STEP 1 Convert the mixed numbers to improper fractions.

$$3\frac{1}{3} = \frac{10}{3}$$

$$6\frac{1}{4} = \frac{25}{4}$$

STEP 2 Find the reciprocal of the divisor.

The reciprocal of $\frac{25}{4}$ is $\frac{4}{25}$.

STEP 3 Simplify if possible.

$$\frac{\overset{2}{\cancel{10}}}{3} \times \frac{4}{\underset{5}{\cancel{25}}}$$

STEP 4 Multiply.

$$\frac{2}{3} \times \frac{4}{5} = \frac{8}{15}$$

SOLUTION $3\frac{1}{3} \div 6\frac{1}{4} = \frac{8}{15}$

COACHED EXAMPLE

Colette has a piece of yarn that is 24 inches long. She needs to cut it into $\frac{3}{4}$-inch pieces. How many pieces will she have?

THINKING IT THROUGH

Write the dividend as a fraction. ______

Find the reciprocal of the divisor. ______

Simplify. ______

Multiply the fractions. ______

The product is ______.

So, Colette will have ______ $\frac{3}{4}$-inch pieces of yarn.

Lesson Practice

Choose the correct answer.

1. What is $\frac{3}{4} \div \frac{5}{8}$?

A $\frac{15}{32}$

B $\frac{4}{5}$

C $1\frac{1}{5}$

D $1\frac{2}{5}$

2. What is true about the quotient of $\frac{1}{3} \div 3\frac{4}{5}$?

A It will be less than both the dividend and divisor.

B It will be greater than both the dividend and divisor.

C It will be greater than the divisor, but less than the dividend.

D It will be greater than the dividend, but less than the divisor.

3. Judy needs to measure 4 cups of oatmeal with a $\frac{1}{3}$-cup measure. She wants to know how many times she must fill the $\frac{1}{3}$-cup measure. What number sentence can you write to represent the situation?

A $\frac{1}{4} \times \frac{1}{3}$?

B $4 \times \frac{1}{3}$?

C $\frac{1}{3} \div 4$?

D $4 \div \frac{1}{3}$?

4. Russell volunteers at the animal shelter 6 hours each month. He stays for $\frac{3}{4}$ hour each time. How many times does he volunteer each month?

A 6

B 8

C $8\frac{1}{4}$

D $8\frac{1}{2}$

5. What is $10\frac{1}{2} \div 3$?

A $2\frac{1}{2}$

B $3\frac{1}{4}$

C $3\frac{1}{2}$

D $3\frac{3}{4}$

6. Which division problem has the *greatest* quotient?

A $5 \div \frac{2}{3}$

B $\frac{2}{3} \div 5$

C $4 \div \frac{5}{6}$

D $\frac{5}{6} \div 4$

7. The nature trail in the park is $2\frac{2}{5}$ miles long. There are 6 benches spaced evenly along the trail. What is the distance between benches?

A $\frac{1}{5}$ mile

B $\frac{2}{5}$ mile

C $\frac{7}{12}$ mile

D $\frac{2}{3}$ mile

8. When you divide a whole-number by a divisor less than 1, which sentence is true?

A The quotient will be greater than the divisor and the dividend.

B The quotient will be less than the dividend and the divisor.

C The quotient will be less than the divisor, but greater than the dividend.

D The quotient will be greater than the divisor, but less than the dividend.

OPEN-ENDED ITEM

9. Rosie is making a cross-stitch wall hanging that is 9 feet long. Every $\frac{1}{3}$ foot, she wants to change colors.

How many times will Rosie change colors? ________

Explain how you determined your answer.

____

____

____

____

8 Estimation with Whole Numbers

GLCEs: N.FL.06.14

Getting the Idea

Sometimes it is not necessary to know an exact answer. In those situations, an **estimate**, an answer close to the exact answer, is all that is needed. One way to estimate is to **round** numbers to a specific place.

To round a number, look at the digit to the right of the place that you are rounding. If the digit is 5 or greater, round up to the next digit in that place. If the digit is less than 5, round down. In either case, replace the lesser digits with zeros.

When rounded to the nearest thousand, 4,527 rounds to 5,000 because the hundreds digit is 5. When rounded to the nearest hundred, 4,527 rounds to 4,500 because the tens digit is less than 5.

EXAMPLE 1

The population of Burton is 30,926. The population of East Grand Rapids is 10,482. About what is the total population of both towns?

STRATEGY **Round each number to the ten thousands and then compute.**

STEP 1 Choose an operation.

"Total" indicates addition.

STEP 2 Round each number to the ten thousands.

Look at the digit in the thousands place.

30,926 rounds to 30,000 because $0 < 5$.

10,482 rounds to 10,000 because $0 < 5$.

STEP 3 Add the rounded numbers.

$30{,}000 + 10{,}000 = 40{,}000$

SOLUTION **The total population of Burton and East Grand Rapids is about 40,000.**

EXAMPLE 2

Room and board at the University of Chicago costs $9,623 per year. At Philadelphia University, room and board costs $7,782 per year. About how much more does room and board cost at the University of Chicago than at Philadelphia University?

STRATEGY **Round each number to its greatest place and then compute.**

STEP 1 Choose an operation.

"How much more" indicates subtraction.

STEP 2 Round each number to its greatest place: thousands.

Look at the digits in the hundreds place.

9,623 rounds to 10,000 because $6 > 5$.

7,782 rounds to 8,000 because $7 > 5$.

STEP 3 Subtract the rounded numbers.

$10{,}000 - 8{,}000 = 2{,}000$.

SOLUTION **Room and board costs about $2,000 more at the University of Chicago than at Philadelphia University.**

Sometimes it is only necessary to find an estimate of a product. Estimates of products can be found by rounding.

To estimate the product of a 2-digit factor by a 1-digit factor, round the 2-digit number to the nearest ten and then multiply by the 1-digit factor. To estimate the product of greater numbers, you can round each factor to its greatest place.

EXAMPLE 3

The local ice rink can seat 275 people. If the seats are filled for 34 hockey games in a row, about how many people attended these games?

STRATEGY **Round each number to its greatest place and then multiply.**

STEP 1 Round the 3-digit factor to its greatest place: hundreds.

275 rounds to 300 because $7 > 5$.

STEP 2 Round the 2-digit factor to its greatest place: tens.

34 rounds to 30 because $4 < 5$.

STEP 3 Multiply the rounded numbers.

$300 \times 30 = 9{,}000$

SOLUTION **About 9,000 people attended the hockey games.**

To estimate quotients in division problems, use **compatible numbers**. Compatible numbers are numbers that can easily be divided mentally.

EXAMPLE 4

A bookstore made $1,426 in one week selling a new author's book. The book cost $23. About how many copies were sold that week?

STRATEGY **Find compatible numbers and then divide.**

STEP 1 Find a pair of compatible numbers for 23 and 1426.

20 is close to 23.

1,400 is close to 1,426.

STEP 2 Divide the compatible numbers.

$1{,}400 \div 20 = 70$

SOLUTION **The bookstore sold about 70 of the new author's books.**

You can use estimation to check if answers are reasonable. You can quickly tell if you made a place-value error when computing.

EXAMPLE 5

Stella said that 59,154 + 35,728 is equal to 84,882. Is her sum reasonable?

STRATEGY **Estimate to see if an answer is reasonable.**

STEP 1 Round each addend to its second greatest place to get an estimate.

Round to the nearest thousand. Look at the digits in the hundreds place.

59,154 rounds to 59,000 because $1 < 5$.

35,728 rounds to 36,000 because $7 > 5$.

STEP 2 Add the rounded numbers.

59,000 + 36,000 = 95,000

SOLUTION **Stella's sum is not reasonable.**

COACHED EXAMPLE

In 2004 in the United States, there were 56,514 people employed by the Department of Transportation and 32,693 people employed in the U.S. courts. About how many more people worked for the Department of Transportation than for the courts?

THINKING IT THROUGH

Which word indicates an estimate? ____________

Do you need to add or subtract? ____________

Which place will you round to? ____________

What does 56,514 round to? ____________

What does 32,693 round to? ____________

Subtract the rounded numbers. ____________ – ____________ = ____________

So, there were about ____________ more people employed by the Department of Transportation than by the U.S. courts in 2004.

Lesson Practice

Choose the correct answer.

1. In 2002, China's commercial catch of fish was 45,869. In 2003, the catch was 47,298. Which is the *best* estimate of the total catch for both years?

A 90,000

B 91,000

C 92,000

D 93,000

2. The population of Montana in 2004 was 926,865. The population of Alaska was 655,435. To the nearest ten thousand, about how many more people lived in Montana than Alaska?

A 260,000

B 270,000

C 280,000

D 290,000

3. Stuart multiplied $583 \times 47 = 27{,}401$. Using estimation, which sentence is correct?

A Stuart's product is reasonable.

B Stuart's product is not reasonable because the estimated product is in hundred thousands.

C Stuart's product is not reasonable because the estimated product is in thousands.

D Stuart's product is not reasonable because he picked the wrong numbers to round.

4. There were 18 performances of a summer concert, which were attended by a total of 4,770 people. About the same number of people attended each concert. Which is the *best* estimate for the number of people who attended each concert?

A 200

B 220

C 240

D 300

5. Miguel scored 4,650 points while playing a video game on Saturday. On Sunday, he scored 6,435 points. Which is the *best* estimate for the number of points he scored that weekend?

A 10,000

B 11,000

C 12,000

D 13,000

6. The population density of the country Vanuatu is 44 people per square mile. It has an area of 4,710 square miles. Which is the *best* estimate for the number of people who live in Vanuatu?

A 160,000

B 180,000

C 200,000

D 250,000

7. Which is the *best* estimate for the product 583 × 72?

   A 3,500
   B 4,200
   C 35,000
   D 42,000

8. In 2005, the median price of a house in Detroit was $169,200. The median price of a house in Lansing was $143,600. Which is the *best* estimate for how much more did the median price of a house cost in Detroit than in Lansing?

   A $20,000
   B $25,000
   C $30,000
   D $35,000

OPEN-ENDED ITEM

9. In 1990, the population of Gladwin was 21,896. In 2004, the population was 27,172.

   Which will give a better estimate for how much the population grew between 1990 and 2004, rounding to the nearest ten thousand or to the nearest thousand?

   ____

   Explain your answer.

   ____
   ____
   ____
   ____
   ____
   ____

9 Estimation with Decimals

GLCEs: N.FL.06.14

Getting the Idea

To estimate with decimals, round as you would with whole numbers. You can round to any place value.

EXAMPLE 1

A new clothing store made $4,725.28 the first day it was open. The second day, it made $3,895.62. Estimate, to the nearest hundred, the total amount the store made in the first two days.

STRATEGY **Round to the nearest hundred and then add.**

STEP 1 Round 4,725.28 to the nearest hundred.

The number to the right of the hundreds place is 2.

$2 < 5$, so 4,725.28 rounds to 4,700.

STEP 2 Round 3,895.62 to the nearest hundred.

The number to the right of the hundreds place is 9.

$9 > 5$, so 3,895.62 rounds to 3,900.

STEP 3 Add the rounded numbers.

$4{,}700 + 3{,}900 = 8{,}600$

SOLUTION **The store made about $8,600.00 the first two days it was open.**

Remember that rounding to a lesser place value will give a more precise estimate.

EXAMPLE 2

Ali had \$27.54 when she went to the mall. She bought a book for \$8.95. About how much does she have left?

STRATEGY **Round to the nearest dollar and then subtract.**

STEP 1 Round \$27.54 to the nearest dollar.

The number to the right of the ones place is 5.

$5 = 5$, so \$27.54 rounds to \$28.

STEP 2 Round \$8.95 to the nearest dollar.

The number to the right of the ones place is 9.

$9 > 5$, so \$8.95 rounds to \$9.

STEP 3 Subtract the rounded numbers.

$\$28 - \$9 = \$19$

SOLUTION **Ali has about \$19.00 left.**

EXAMPLE 3

Mr. Washington earns \$32.85 per hour. If he worked 35.25 hours last week, about how much money did he earn?

STRATEGY **Round to the nearest ten dollars and then multiply.**

STEP 1 Round \$32.85 to the nearest ten dollars.

The number to the right of the tens place is 2.

$2 < 5$, so \$32.85 rounds to \$30.

STEP 2 Round \$35.25 to the nearest ten dollars.

The number to the right of the tens place is 5.

$5 = 5$, so \$35.25 rounds to \$40.

STEP 3 Multiply the rounded numbers.

$\$30 \times \$40 = \$1,200$

SOLUTION **Mr. Washington made about \$1,200.00 last week.**

To estimate quotients, use compatible numbers. Compatible numbers are numbers that can easily be divided mentally.

EXAMPLE 4

The Nolan family drove 473.25 miles on vacation. Their average speed was 57.3 miles per hour. About how many hours did they drive?

STRATEGY **Find compatible numbers and then divide.**

STEP 1 Find a pair of compatible numbers for 473.25 and 57.3

480 is close to 473.28.

60 is close to 57.3.

STEP 2 Divide the compatible numbers.

$480 \div 60 = 8$

SOLUTION **The Nolan family drove about 8 hours.**

COACHED EXAMPLE

Amanda's town got 1.85 inches of rain in March. Her friend Emily's town got 3.24 inches of rain the same month. About how much more rain did Emily's town get in March than Amanda's town?

THINKING IT THROUGH

Will rounding to the nearest whole number give a reasonable estimate? ______

Which place will you round to? ______

What does 1.85 round to? ______

What does 3.24 round to? ______

Subtract the rounded numbers. ☐ − ☐ = ☐

So, Emily's town got about ______ more rain in March than Amanda's town.

Lesson Practice

Choose the correct answer.

1. Mrs. Warren spent $150.82 at the grocery store, $19.56 at the hardware store, and $24.12 at the drugstore. Which is the *best* estimate for the total amount that she spent?

A $194.00

B $195.00

C $196.00

D $197.00

2. The average annual precipitation for Sault Ste. Marie, Michigan, was 34.67 inches. The average annual precipitation for Denver, Colorado, was 15.81 inches. Which is the *best* estimate for the difference in precipitation between the two towns?

A 17 inches

B 18 inches

C 19 inches

D 20 inches

3. Lisa wants to exchange $65.57 in American dollars for Indian rupees. One American dollar is worth 45.26 rupees. Which is the *best* estimate for the rupees Lisa will receive?

A 2,970

B 2,990

C 3,000

D 3,050

4. A music CD is 57.54 minutes long. If there are 17 songs of about the same length, about how long is each song?

A 2 minutes

B 3 minutes

C 4 minutes

D 5 minutes

5. The greatest annual precipitation in South America was 523.6 inches. The greatest annual precipitation in Asia was 467.4 inches. Which is the *best* estimate for the difference between the greatest annual precipitation on the two continents?

A 45 inches

B 48 inches

C 50 inches

D 57 inches

6. An ERJ-135 aircraft can fly 357 miles per hour. About how far could it fly in 2.8 hours?

A 9,000 miles

B 1,080 miles

C 1,020 miles

D 1,400 miles

7. Oliver's family drove 266 miles from Detroit to Chicago. Their average speed was 59.7 miles per hour. Which is the *best* estimate for how long the trip took?

A 2 hours

B 3 hours

C 5 hours

D 6 hours

8. A movie was 2.15 hours long. About how many minutes long was the movie?

A 120 minutes

B 150 minutes

C 160 minutes

D 180 minutes

OPEN-ENDED ITEM

9. In 2004, Americans spent $91.6 billion on foreign travel and $37.4 billion on recreation.

Which will give a better estimate for how much more was spent on foreign travel than recreation, rounding to the nearest ten billion or to the nearest one billion?

____

Explain your answer.

____

____

____

____

____

____

Lesson

10 Estimation with Mixed Numbers

GLCEs: N.F.L.06.14

Getting the Idea

To estimate sums and differences with mixed numbers, you can round to the nearest $\frac{1}{2}$ or whole number. To round a mixed number to the nearest whole number, use $\frac{1}{2}$ as a benchmark. If the fraction part is $\frac{1}{2}$ or greater, round up to the next whole number. Otherwise, simply remove the fraction part.

EXAMPLE 1

A jewelry maker is making two necklaces. She needs $16\frac{3}{4}$ inches of chain for one and $12\frac{1}{8}$ inches for the other. About how much chain does she need altogether?

STRATEGY **Round to the nearest whole number and then compute.**

STEP 1 Round $16\frac{3}{4}$ to the nearest whole number.

$\frac{3}{4} > \frac{1}{2}$, so $16\frac{3}{4}$ rounds to 17.

STEP 2 Round $12\frac{1}{8}$ to the nearest whole number.

$\frac{1}{8} < \frac{1}{2}$, so $12\frac{1}{8}$ rounds to 12.

STEP 3 Add the rounded numbers.

$17 + 12 = 29$

SOLUTION **The jewelry maker needs about 29 inches of chain.**

To round to the nearest $\frac{1}{2}$, follow these rules:

If the fraction part is less than $\frac{1}{4}$, remove the fraction part of the mixed number.

If the fraction part is $\frac{3}{4}$ or greater, round to the next whole number.

If the fraction part is equal to or greater than $\frac{1}{4}$ but less than $\frac{3}{4}$, round to $\frac{1}{2}$.

EXAMPLE 2

Tessa decided to keep track of the growth of the sunflowers in her garden. One day the tallest sunflower was $12\frac{2}{5}$ cm, and the shortest was $4\frac{7}{8}$ cm. To the nearest $\frac{1}{2}$ cm, estimate the difference in height between the two sunflowers.

STRATEGY **Round to the nearest $\frac{1}{2}$ and then compute.**

STEP 1 Round $12\frac{2}{5}$ to the nearest $\frac{1}{2}$.

Since $\frac{2}{5}$ is greater than $\frac{1}{4}$ but less than $\frac{3}{4}$, round $12\frac{2}{5}$ to $12\frac{1}{2}$.

STEP 2 Round $4\frac{7}{8}$ to the nearest $\frac{1}{2}$.

Since $\frac{7}{8}$ is greater than $\frac{3}{4}$, round $4\frac{7}{8}$ to 5.

STEP 3 Subtract the rounded numbers.

$12\frac{1}{2} - 5 = 7\frac{1}{2}$

SOLUTION **The difference in height between Tessa's tallest and shortest sunflowers was $7\frac{1}{2}$ cm.**

When estimating the product or quotient of a mixed number and a whole number, you can round or use compatible numbers.

EXAMPLE 3

Florence earns \$23 per hour. When she gets a raise, she will earn $1\frac{2}{3}$ times that amount. About how much will Florence earn per hour after getting a raise?

STRATEGY **Round each factor to its greatest place. Then multiply.**

STEP 1 Round each factor to its greatest place.

23 rounds to 20.

$1\frac{2}{3}$ rounds to 2.

STEP 2 Multiply the rounded numbers.

$20 \times 2 = 40$

SOLUTION **Florence will earn about \$40 per hour after her raise.**

EXAMPLE 4

Mr. Ziel has an 11-foot-long piece of corkboard in his classroom. He wants to put up a piece of artwork every $2\frac{2}{5}$ feet. About how many pieces of artwork can Mr. Ziel put up?

STRATEGY **Find compatible numbers and then divide.**

STEP 1 Write the problem.

$11 \div 2\frac{2}{5}$

STEP 2 Use compatible numbers to estimate.

10 is close to 11.

2 is close to $2\frac{2}{5}$.

STEP 3 Divide the compatible numbers.

$10 \div 2 = 5$

SOLUTION **Mr. Ziel can put up about 5 pieces of artwork.**

COACHED EXAMPLE

Nathan has $26 in his savings account. He plans to have $3\frac{3}{4}$ of this amount in two months. About how much money will Nathan have in two months?

THINKING IT THROUGH

First, find a ______ number for ______.

______ is close to 26.

Find a compatible number for ______.

Multiply. ______ × ______ = ______

So, Nathan will have about ______ in two months.

Lesson Practice

Choose the correct answer.

1. On a camping trip, Bill and Ted hiked $3\frac{5}{8}$ miles in the morning and $5\frac{2}{3}$ miles in the afternoon. About how far did they hike that day, rounded to the nearest $\frac{1}{2}$?

A $8\frac{1}{2}$ miles

B 9 miles

C $9\frac{1}{2}$ miles

D 10 miles

2. Javier is baking with a recipe that calls for $6\frac{3}{4}$ cups of flour. The first step in the recipe is to set aside $2\frac{1}{3}$ cups of the flour for later. To the nearest $\frac{1}{2}$ cup, about how much flour will Javier use for the first part of the recipe?

A 3 cups

B $3\frac{1}{2}$ cups

C 4 cups

D $4\frac{1}{2}$ cups

3. Patrick is knitting a scarf. So far, it is 18 inches long. He plans to keep knitting until it is $2\frac{7}{8}$ times that long. Using compatible numbers, about how long will the scarf be when Patrick is done?

A 50 inches

B 60 inches

C 65 inches

D 70 inches

4. A small film festival lasted $15\frac{2}{3}$ hours. Each film was $2\frac{1}{4}$ hours long. About how many films were shown at the festival?

A 6

B 7

C 8

D 9

5. Valerie helps out at her mother's bakery. One day she packed cupcakes into boxes. She filled $6\frac{1}{5}$ boxes, then she had to wait for more cupcakes to cool. After the cupcakes cooled, she filled $10\frac{9}{10}$ boxes. About how many boxes did Valerie fill altogether?

A 16

B 17

C 18

D 19

6. The French club made $42 at its first fundraiser. The club hopes to make $4\frac{2}{3}$ times that amount at the next fundraiser. About how much does the club hope to make?

A $200

B $250

C $300

D $325

7. Stacey noticed that there were $6\frac{5}{8}$ packages of English muffins in the refrigerator on Monday. On Thursday, there were $3\frac{3}{8}$ packages left. To the nearest $\frac{1}{2}$, about how many packages of English muffins were eaten between Monday and Thursday?

A 2

B $2\frac{1}{2}$

C 3

D 4

8. A bakery made 32 cakes to sell by the slice. If $2\frac{2}{3}$ cakes were sold per hour, about how many hours did it take to sell all 32 cakes?

A 19

B 10

C 11

D 12

OPEN-ENDED ITEM

9. Pizza Planet hosted 3 birthday parties one weekend. At the first party, $5\frac{1}{6}$ pizzas were eaten. At the second party, $8\frac{3}{8}$ pizzas were eaten. At the third party, $3\frac{3}{4}$ pizzas were eaten.

To the nearest $\frac{1}{2}$, about how many pizzas were eaten at all three parties?

____

Explain how you determined your answer.

____

____

____

____

____

____

11 Percents

GLCEs: N.FL.06.12, N.FL.06.13

Getting the Idea

Percent means per hundred. To convert a percent to a fraction in simplest form, write the percent as the numerator over a denominator of 100. Then simplify the fraction using the GCF.

EXAMPLE 1

How can you write 75% as a fraction in simplest form?

STRATEGY **Write the percent as a fraction with a denominator of 100. Simplify.**

STEP 1 Remove the percent sign. Write the percent as a numerator over a denominator of 100.

$75\% = \frac{75}{100}$

STEP 2 Simplify the fraction using the GCF.

The GCF of 75 and 100 is 25.

Divide by $\frac{25}{25}$.

$\frac{75}{100} \div \frac{25}{25} = \frac{3}{4}$

SOLUTION $\mathbf{75\% = \frac{3}{4}}$

To convert a percent to a decimal, divide the percent by 100 and remove the percent sign. Dividing a percent by 100 is like moving the decimal point 2 places to the left. In the example above, 75% = 0.75.

To find the percent of a number, rename the percent as a decimal or a fraction. Then multiply the number by that decimal or fraction.

EXAMPLE 2

What is 30% of 120?

STRATEGY **Write the percent as a decimal and multiply.**

STEP 1 Rename 30% as a decimal.

Divide the percent by 100 and remove the percent sign.

$30 \div 100 = 0.3$

STEP 2 Multiply.

$0.3 \times 120 = 36$

SOLUTION **30% of 120 is 36.**

EXAMPLE 3

Cassie bought a book that cost $12. The tax was 5%. How much did the book cost with tax?

STRATEGY **Write the percent as a decimal and multiply. Then add the tax to the cost of the book**

STEP 1 Rename 5% as a decimal.

Divide the percent by 100 and remove the percent sign.

$5 \div 100 = 0.05$

STEP 2 Multiply.

$0.05 \times 12 = 0.6$

5% of $12 is $0.60.

STEP 3 Add the tax to the cost of the book.

$\$12 + \$0.60 = \$12.60$

SOLUTION **The book cost $12.60 with tax.**

EXAMPLE 4

An item that originally sells for $200 is on sale at 25% off. What is the sale price?

STRATEGY **Write the percent as a fraction and multiply.**

STEP 1 Rename 25% as a fraction in simplest form. $\frac{25}{100} = \frac{1}{4}$

STEP 2 Multiply. $\frac{1}{4} \times \frac{200}{1} = \frac{200}{4} = 50$

STEP 3 Subtract the discount from the original price. $200 − $50 = $150

SOLUTION **The sale price is $150.**

EXAMPLE 5

Amber wants to leave a 20% tip on a restaurant check that came to $17. How much should she leave for a tip?

STRATEGY **Write the percent as a decimal and multiply.**

STEP 1 Rename 20% as a decimal. $20\% = 0.2$

STEP 2 Multiply. $0.2 \times 17 = 3.4$

SOLUTION **A 20% tip on $17 is $3.40.**

COACHED EXAMPLE

Raina bought some new clothes for school. The total was $86.00. Sales tax was 6%. How much did Raina spend including the tax?

THINKING IT THROUGH

Convert the percent to a ______.

6 ÷ 100 = ______

______ × 86 = ______

86 + ______ = ______

So, Raina spent ______ including the tax.

Lesson Practice

Choose the correct answer.

1. What is 40% of 76?

   A 3.04
   B 23.4
   C 28.4
   D 30.4

2. Melinda's parents took her and her sister out for lunch. The bill came to \$45. If they left a 15% tip, which of the following shows how much money they left for a tip?

   A \$6.00
   B \$6.75
   C \$7.00
   D \$7.25

3. A stereo system that originally cost \$540 is on sale at 35% off. What is the sale price of the stereo system?

   A \$351
   B \$461
   C \$500
   D \$521

4. Mrs. Kim bought several items at a department store that totaled \$134.50. After the 4% tax was added, how much did Mrs. Kim spend?

   A \$137.88
   B \$138.76
   C \$139.88
   D \$188.30

5. What is 28% of 50?

   A 12
   B 14
   C 16
   D 18

6. Anne had her hair cut and colored, which cost \$70. She wants to give the stylist an 18% tip. How much will the tip be?

   A \$ 7.60
   B \$11.20
   C \$12.60
   D \$13.00

7. Terrence's father bought a new computer for $1,299. The sales tax was 6%. How much did he spend altogether?

A $1,376.94

B $1,378.94

C $1,476.94

D $2,078.40

8. Jenny's favorite store was having a 15% off sale. If she bought 2 shirts that cost $18.70 each, how much would she save?

A $4.50

B $4.61

C $5.40

D $5.61

OPEN-ENDED ITEM

9. The original price of an outdoor grill was $249. It was on sale for 20% off. Sales tax was 5%.

What was the sale price of the grill before tax? ____________

What was the total price once the tax was added? ____________

Explain the steps you took to find your answers.

____

____

____

____

Lesson

12 Represent Rational Numbers

GLCEs: N.ME.06.17, N.ME.06.18, N.ME.06.19, N.ME.06.20

Getting the Idea

A **rational number** is a number that can be written as a fraction with an integer in the numerator and a positive integer in the denominator. So a rational number is either a fraction or a negative fraction. Zero is a rational number, but it is neither negative nor positive.

EXAMPLE 1

What rational number is represented by the point on this number line?

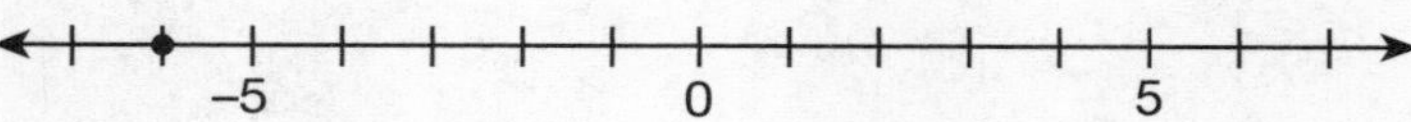

STRATEGY **Think: On a number line, negative numbers are to the left of 0.**

The point is to the left of 0, so the number is negative.

Count how many tick marks the point is from 0: 6.

SOLUTION **The point on the number line represents −6.**

EXAMPLE 2

What rational number is represented by the point on this number line?

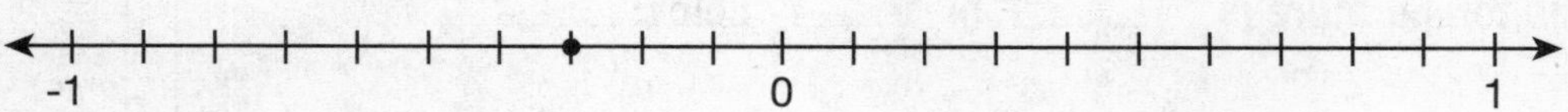

STRATEGY **First determine whether the number is positive or negative.**

The point is to the left of 0, so the number is negative.

Each time you go from one tick mark to the next it represents $\frac{1}{10}$.

Count how many tick marks the point is from 0: 3.

SOLUTION **The point on the number line represents $-\frac{3}{10}$.**

The **absolute value** of a number is the distance the number is from 0 on a number line. You can also determine the absolute value of a number by ignoring the sign. For example, the absolute value of −5 is 5. The sum of a number and its opposite is zero. For example, −3 + 3 = 0.

EXAMPLE 3

What is the absolute value of −8?

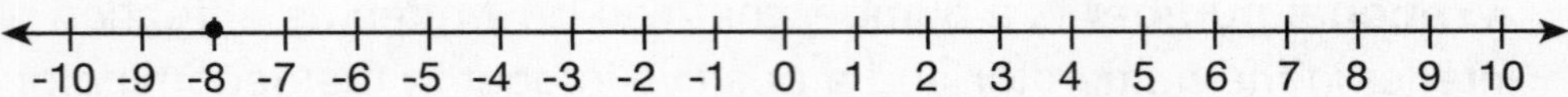

STRATEGY **Find the absolute value by determining the distance from 0 on a number line.**

STEP 1 Count the number of units −8 is from 0.

−8 is 8 units from 0.

SOLUTION **So, the absolute value of −8 is 8.**

COACHED EXAMPLE

What temperature is shown on this thermometer?

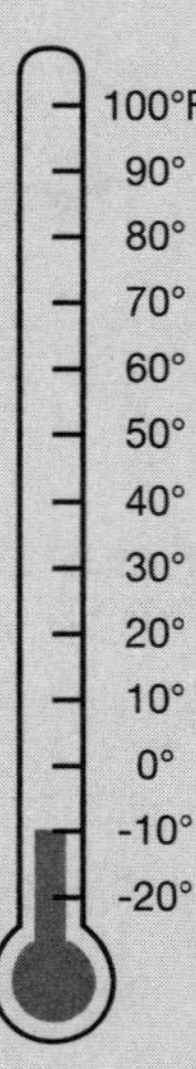

THINKING IT THROUGH

You can read the thermometer like a ____________ line.

What rational number is shown on the thermometer? ______

How do you read the temperature? ______ below ______

So, the temperature is ______°F, or ______ below ______.

Lesson Practice

Choose the correct answer.

1. What is the absolute value of -10?

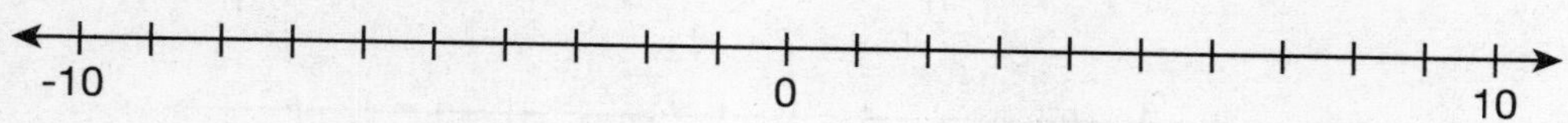

A -1

B -10

C 1

D 10

---

2. What rational number is represented by the point on this number line?

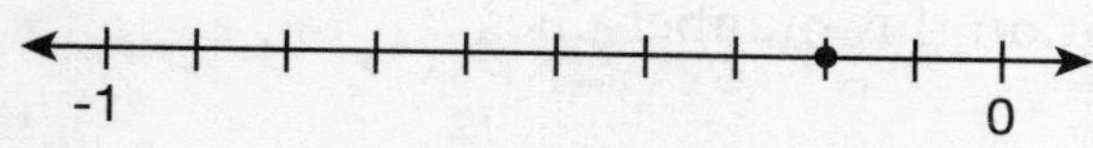

A $-\frac{3}{10}$

B $-\frac{2}{10}$

C $\frac{2}{10}$

D $\frac{3}{10}$

3. Which of the following is **NEITHER** a positive **NOR** a negative rational number?

A -3

B 0

C 1

D 10

4. Which is **NOT** a rational number?

A -4.85

B $-\frac{9}{10}$

C $\frac{6}{0}$

D 3.14

5. What is $-9 + 9$?

A 0

B 9

C 10

D 18

6. Which number line shows the absolute value of -7?

A 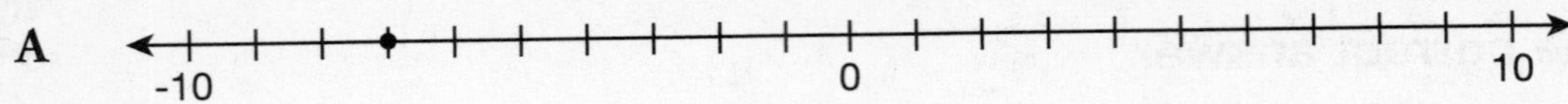

B 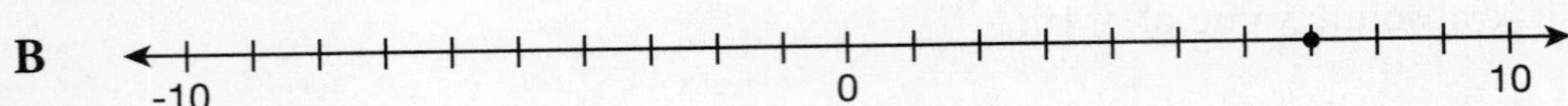

C 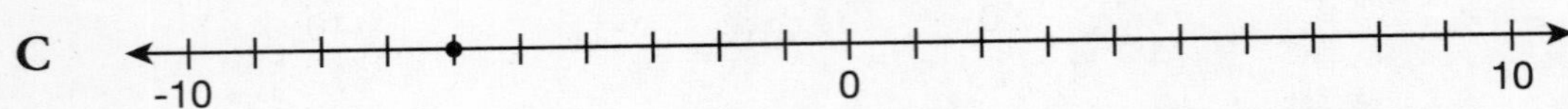

D 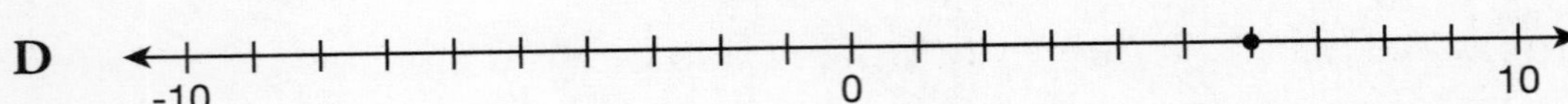

OPEN-ENDED ITEM

7. What rational number is represented by the point on this number line?

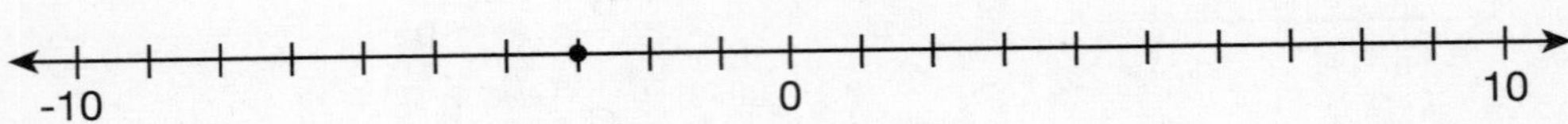

____

What is its absolute value?

____

Explain why.

____

____

____

Write a situation using the rational number.

____

____

____

Lesson

13 Order Rational Numbers

GLCEs: N.ME.06.05, N.ME.06.06

Getting the Idea

Rational numbers, can be compared and ordered by using a number line. The farther a number is to the right on a number line, the greater its value. Therefore, any positive number is greater than any negative number.

EXAMPLE 1

Order the following numbers from least to greatest by placing them on the number line: $\frac{5}{10}$, $-\frac{1}{10}$, $-\frac{5}{10}$, $\frac{8}{10}$.

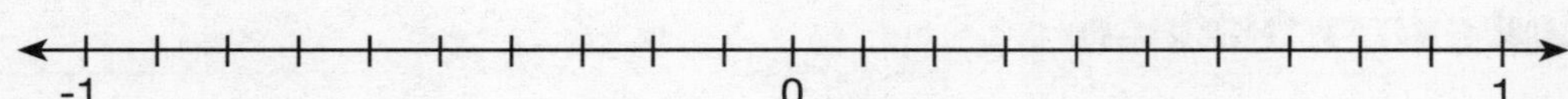

STRATEGY **Place the numbers on the number line to determine their order.**

STEP 1 Place $\frac{5}{10}$ on the number line.

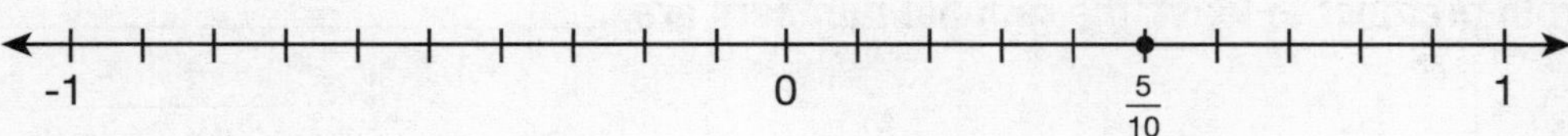

STEP 2 Place $-\frac{1}{10}$ on the number line.

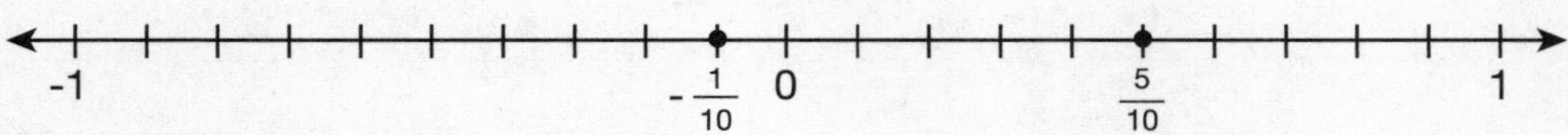

STEP 3 Place $-\frac{5}{10}$ on the number line.

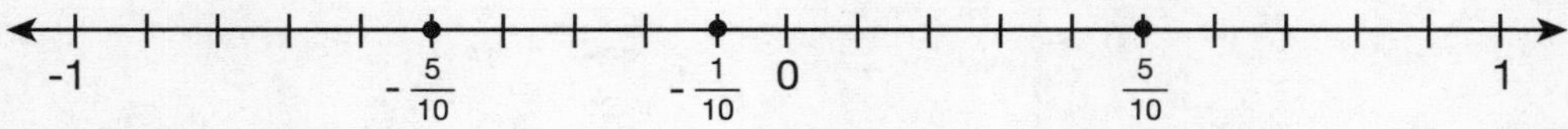

STEP 4 Place $\frac{8}{10}$ on the number line.

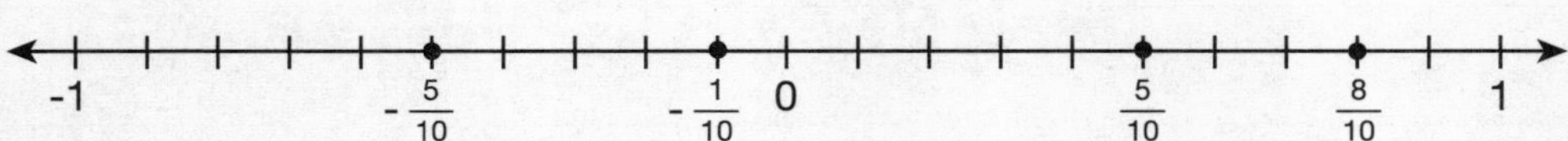

SOLUTION **The order of the numbers from least to greatest is $-\frac{5}{10}$, $-\frac{1}{10}$, $\frac{5}{10}$, $\frac{8}{10}$.**

EXAMPLE 2

What is another way to represent the rational numbers in Example 1?

STRATEGY **Rename the fractions as decimals.**

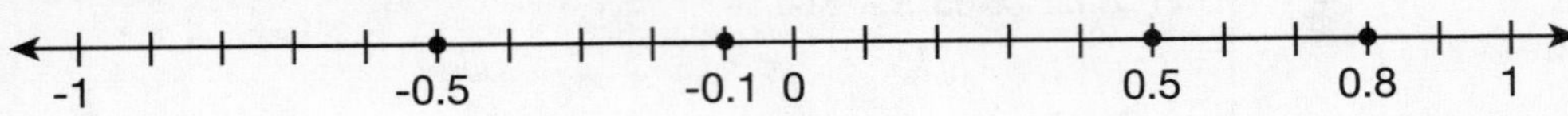

SOLUTION **So, the rational numbers can also be represented as −0.5, −0.1, 0.5, 0.8.**

COACHED EXAMPLE

Use a number line to order these rational numbers from greatest to least. −4, 6, −3, 2, −1, 7

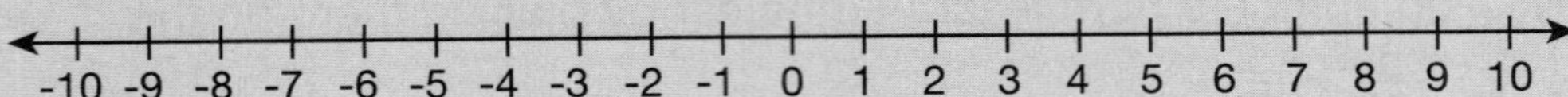

THINKING IT THROUGH

How do you know which side of 0 to put the numbers? ______________________

How does the question ask you to order the numbers?
from ____________ to ____________

From greatest to least, the rational numbers are ______________________.

Lesson Practice

Choose the correct answer.

1. Which shows the rational numbers in order from *least* to *greatest*?

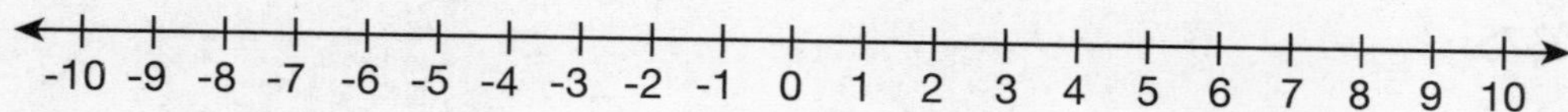

A 0.9, 0.7, −0.1, −0.7, −0.9

B −0.9, −0.7, −0.1, 0.7, 0.9

C −0.1, −0.7, −0.9, 0.7, 0.9

D −0.1, −0.7, 0.7, −0.9, 0.9

2. The table shows some high temperatures in Jorge's town. Which day was the temperature the lowest?

Day	High Temperatures
Monday	10°F
Tuesday	0°F
Wednesday	-12°F
Thursday	-6°F
Friday	2°F

A Tuesday

B Wednesday

C Thursday

D Friday

3. Which shows the rational numbers in order from *least* to *greatest*?

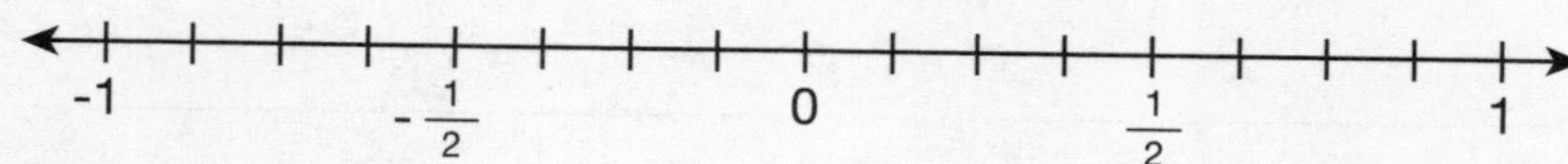

A $-\frac{5}{8}, -\frac{1}{4}, \frac{3}{4}, 0.25$

B $-\frac{5}{8}, -\frac{1}{4}, 0.25, \frac{3}{4}$

C $\frac{3}{4}, 0.25, -\frac{1}{4}, -\frac{5}{8}$

D $-\frac{5}{8}, -\frac{1}{4}, 0.25, \frac{3}{4}$

4. Which is $3\frac{1}{8}$ written as a decimal?

A 3.125

B 3.18

C 3.2

D 3.375

5. How is -2.6 represented as a mixed number in simplest form?

A $-2\frac{3}{50}$

B $-2\frac{3}{25}$

C $-2\frac{1}{2}$

D $-2\frac{3}{5}$

OPEN-ENDED ITEM

6. Carl says these numbers are in order from *greatest* to *least.*

$-5, 4, 3, -2, -1$

Place the numbers on the number line to see if Carl is correct.

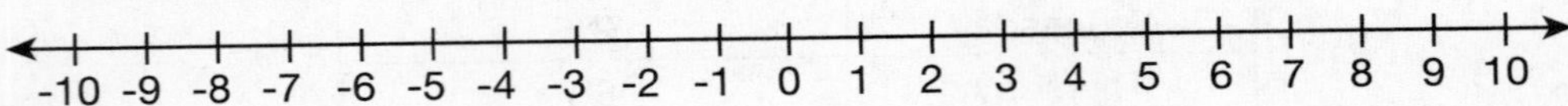

Is Carl correct? ____________

Why or why not?

____

____

____

Write the numbers in order from *least* to *greatest.*

____

Lesson

14 Add Integers

GLCEs: N.MR.06.08, N.FL.06.09

Getting the Idea

Integers are the whole numbers and their opposites.

EXAMPLE 1

What is $-4 + 6$?

STRATEGY **Use a number line to add integers.**

Start at -4. Since 6 is positive, move to the right 6 units.

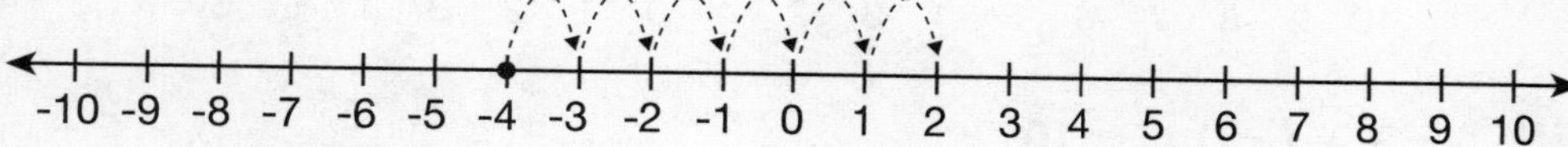

SOLUTION $\mathbf{-4 + 6 = 2}$

EXAMPLE 2

What is $-5 + 9$?

STRATEGY **Use positive and negative counters to add integers.**

STEP1 Use negative counters to represent -5. Use positive counters to represent 9.

STEP 2 The sum of an integer and its opposite is 0, so remove all the positive/negative pairs. Count the counters that are left.

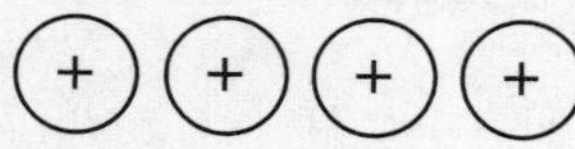

SOLUTION $\mathbf{-5 + 9 = 4}$

As the examples show, when you add a positive and a negative integer, the sign of the sum will be the same as the sign of the addend with the greatest absolute value. Two positive integers will always give a positive sum. What happens when you add two negative integers?

EXAMPLE 3

What is $-3 + (-7)$?

STRATEGY **Use the number line to add integers.**

STEP 1 Start at -3.

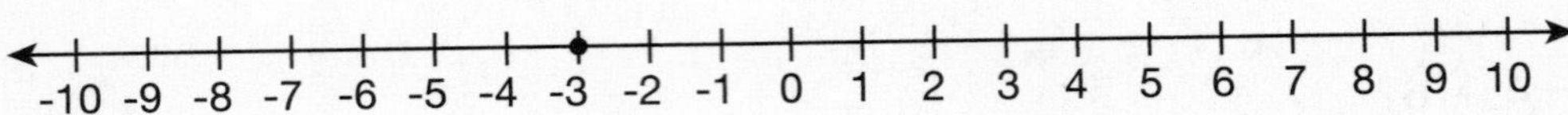

STEP 2 Since 7 is negative, move to the left 7 units.

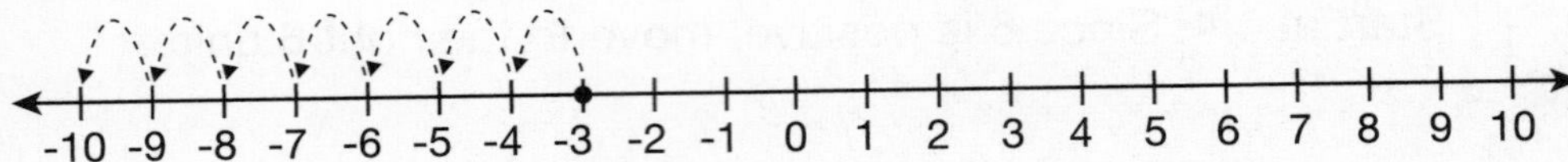

SOLUTION $\mathbf{-3 + (-7) = -10}$

When you add two negative integers, the sum is always negative.

COACHED EXAMPLE

The temperature on Monday morning was -5°F. By noon, it rose by 10°, then dropped by 6° in the evening. What was the temperature in the evening?

THINKING IT THROUGH

What is the first step to solve this problem? Add ______ + ______.

What is the next step? Add ______ to the sum.

In the evening the temperature was ______.

Lesson Practice

Choose the correct answer.

1. What is $9 + (-10)$?

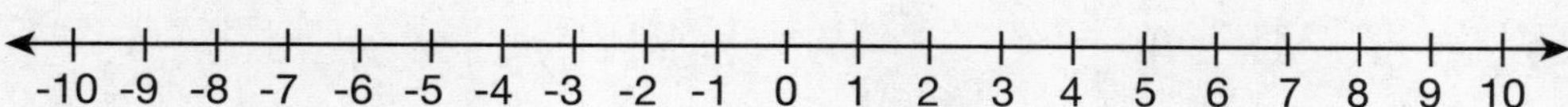

A 0

B -1

C 1

D 10

2. Frank scored 7 points in a game. Then he lost 9 points. Which number sentence represents the situation?

A $-7 + 9$

B $9 - 7$

C $7 + 9$

D $7 + (-9)$

3. Ethan is using this number line to solve $3 + (-8)$. What should his next step be?

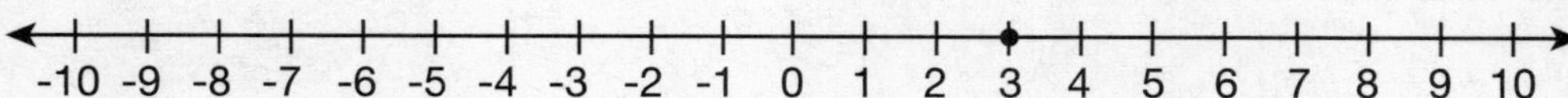

A Count 8 units to the right.

B Count 8 units to the left.

C Count 3 units to the right.

D Count 3 units to the left.

4. Which is **NOT** true?

A Adding two positive integers will give a positive sum.

B Adding a positive and a negative integer will give a sum with the sign of the number with the greater absolute value.

C Adding a positive and a negative integer will give a sum with the sign of the number with the lesser absolute value.

D Adding two negative integers will give a negative sum.

5. What is $-2 + -6$?

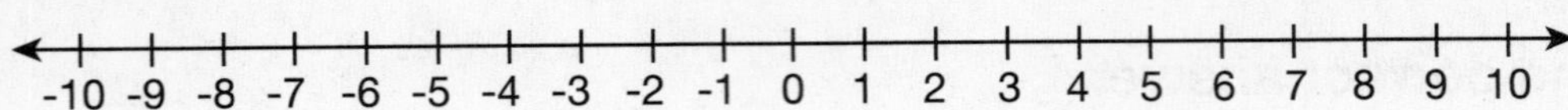

A -8 C 4

B -4 D 8

6. Which number sentence do the counters represent?

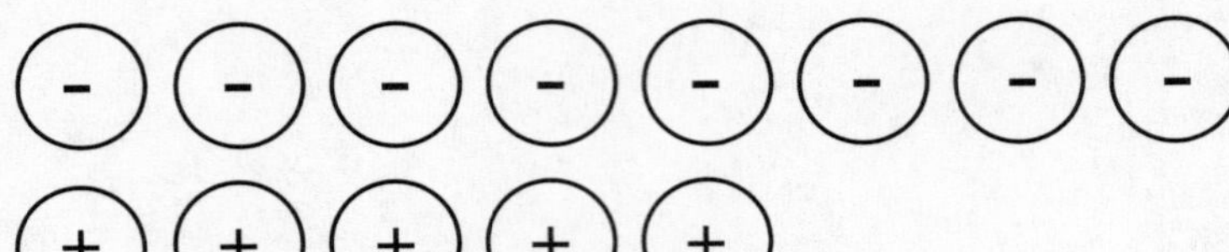

A $8 + 5$

B $-5 + 8$

C $8 - 5$

D $-8 + 5$

OPEN-ENDED ITEM

7. Keri borrowed some money from her brother. She is now $8 in debt. If she earns $10 babysitting, how much money will she have?

____

What number sentence did you write to solve the problem?

____

Explain why you solved the problem the way you did.

____

____

____

15 Subtract Integers

GLCEs: N.MR.06.08, N.FL.06.09

Getting the Idea

You can use the same methods to subtract integers that you did to add them.

EXAMPLE 1

What is 4 − 8?

STRATEGY **Use a number line to subtract integers.**

Start at 4. Move to the left 8 units.

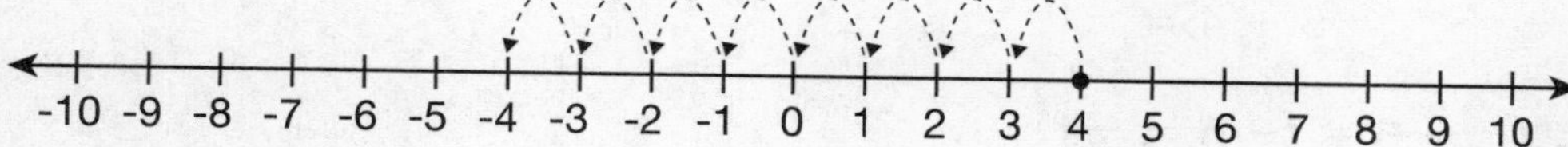

SOLUTION **4 − 8 = −4**

EXAMPLE 2

What is −6 − 2?

STRATEGY **Use negative counters.**

STEP 1 Use negative counters to represent −6.

(-) (-) (-) (-) (-) (-)

STEP 2 Add 2 negative counters. Count the total number of negative counters.

(-) (-) (-) (-) (-) (-) (-) (-)

SOLUTION **−6 − 2 = −8**

When you subtract a positive from a positive, the difference can be positive, negative, or 0. When you subtract a positive from a negative, the difference will be negative. When you subtract a negative from a positive, the difference will be positive. Subtracting a negative number is like adding a positive number.

EXAMPLE 3

What is $-5 - (-4)$?

STRATEGY **Change the subtraction problem to an addition problem.**

STEP 1 Rewrite $-5 - (-4)$ as an addition problem.

$-5 + 4$

STEP 2 Use a number line to solve the problem.

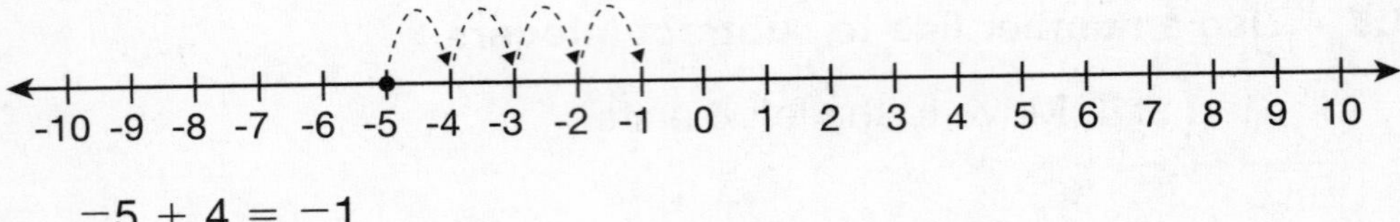

$-5 + 4 = -1$

SOLUTION $\mathbf{-5 - (-4) = -1}$

COACHED EXAMPLE

The highest recorded temperature for Sault Ste. Marie was 98°F. The lowest recorded temperature was −36°F. What is the difference between the highest and lowest temperatures?

THINKING IT THROUGH

What number sentence should you write to solve this problem? _______ − _______

Rewrite ____________ as ____________.

The difference in Sault Ste. Marie's highest and lowest temperatures is _______.

Lesson Practice

Choose the correct answer.

1. What is 6 − 10?

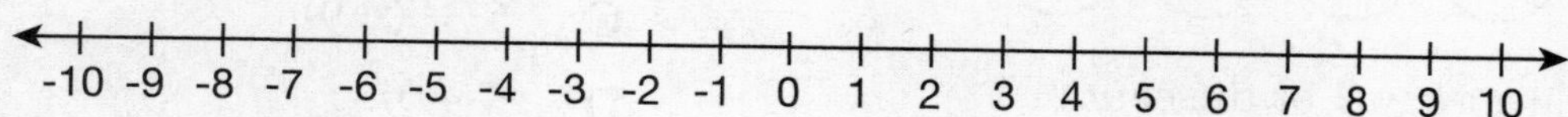

A −10
B − 4
C 0
D 4

2. Which number line represents 1 − (−5)?

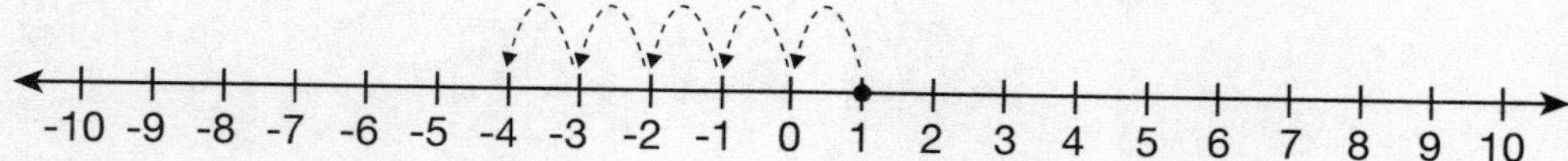

B

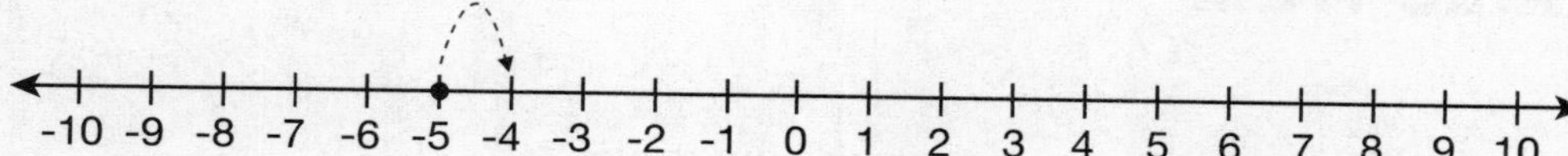

C

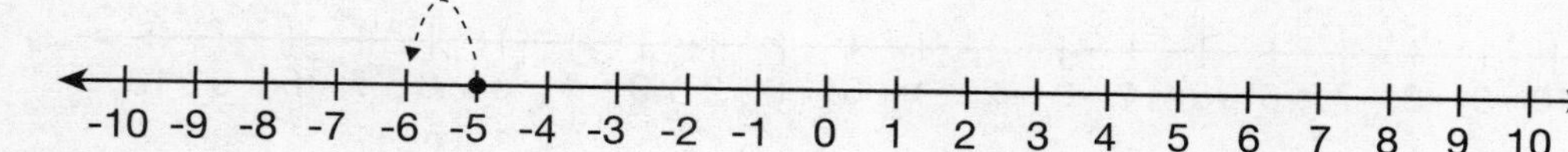

D

3. The temperature at 9 A.M. was −4°F. By noon, the temperature had decreased 5 degrees. What was the temperature at noon?

A −9°F
B −1°F
C 1°F
D 9°F

4. What is −2 − (−8)?

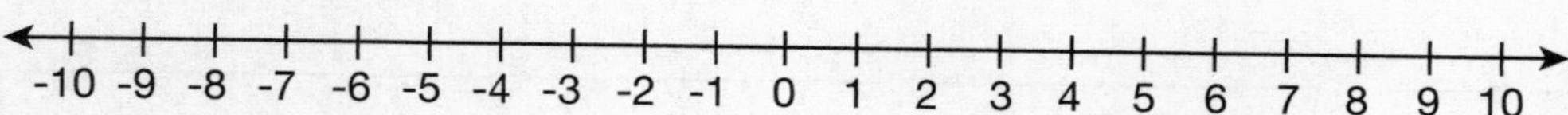

A −10
B − 6
C 6
D 10

5. Ned wants to use counters to solve $-5 - 2$. He starts with these counters. What should he do next?

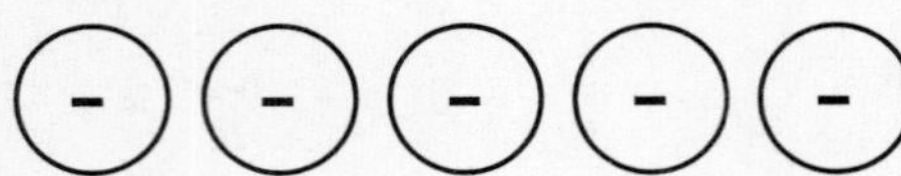

A Take away 2 of the counters.

B Add 2 positive/negative pairs of counters.

C Add 2 negative counters.

D Add 2 positive counters.

6. Which is another way to write $5 - (-9)$?

A $5 - 9$

B $9 - 5$

C $5 + (-9)$

D $5 + 9$

OPEN-ENDED ITEM

7. Use the number line to help you answer the questions.

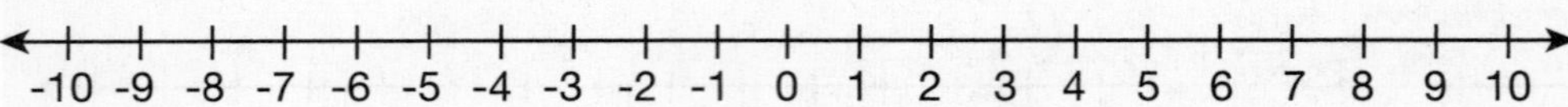

Lorie scored 4 points in a game, then she lost 9 points. How many points does she have now?

____

How many points does Lorie need to score to have a positive score again?

____

Explain how you solved the problems.

____

____

____

____

Lesson

16 Multiply and Divide Integers

GLCEs: N.FL.06.09

Getting the Idea

When multiplying integers, multiply as you would with whole numbers. The signs of the factors will determine the sign of the product. If the two factors have the same sign, the product will be positive. If the two factors have different signs, the product will be negative.

EXAMPLE 1

What is $-4 \times (-8)$?

STRATEGY **Look at the signs of the factors to determine the sign of the product.**

STEP 1 Multiply the numbers.

$4 \times 8 = 32$

STEP 2 Determine the sign of the product.

-4 and -8 have the same sign, so the product will be positive.

SOLUTION $\mathbf{-4 \times (-8) = 32}$

EXAMPLE 2

What is -5×7?

STRATEGY **Look at the signs of the factors to determine the sign of the product.**

STEP 1 Multiply the numbers.

$5 \times 7 = 35$

STEP 2 Determine the sign of the product.

-5 and 7 have different signs, so the product will be negative.

SOLUTION $\mathbf{-5 \times 7 = -35}$

The rules for dividing integers are the same as for multiplying integers.

EXAMPLE 3

What is $-10 \div (-2)$?

STRATEGY **Look at the signs of the dividend and divisor to determine the sign of the quotient.**

STEP 1 Divide the numbers.

$10 \div 2 = 5$

STEP 2 Determine the sign of the quotient.

-10 and -2 have the same sign, so the quotient will be positive.

SOLUTION $\mathbf{-10 \div (-2) = 5}$

EXAMPLE 4

What is $9 \div (-3)$?

STRATEGY **Look at the signs of the dividend and divisor to determine the sign of the quotient.**

STEP 1 Divide the numbers.

$9 \div 3 = 3$

STEP 2 Determine the sign of the quotient.

9 and -3 have different signs, so the quotient will be negative.

SOLUTION $\mathbf{9 \div (-3) = -3}$

COACHED EXAMPLE

When Eric woke up, the temperature was 0°F. The temperature fell by 3° per hour for 4 hours. What was the temperature after 4 hours?

THINKING IT THROUGH

What number sentence should you write to solve this problem? ____________.

What is the product of the numbers? ____________

Are the signs of the factors the same or different? ____________

So, the temperature was ______ after 4 hours.

Lesson Practice

Choose the correct answer.

1. What is $-26 \div -2$?

A -14
B -13
C 13
D 14

2. If a diver dove 3 feet per second, how far under water would she be after 12 seconds?

A -38 feet
B -36 feet
C 36 feet
D 38 feet

3. Harold is going to spin both spinners and then multiply the integers. Which is **NOT** a product that he could get?

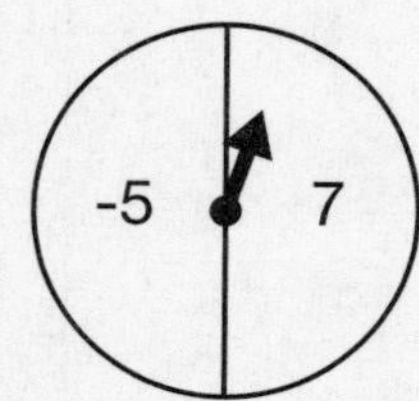

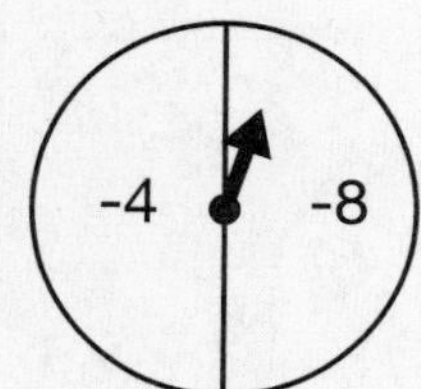

A -56
B -28
C 20
D 28

4. What is -6×9?

A -54
B -45
C 45
D 54

5. What is the missing number in the table?

Rule: Divide by 3	
-21	?
-12	-4
9	3
18	6

A -8
B -7
C 7
D 8

6. After a 4-month period, Mr. Frankel's company was \$348 in debt. If the company accumulated an equal amount of debt each month, how much was the company's debt in 1 month?

A $-\$87$
B $-\$77$
C \$77
D \$87

OPEN-ENDED ITEM

7. What is the rule for this table?

Rule:	
-10	50
-5	25
15	-75
20	-100

____

Explain how you found your answer.

____

____

____

____

MEAP Review

Choose the correct answer.

1 Hannah travels $9\frac{1}{2}$ miles to school each day. Her friend Beth travels $5\frac{3}{4}$ miles to school. How much closer does Beth live to school than Hannah?

A $2\frac{3}{4}$ miles

B $3\frac{1}{2}$ miles

C $3\frac{3}{4}$ miles

D $4\frac{1}{4}$ miles

2 Which shows the rational numbers in order from *least* to *greatest*?

A −5, −7, −9, 6, 8

B −5, 6, −7, 8, −9

C −9, 8, −7, 6, −5

D −9, −7, −5, 6, 8

3 A pilot flew 3,469 miles from New York to London. Then she flew 1,564 miles from London to Moscow. How far did the pilot fly altogether?

A 5,033 miles

B 5,034 miles

C 5,035 miles

D 5,036 miles

4 Felicity wants to read 7 books over the summer. She plans to read $\frac{2}{3}$ of a book each week. How many weeks will it take her to read the 7 books?

A 10 weeks

B $10\frac{1}{2}$ weeks

C 11 weeks

D $11\frac{1}{2}$ weeks

5 Which of the following is **NEITHER** a positive **NOR** a negative rational number?

A $-\frac{7}{8}$

B −0.09

C 0

D 10.22

6 Which is another way to write 3 − (−10)?

A 3 + 10

B 10 − 3

C 3 − 10

D 3 + (−10)

7 Daniel needs to measure 6 cups of water with a $\frac{1}{4}$-cup measure. He wants to know how many times he must fill the $\frac{1}{4}$-cup measure. Which expression can you use to represent the situation?

A $\frac{6}{1} \div \frac{1}{4}$

B $\frac{1}{4} \div 6$

C $\frac{6}{1} \times \frac{1}{4}$

D $\frac{4}{1} \times \frac{1}{6}$

8 The average depth of the Pacific Ocean is 12,925 feet. The average depth of the South China Sea is 4,802 feet. About how much deeper is the Pacific Ocean than the South China Sea?

A 7,000 feet

B 8,000 feet

C 9,000 feet

D 10,000 feet

9 What is $2\frac{2}{3} \times 10\frac{1}{8}$?

A 27

B $27\frac{1}{3}$

C $27\frac{2}{3}$

D 28

10 Which is another way to represent the rational number $\frac{8}{10}$?

A 0.008

B 0.08

C 0.8

D 8.1

11 Which rational number is represented by the point on this number line?

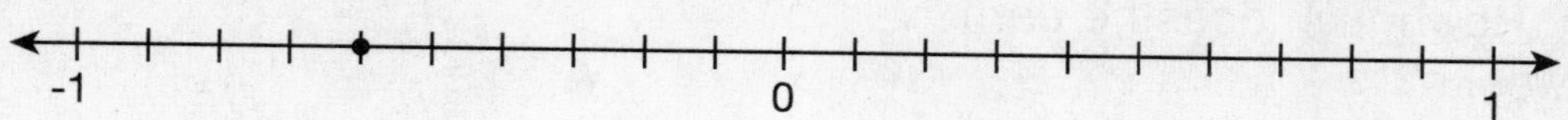

A −0.7

B −0.6

C −0.5

D 0.6

12 What is 258.94 ÷ 2.5?

A 10.36

B 103.576

C 104.476

D 1,035.76

13 What is the absolute value of −2?

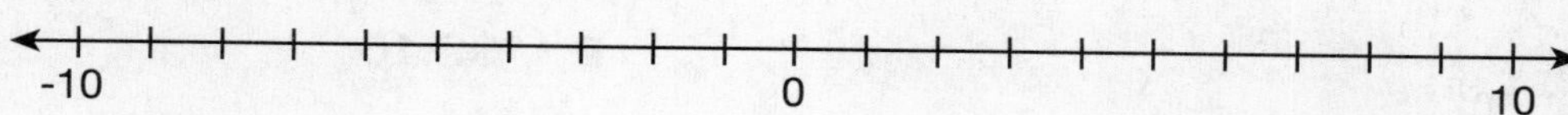

A −0.2

B −2

C 0.2

D 2

14 Which is **NOT** a rational number?

A −3.02

B $-\frac{5}{9}$

C $\frac{8}{0}$

D 12.25

15 What is 48 ÷ −6?

A −8

B −7

C 7

D 8

16 Mr. Vargas earns $876.35 per week. How much does he earn in 6 weeks?

A $ 4,926.80

B $ 5,258.10

C $19,710.20

D $21,032.40

17 Pauline's mother drives $12\frac{3}{5}$ miles to work each day. After driving $\frac{2}{3}$ of the distance, she drops Pauline off at school. How far does Pauline live from school?

A 5 miles

B $8\frac{1}{5}$ miles

C $8\frac{2}{5}$ miles

D $8\frac{4}{5}$ miles

18 Ingrid is on vacation in Mexico and needs to exchange $35 for new pesos. One American dollar equals 11.29 new pesos. How many new pesos will Ingrid receive?

A 88.62

B 90.32

C 381.75

D 395.15

19 What is $\frac{5}{8} + \frac{3}{4}$?

A $\frac{2}{3}$

B $1\frac{3}{8}$

C $1\frac{1}{2}$

D $2\frac{3}{8}$

20 Wanda took a taxi while on vacation. The fare was $12.80, and she wanted to tip the cabdriver 15%. How much was the tip?

A $1.52

B $1.85

C $1.92

D $2.10

21 Bernie takes Spanish classes for 10 hours each month. Each class is $1\frac{1}{4}$ hours long. How many classes does Bernie take each month?

A 6

B 7

C 8

D 9

22 What is 43% of 258?

A 11.1

B 18.06

C 86.82

D 110.94

23 In 2004, the population of Muskegon was 174,401. The population of Marquette was 64,874. How many more people lived in Muskegon than in Marquette?

A 109,527

B 109,627

C 110,637

D 110,647

24 In the Netherlands, cell phone use per 100 people is 76.8. In the United States, it is 54.3. Which is the *best* estimate for the difference in cell phone use between the two countries?

A 22 per 100 people

B 23 per 100 people

C 24 per 100 people

D 25 per 100 people

OPEN-ENDED ITEM

25 Mr. Goldstein took his family out for dinner. The check came to $124.00. He had a coupon for 20% off, and he wanted to leave a 15% tip.

How much was the check after the discount?

____

About how much tip did Mr. Goldstein leave?

____

Explain how you found your answers.

____

____

____

____

26 Mr. Clark worked 42 hours last week at $28.50 per hour.
Mr. Walt worked 35 hours at $32.44 per hour.

Who earned more money, Mr. Clark or Mr. Walt?

____

How much more?

____

Explain how you found your answer.

____

____

____

____

____

CHAPTER 2 Algebra

17 Expressions and Equations

GLCEs: A.FO.06.03, A.FO.06.04, A.FO.06.05, A.FO.06.06, A.FO.06.07

Getting the Idea

An **expression** is a group of numbers and symbols that shows a mathematical quantity. An **equation** is a statement that says two quantities are equal. A **variable** can be used to represent a number in an expression or equation.

EXAMPLE 1

Michelle writes 15 pages in her journal each week, plus an extra 5 pages on her birthday. Write an expression to represent the situation.

STRATEGY **Use a variable to write an expression.**

STEP 1 Choose a variable for the unknown number.

Let w equal the number of weeks Michelle has been writing.

STEP 2 Write the expression.

$15w + 5$

SOLUTION **The expression is $15w + 5$.**

You can evaluate an expression by substituting a number for the variable. If an expression contains more than one operation, follow the **order of operations**.

EXAMPLE 2

Evaluate $7x - 5$ for $x = 4$.

STRATEGY **Substitute a number for a variable to evaluate an expression.**

STEP 1 Rewrite the expression, substituting 4 for x.

$7 \times 4 - 5$

STEP 2 Evaluate the expression.

$7 \times 4 - 5 =$

$28 - 5 = 23$

SOLUTION $7x - 5 = 23$ **when** $x = 4$.

An expression can be simplified by combining **like terms**.

EXAMPLE 3

Simplify $10x + 6y + 4x$.

STRATEGY **Simplify using like terms.**

STEP 1 Find the variable that occurs more than once.

x

STEP 2 Add the parts of the expression that contain the variable x.

$10x + 4x = 14x$

STEP 3 Rewrite the expression.

$14x + 6y$

SOLUTION $10x + 6y + 4x$ **can be simplified as** $14x + 6y$.

COACHED EXAMPLE

Mr. Alvarez bought concert tickets for his family from an Internet site. Each ticket cost $65, and there was an $8 handling fee per order. If he bought 6 tickets, how much did Mr. Alvarez spend?

THINKING IT THROUGH

Write an expression to represent the situation. ____________________

Substitute ______ for the variable.

Solve the equation: 65 × ______ + ______ = __________.

So, Mr. Alvarez spent __________.

Lesson Practice

Choose the correct answer.

1. Which situation can be represented by the expression $4d + 6$?

- **A** Kristin worked 10 hours each day.
- **B** Kristin worked 6 hours each day after working 4 hours the first day.
- **C** Kristin worked 4 hours the first day and 6 hours the second day.
- **D** Kristin worked 4 hours each day after working 6 hours the first day.

2. What is $6p + 50r + 12p$, simplified using like terms?

- **A** $18p + 50r$
- **B** $65r + 12p$
- **C** $6p + 62r$
- **D** $5r - 12$p

Use the information to answer questions 3 and 4.

Pete has 5 less than 4 times as many model cars as Horatio.

3. Which expression represents this situation?

- **A** $5h - 4$
- **B** $4h - 5$
- **C** $5h + 4$
- **D** $4h + 5$

4. If Horatio has 3 model cars, how many model cars does Pete have?

- **A** 7
- **B** 11
- **C** 17
- **D** 19

5. Evaluate $20x + 8$ for $x = 3$.

- **A** 31
- **B** 52
- **C** 68
- **D** 84

6. Bianca puts $10 in a savings account each month and an extra $20 when she received money for her birthday. Which expression represents the situation?

- **A** $20m + 10$
- **B** $20m - 10$
- **C** $10m - 20$
- **D** $10m + 20$

Use the information to answer questions 7 and 8.

The Downtown Theater has 8 more than 3 times as many seats as the Uptown Theater.

7. Which expression represents this situation?

   A $3u - 8$

   B $8u - 3$

   C $3u + 8$

   D $8u + 3$

8. If the Uptown Theater has 40 seats, how many seats does the Downtown Theater have?

   A 112

   B 128

   C 312

   D 328

OPEN-ENDED ITEM

9. Bill rides his bicycle 8 miles each day. One day it rained, so he only rode 5 miles.

   Write an expression to represent the situation.

   ____

   If Bill rode for 12 days, how many miles did he ride?

   ____

   Explain how you found your answers.

   ____

   ____

   ____

   ____

18 Ordered Pairs

GLCEs: A.RP.06.02

Getting the Idea

Ordered pairs are used to name the points on a coordinate grid. A coordinate grid is divided into 4 quadrants. The quadrants are labeled on this grid.

The first number in an ordered pair tells the *x*-coordinate on the ***x*-axis**. The second number tells the *y*-coordinate on the ***y*-axis**. When plotting a point, start at the **origin**, (0, 0).

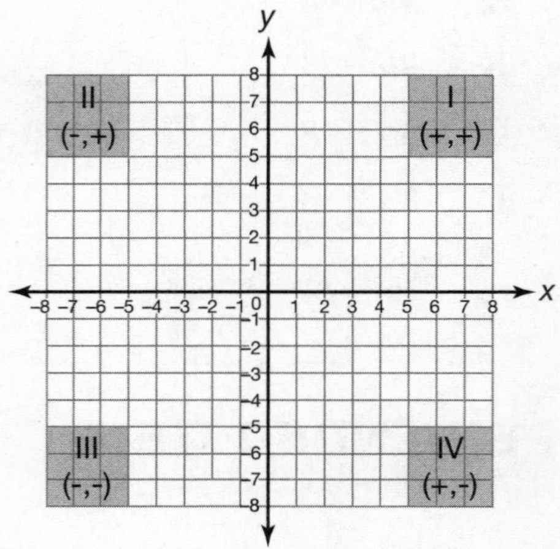

EXAMPLE 1

Plot point *A* at (4, 6) on the coordinate grid.

STRATEGY **Use ordered pairs to plot a point.**

STEP 1 Start at the origin. The first number is positive. Count 4 units to the right.

STEP 2 From 4 on the *x*-axis, count up 6 units and place point *A*.

SOLUTION

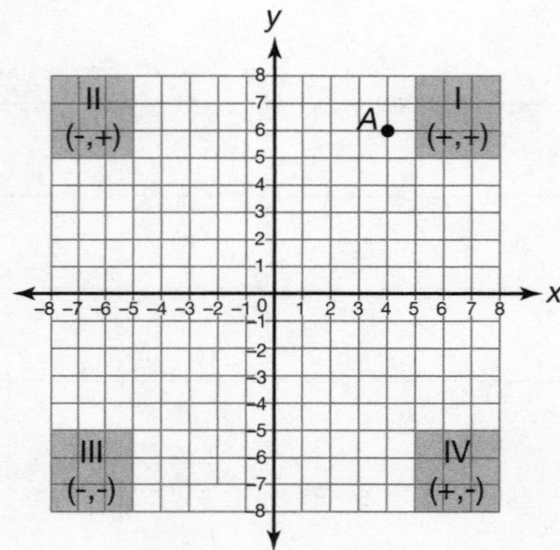

EXAMPLE 2

What ordered pair names point *B*?

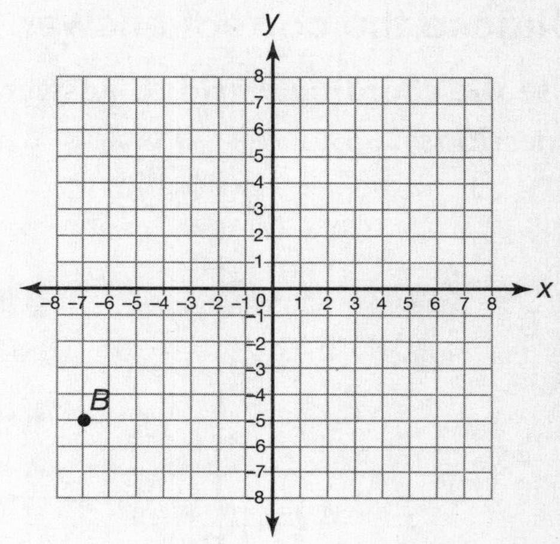

STRATEGY **Read the coordinate grid to find the ordered pair for point *B*.**

STEP 1 Since the point is to the left of the origin, the first number is negative. Determine how many units point *B* is to the left of 0.

−7

STEP 2 Since the point is below the origin, the second number is negative. Determine how many units point *B* is below 0.

−5

SOLUTION **So, the coordinate pair that names point *B* is (−7, −5).**

COACHED EXAMPLE

The grid represents streets in Brad and Cara's town. Brad's house is at (−6, 8). Cara's house is at (4, −5). Plot and label the points for both houses.

THINKING IT THROUGH

In which direction should you count for the first number in the first ordered pair? ______

In which direction should you count for the second number in the first ordered pair? ______

In which direction should you count for the first number in the second ordered pair? ______

In which direction should you count for the second number in the second ordered pair? ______

So, the points for Brad and Cara's houses look like this:

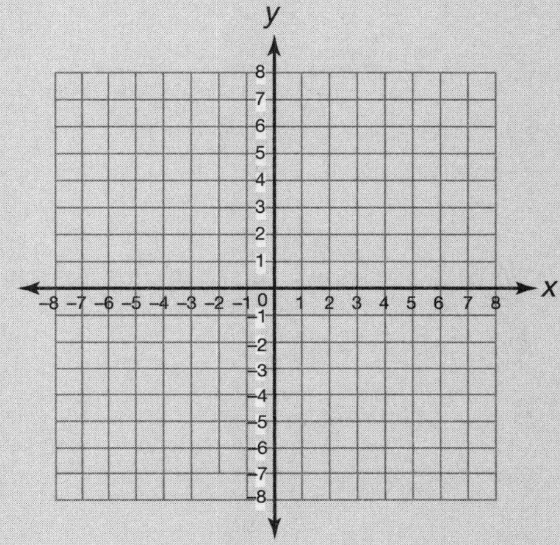

Lesson Practice

Choose the correct answer.

Use the coordinate grid to answer questions 1–3.

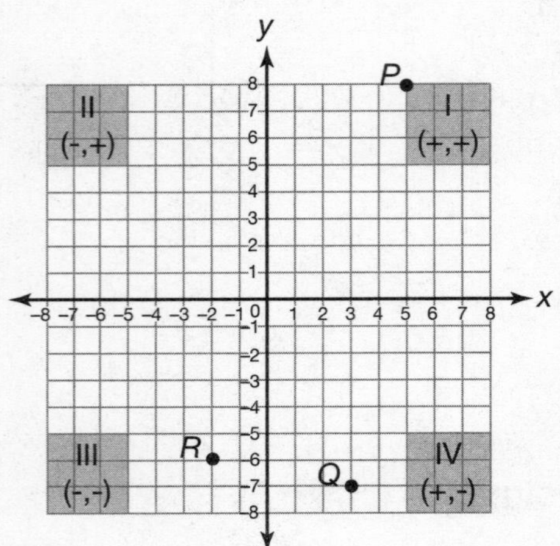

1. Which ordered pair names point P?

   A (4, 8)

   B (5, 8)

   C (4, 9)

   D (5, 9)

2. Which ordered pair names point Q?

   A (3, 7)

   B (−3, 7)

   C (3, −6)

   D (3, −7)

3. Which ordered pair names point R?

   A (−2, −6)

   B (2, −6)

   C (2, 6)

   D (−2, 6)

4. Which shows point H at (3, −5)?

   A

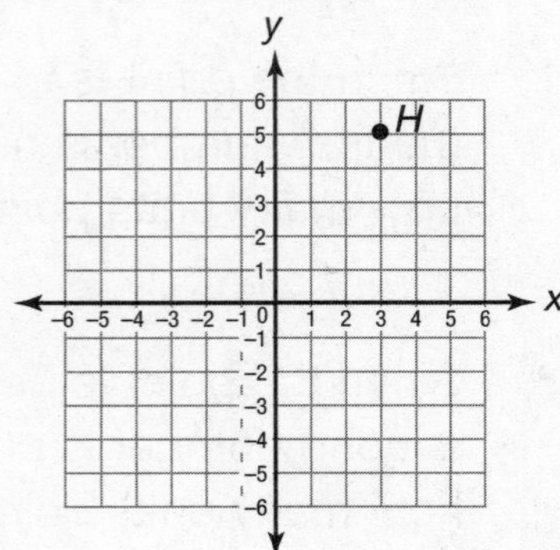

   B

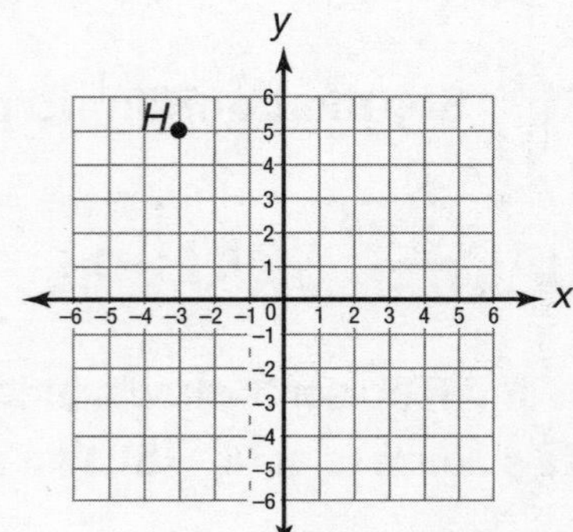

   C

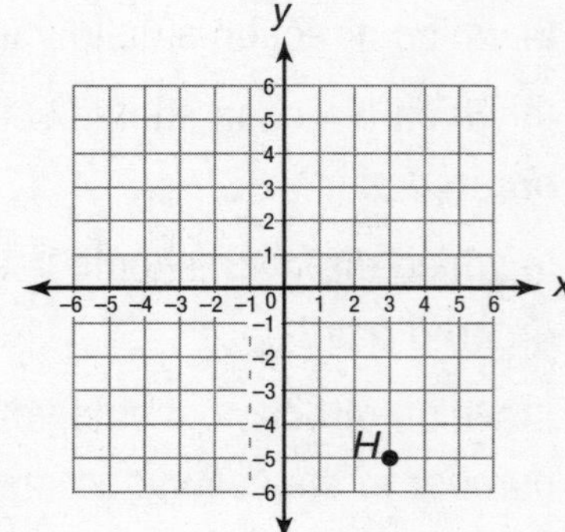

   D

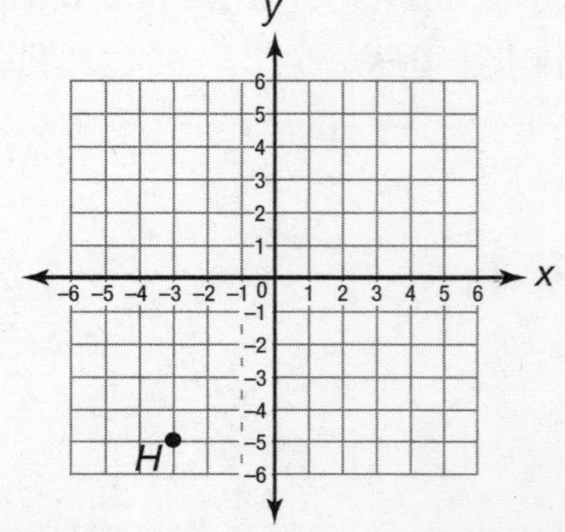

Use the coordinate grid to answer questions 5–6.

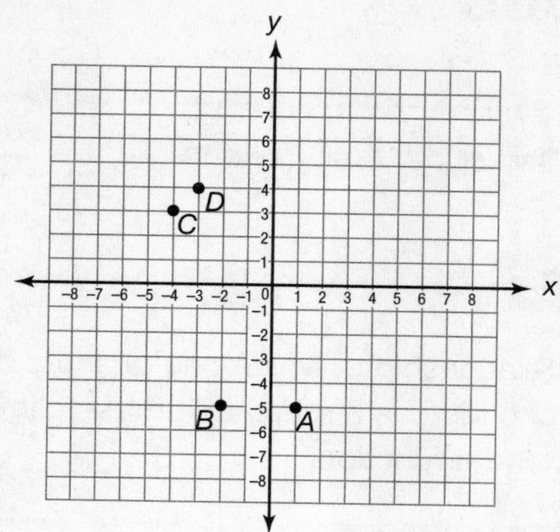

5. Which point is at $(-2, -5)$?

   A point *A** **C** point *C*
   B point *B* **D** point *D*

6. Which point is at $(-3, 4)$?

   A point *A* **C** point *C*
   B point *B* **D** point *D*

OPEN-ENDED ITEM

7. Plot the following points on the coordinate grid: $F\,(10, 8)$, $G\,(-5, 6)$, $H\,(-7, -7)$, $J\,(3, -2)$.

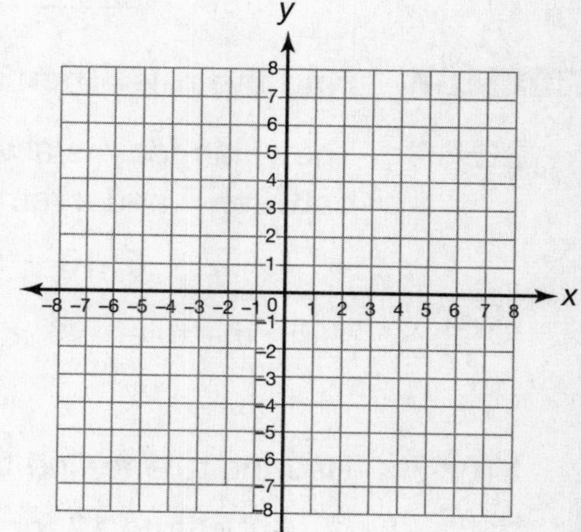

Explain how you knew which quadrant to plot the points in.

19 Functions

GLCEs: A.RP.06.08, A.PA.06.09, A.RP.06.10

Getting the Idea

A **function** is a relationship in which one quantity depends on another quantity. Each function has a rule that it must follow. You can use the rule of a function to extend a function.

EXAMPLE 1

What is the missing number in this function?

x	y
2	7
5	10
8	13
12	?

STRATEGY **Find the rule. Then use the rule to find the missing number.**

STEP 1 The value for y is always greater than the value for x. See if the difference between y and x remains the same. If it does, it is an addition function.

$7 - 2 = 5$, $10 - 5 = 5$, $13 - 8 = 5$

STEP 2 Write the rule.

$y = x + 5$

STEP 3 Use the rule to find the missing value.

Substitute 12 for x.

$y = 12 + 5$

$y = 17$

SOLUTION **The missing number is 17.**

A function can show the relationship between real-life quantities.

EXAMPLE 2

This function shows the relationship between inches and feet. If there are 168 inches, how many feet are there?

Inches	Feet
36	3
60	5
84	7
108	9

STRATEGY **Find the pattern. Then write the rule.**

STEP 1 The number of feet is less than the number of inches. The function is probably a division or a subtraction rule. Try division.

$36 \div 3 = 12$, $60 \div 5 = 12$, $84 \div 7 = 12$, $108 \div 9 = 12$

The rule is Feet = Inches ÷ 12

STEP 2 Use the rule to find the number of feet in 168 inches.

$168 \div 12 = 14$

SOLUTION **If there are 168 inches, then there are 14 feet.**

Functions can be graphed on a coordinate grid.

EXAMPLE 3

The graph shows the number of miles that a walking club walked on a Saturday. What function is represented by the graph?

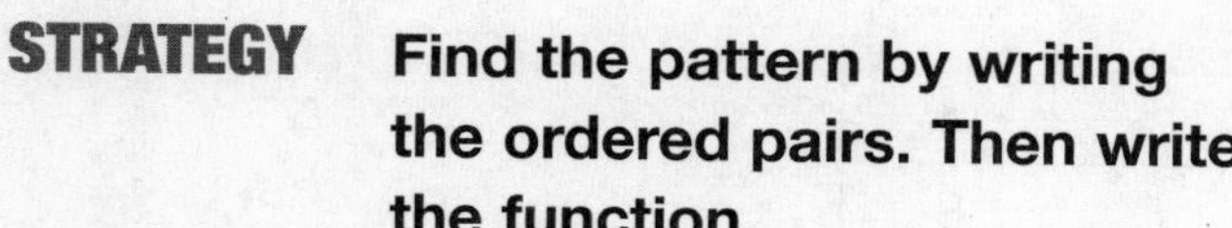

STRATEGY **Find the pattern by writing the ordered pairs. Then write the function.**

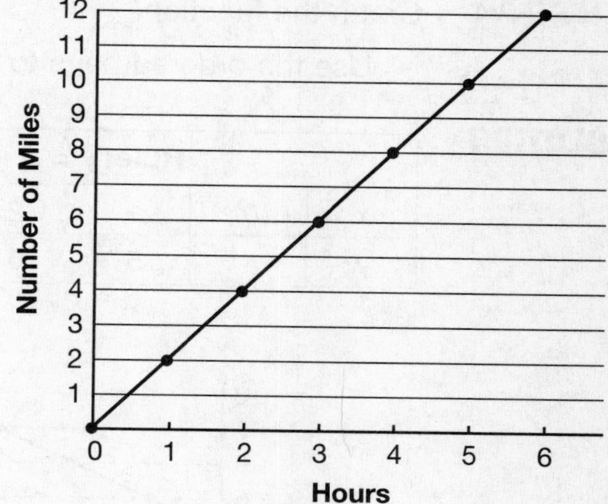

STEP 1 Write the ordered pairs using the whole number of hours.

(0, 0), (1, 2), (2, 4), (3, 6), (4, 8), (5, 10), (6, 12)

STEP 2 Find the pattern.

The value of y is 2 times the value of x.

SOLUTION **The graph represents the function $y = 2x$.**

You can use the rule of a function to complete a function table and then graph the function.

EXAMPLE 4

The rule of a function is $y = x + 4$.
Complete the function table.
Then graph the function.

Rule: $y = x + 4$					
x	0	1	2	3	4
y					

STRATEGY **Substitute each value in the table for *x* to create ordered pairs. Then graph the function.**

STEP 1 Substitute each value of *x* to find *y*.

$y = 0 + 4 = 4$, $y = 1 + 4 = 5$, $y = 2 + 4 = 6$,
$y = 3 + 4 = 7$, $y = 4 + 4 = 8$

STEP 2 Fill in the function table.

Rule: $y = x + 4$					
x	0	1	2	3	4
y	4	5	6	7	8

STEP 3 Write the ordered pairs.

(0, 4), (1, 5), (2, 6), (3, 7), (4, 8)

STEP 4 Graph the function.

Use the ordered pairs to graph the function.

SOLUTION

Rule: $y = x + 4$					
x	0	1	2	3	4
y	4	5	6	7	8

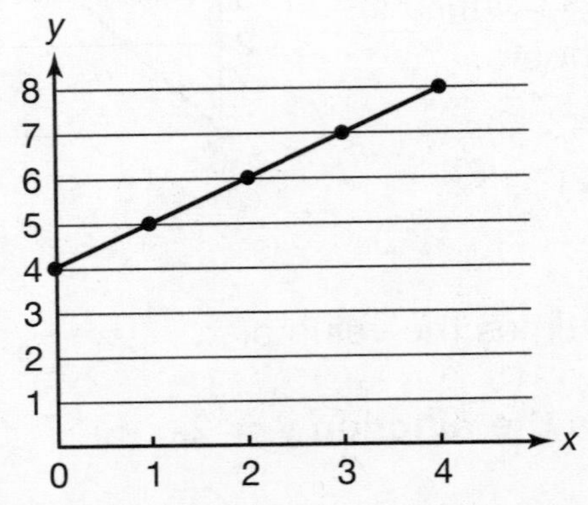

COACHED EXAMPLE

Each time the dogs at Dougie's Doggie Day Care come in from the rain, their paws are wiped clean. Write a function and then graph it to represent the number of paws that are wiped for each number of dogs up to 6 dogs.

THINKING IT THROUGH

How many paws does a dog have? ____________

What is the rule of the function? ____________

What interval will you use for the *x*-axis? ____________

What interval will you use for the *y*-axis? ____________

Complete the function table.

Dogs	1	2	3	4	5	6
Paws						

What ordered pairs can you write?

____

Graph the function.

Lesson Practice

Choose the correct answer.

1. What is the missing number in this function table?

x	*y*
8	2
12	6
20	?
28	22

A 5
B 10
C 12
D 14

2. What is the rule of this function?

x	*y*
9	3
15	5
24	8
36	12

A $y = x + 3$
B $y = x \div 3$
C $y = x - 6$
D $y = 3x$

3. Which function would you write to represent the number of fingers on a set of hands?

A $y = 5x$
B $y = 5 \div x$
C $y = 5 + x$
D $y = 5 - x$

Use the graph to answer questions 4 and 5.

The graph shows the number of miles a cycling club rode.

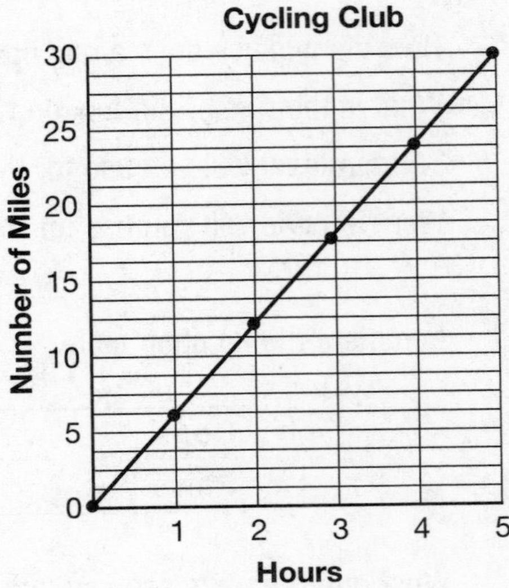

4. What is the rule of the function?

A Miles = Hours + 6
B Miles = Hours × 6
C Miles = Hours − 6
D Miles = Hours ÷ 6

5. If the members of the club cycled for a total of 8 hours, how many miles would they have cycled altogether?

A 40 miles
B 48 miles
C 56 miles
D 64 miles

6. Which is **NOT** one of the values of this function table?

Rule: $y = x \div 4$					
x	0	1	2	3	4
y					

A 0

B 0.5

C 0.8

D 1

OPEN-ENDED ITEM

7. A regular hexagon has six sides of the same length. Complete the function table for the relationship between the length of a side of a regular hexagon and its perimeter. Then graph the function for the values given.

Length of Side (in cm)	2	4	6	8	10
Perimeter (in cm)					

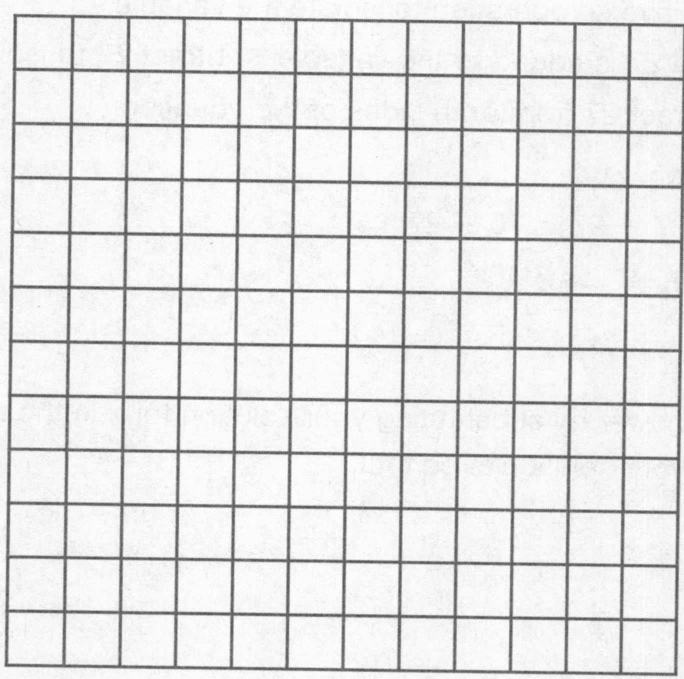

20 One-Step Equations

GLCEs: A.FO.06.11, A.FO.06.12, A.FO.06.13

Getting the Idea

An **equation** is a statement that two quantities are equal. To solve an equation requires finding what value a variable has. The strategy that is often used to solve equations is to isolate the variable. To isolate a variable in a one-step equation, use the **inverse operation** of the operation used in the equation.

When you use an inverse operation you are writing a new equation that has the same solution.

EXAMPLE 1

What is the value of x in the equation $x + 27 = 75$?

STRATEGY **Isolate the variable.**

STEP 1 Use the inverse operation to isolate the variable.

Since 27 is added to the variable, subtract 27 to isolate the variable.

Subtract 27 from both sides of the equation.

STEP 2 Subtract.

$$x + 27 - 27 = 75 - 27$$
$$x = 48$$

SOLUTION $\mathbf{x = 48}$

You can check your answer by substituting your solution for x in the original equation. Since $48 + 27 = 75$, your solution is correct.

You can use addition to solve a subtraction equation.

EXAMPLE 2

What is the value of y in the equation $y - 19 = 24$?

STRATEGY **Isolate the variable.**

STEP 1 Use the inverse operation to isolate the variable.

Since 19 is subtracted from the variable, add 19 to isolate the variable.

Add 19 to both sides of the equation.

STEP 2 Add.

$$y - 19 + 19 = 24 + 19$$

$$y = 43$$

SOLUTION $\mathbf{y = 43}$

Multiplication and division one-step equations are solved the same way as addition and subtraction one-step equations. As with addition and subtraction, when you use an inverse operation, you are writing a new equation that has the same solution.

EXAMPLE 3

What is the value of z in the equation $16z = 192$?

STRATEGY **Isolate the variable.**

STEP 1 Use the inverse operation to isolate the variable.

Since the variable is multiplied by 16, divide by 16 to isolate the variable.

Divide both sides of the equation by 16.

STEP 2 Divide.

$$16z \div 16 = 192 \div 16$$

$$z = 12$$

SOLUTION $\mathbf{z = 12}$

EXAMPLE 4

What is the value of a in the equation $a \div 7 = 36$?

STRATEGY **Isolate the variable.**

STEP 1 Use the inverse operation to isolate the variable.

Multiply both sides of the equation by 7.

STEP 2 Multiply.

$$a \div 7 \times 7 = 36 \times 7$$
$$a = 252$$

SOLUTION $a = 252$

COACHED EXAMPLE

Solve for b: $3b = 45$

THINKING IT THROUGH

You need to use the inverse operation.

Since b is multiplied by 3, you need to ____________ both sides of the equation by 3 to get b by itself.

The value of b is ______.

Lesson Practice

Choose the correct answer.

1. What is the value of c in the following equation?

$$19 + c = 62$$

A $c = 43$

B $c = 53$

C $c = 71$

D $c = 81$

2. What is the value of d in the following equation?

$$75 \div d = 5$$

A $d = 15$

B $d = 25$

C $d = 355$

D $d = 375$

3. What is the value of e in the following equation?

$$e - 38 = 17$$

A $e = 11$

B $e = 21$

C $e = 45$

D $e = 55$

4. What is the value of f in the following equation?

$$19f = 152$$

A $f = 6$

B $f = 7$

C $f = 8$

D $f = 9$

5. What is the value of g in the following equation?

$$g \div 7 = 12$$

A $g = 19$

B $g = 72$

C $g = 84$

D $g = 96$

6. What is the value of h in the following equation?

$$172 + h = 421$$

A $h = 249$

B $h = 259$

C $h = 593$

D $h = 603$

7. What is the value of j in the following equation?

$$j - 87 = 165$$

A $j = 78$

B $j = 88$

C $j = 242$

D $j = 252$

8. What is the value of k in the following equation?

$$22k = 418$$

A $k = 12$

B $k = 14$

C $k = 19$

D $k = 24$

OPEN-ENDED ITEM

9. Trista solved an equation for x. Her solution is shown below.

$x \div 8 = 280$

$x \div 8 - 8 = 280 - 8$

$x = 272$

Trista's solution is incorrect. What is the correct solution to the equation $x \div 8 = 280$? Show your work.

What error did Trista make?

Lesson

21 Two-Step Equations

GLCEs: A.FO.06.14

Getting the Idea

Solving a two-step equation is similar to solving a one-step equation in that it is necessary to isolate the variable. The first step will be to add or subtract the term without the variable to leave one side of the equation with a **coefficient** and variable. If the coefficient is an integer, the second step will be to divide to find the value of the variable.

EXAMPLE 1

What is the value of x in the equation $3x + 7 = 34$?

STRATEGY **Remove the term without a variable and then isolate the variable.**

STEP 1 Subtract 7 from both sides of the equation to remove the term.

$$3x + 7 - 7 = 34 - 7$$
$$3x = 27$$

STEP 2 Divide both sides of the equation by the coefficient to isolate the variable.

$$3x \div 3 = 27 \div 3$$
$$x = 9$$

SOLUTION $\mathbf{x = 9}$

You can check your answer by substituting your solution for x in the original equation. Since $(9 \times 3) + 7 = 34$, your solution is correct.

EXAMPLE 2

What is the value of y in the equation $9y - 6 = 75$?

STRATEGY **Remove the term without a variable and then isolate the variable.**

STEP 1 Add 6 to both sides of the equation to remove the term.

$$9y - 6 + 6 = 75 + 6$$

$$9y = 81$$

STEP 2 Divide both sides of the equation by the coefficient to isolate the variable.

$$9y \div 9 = 81 \div 9$$

$$y = 9$$

SOLUTION $y = 9$

The solution to an equation can be a fraction or a mixed number.

EXAMPLE 3

What is the value of a in the equation $4a + 3 = 16$?

STRATEGY **Remove the term without a variable and then isolate the variable.**

STEP 1 Subtract 3 from both sides of the equation to remove the term.

$$4a + 3 - 3 = 16 - 3$$

$$4a = 13$$

STEP 2 Divide both sides of the equation by the coefficient to isolate the variable.

$$4a \div 4 = 13 \div 4$$

$$a = \frac{13}{4}$$

STEP 3 Write the solution as a mixed number in simplest form.

$$\frac{13}{4} = 3\frac{1}{4}$$

SOLUTION $a = 3\frac{1}{4}$

When the coefficient is a fraction or mixed number, it is necessary to multiply for the second step. The number that is multiplied is the reciprocal of the fraction.

EXAMPLE 4

What is the value of z in the equation $\frac{1}{3}z + 8 = 26$?

STRATEGY **Remove the term without a variable and then isolate the variable.**

STEP 1 Subtract 8 from both sides of the equation to remove the term.

$$\frac{1}{3}z + 8 - 8 = 26 - 8$$

$$\frac{1}{3}z = 18$$

STEP 2 Multiply both sides of the equation by the reciprocal of the coefficient to isolate the variable.

$$\frac{1}{3}z \times 3 = 18 \times 3$$

$$z = 54$$

SOLUTION **So, $z = 54$.**

COACHED EXAMPLE

Solve for b: $4b - 9 = 31$

THINKING IT THROUGH

Which operation do you need to use first? ____________

_______ 9 to both sides of the equation.

To isolate the variable, ________________________ by the coefficient.

Compute. ____________

So, b = _______.

Lesson Practice

Choose the correct answer.

1. What is the first step in solving the equation $2k + 9 = 25$?

A Subtract 9 from both sides of the equation.

B Subtract 2 from both sides of the equation.

C Divide both sides of the equation by 9.

D Divide both sides of the equation by 2.

2. What is the value of c in the following equation?

$$5c + 3 = 38$$

A $c = 4\frac{3}{4}$

B $c = 7$

C $c = 7\frac{3}{5}$

D $c = 8\frac{1}{5}$

3. What is the value of d in the following equation?

$$6d - 5 = 43$$

A $d = 6$

B $d = 7$

C $d = 8$

D $d = 9$

4. What is the value of e in the following equation?

$$12e + 7 = 163$$

A $e = 13$

B $e = 13\frac{7}{12}$

C $e = 14$

D $e = 14\frac{1}{6}$

5. What is the value of g in the following equation?

$$15g - 12 = 192$$

A $g = 12$

B $g = 12\frac{4}{5}$

C $g = 13$

D $g = 13\frac{3}{5}$

6. What is the value of h in the following equation?

$$18h + 32 = 96$$

A $h = 3\frac{5}{9}$

B $h = 5\frac{1}{3}$

C $h = 6$

D $h = 7\frac{1}{9}$

7. What is the value of j in the following equation?

$$\frac{1}{5}j + 9 = 13$$

A $j = 4$

B $j = 16$

C $j = 20$

D $j = 22$

8. What is the value of k in the following equation?

$$\frac{2}{3}k - 5 = 13$$

A $k = 8$

B $k = 12$

C $k = 18$

D $k = 27$

OPEN-ENDED ITEM

9. Mike was given the equation $3x + 8 = 21$ to solve.

What is the solution to Mike's equation? Show your work.

___

Explain your steps in finding the solution.

___

___

___

22 Ratios and Rates

GLCEs: N.ME.06.11, A.PA.06.01

Getting the Idea

A **ratio** compares two quantities. A ratio can compare a part to a part, a part to a whole, or a whole to a part. In Example 1, the ratio is squares to triangles. Other ratios that can be found from the diagram are triangles to squares, squares to total number of figures, triangles to total number of figures, total number of figures to squares, and total number of figures to triangles.

EXAMPLE 1

What is the ratio of squares to triangles?

STRATEGY **Count the number of each shape.**

STEP 1 Count the number of squares.

There are 6 squares.

STEP 2 Count the number of triangles.

There are 2 triangles.

STEP 3 Write a ratio comparing the number of squares to the number of triangles.

There are 6 triangles to 2 triangles.

SOLUTION **So, the ratio of squares to triangles is 6:2.**

You can also write the ratio of squares to triangles as $\frac{6}{2}$ or 6 to 2. You can also write a ratio in simplest form by dividing each quantity by the greatest common factor—in this case, 2. So, the ratio of squares to triangles in simplest form is 3 to 1.

The ratios 6 to 2 and 3 to 1 are **equivalent ratios**. You can find equivalent ratios the same way as you would find equivalent fractions, by either multiplying or dividing the numerator and denominator by the same number.

To find if two ratios are equivalent, find the **cross products**. To find the **cross products**, multiply the numerator of one fraction by the denominator of the other. If the products are equivalent, then the ratios form a **proportion**.

EXAMPLE 2

Are these ratios equivalent?

5:8 and 16:24

STRATEGY **Write as fractions and cross multiply.**

STEP 1 Write the ratios as fractions.

$$\frac{5}{8} \stackrel{?}{=} \frac{16}{24}$$

STEP 2 Cross-multiply.

$$5 \times 24 \stackrel{?}{=} 8 \times 16$$

$$120 \qquad 128$$

SOLUTION **The cross products are not equivalent. Therefore, the ratios are not equivalent.**

To find equivalent ratios, use cross products. This is shown in the following example.

EXAMPLE 3

What number makes this proportion true?

$$\frac{18}{27} = \frac{n}{9}$$

STRATEGY **Use cross products to find the value of *n*.**

STEP 1 Cross-multiply.

$$18 \times 9 = 27 \times n$$

STEP 2 Multiply to find the value of each side.

$$18 \times 9 = 27 \times n$$

$$162 = 27n$$

STEP 3 Divide both sides by the coefficient.

$$162 \div 27 = 27n \div 27$$

$$6 = n$$

SOLUTION **If $n = 6$, the proportion is true.**

A **rate** is a ratio that compares measurements or amounts. Examples of rates are pay rates, speed limits, and exchange rates, which include dollars per hour, miles per hour, and euros per dollar, respectively. Rates are often given as a **unit rate**, which is a rate in which the second measure is 1 unit. A unit rate involving money is a **unit price**.

EXAMPLE 4

Veronica bought 3 pounds of potato salad for $8.97. What is the unit price per pound of the potato salad?

STRATEGY **Divide the cost by the pounds.**

$$\$8.97 \div 3 = \$2.99$$

SOLUTION **The unit price is $2.99 per pound.**

You can use rates to find solutions to applied problems. One application is the speed formula $R = \frac{d}{t}$ or Rate = distance ÷ time.

EXAMPLE 5

Reggie is traveling at 45 miles per hour. How far has he traveled in $2\frac{1}{2}$ hours?

STRATEGY **Substitute the known values in the formula. Then solve.**

STEP 1 Substitute the known values in the formula. Write an equivalent decimal for $2\frac{1}{2}$ hours.

$$45 = \frac{d}{2.5}$$

STEP 2 Multiply both sides of the equation by 2.5 to isolate the variable.

$$45 \times 2.5 = \frac{d}{2.5} \times 2.5$$

$$112.5 = d$$

SOLUTION **Reggie traveled 112.5 miles in $2\frac{1}{2}$ hours.**

COACHED EXAMPLE

Mr. Gonzalez earns $24.75 per hour. If he works 36 hours in a week, how much money will he earn in a week?

THINKING IT THROUGH

What equation can you write to find how much money Mr. Gonzalez will earn in a week?

____

Substitute the known values in your equation. ______________________

What operation do you need to use? ______________________

Compute. ______________________

So, Mr. Gonzalez earns ____________ if he works 36 hours.

Lesson Practice

Choose the correct answer.

1. What is the ratio of stars to hearts?

A 2:3

B 2:5

C 3:2

D 3:5

2. Which ratio is equivalent to 10 to 8?

A $\frac{5}{4}$

B $\frac{15}{10}$

C $\frac{18}{16}$

D $\frac{20}{15}$

3. Which pair of ratios are equivalent?

A 6:9 and 12:16

B 9:15 and 18:30

C 10:18 and 16:27

D 12:15 and 15:20

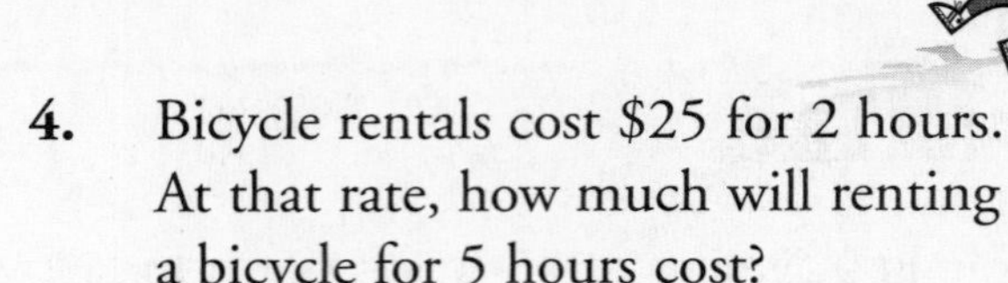

4. Bicycle rentals cost $25 for 2 hours. At that rate, how much will renting a bicycle for 5 hours cost?

A $50

B $57.50

C $62.50

D $75

5. Which number makes this proportion true?

$$\frac{7}{12} = \frac{n}{48}$$

A 21

B 24

C 27

D 28

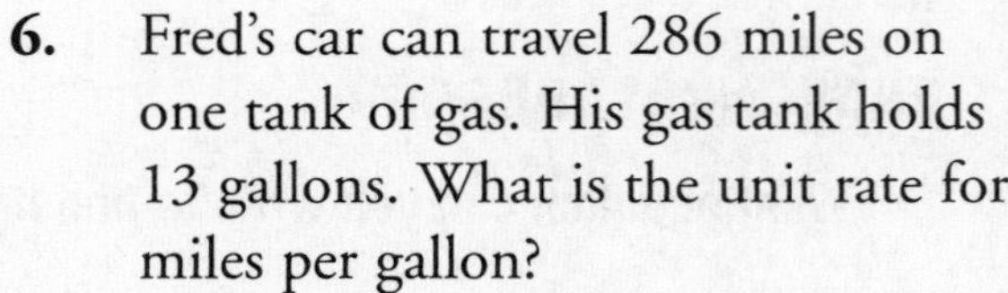

6. Fred's car can travel 286 miles on one tank of gas. His gas tank holds 13 gallons. What is the unit rate for miles per gallon?

A 22 miles per gallon

B 24 miles per gallon

C 26 miles per gallon

D 28 miles per gallon

7. Ms. Corningstone is staying 6 nights at the Carr Memorial Suites for a total of $876. Mr. Tsu is staying 10 nights and will pay the same rate. How much money will Mr. Tsu pay in all?

A $ 584

B $1,314

C $1,460

D $1,752

8. A train is traveling 125 miles per hour. How far will it go in $3\frac{3}{4}$ hours?

A 375 miles

B 406.25 miles

C 437.5 miles

D 468.75 miles

OPEN-ENDED ITEM

9. Ms. Warren earns $912 for working 38 hours each week.

Ms. Warren can only work 28 hours next week. At the same rate, how much money will she earn? Show your work.

Explain how you determined your answer.

MEAP Review

Choose the correct answer.

1 Cole wrote an equation. Which of the following could he have written?

A $3z + 8 = 26$

B $4a - 12$

C $5b + 4b - 6 + 8$

D $6(x + 2)$

2 A plumber earns 80 dollars per hour. He also charges a 35-dollar fee for a house call. If the plumber spends h hours on a house call, which represents the amount of money that he earns?

A $115h$

B $80h + 35$

C $35h + 80$

D $80 + 35 + h$

3 What is the value of x in this equation?

$$16 + x = 43$$

A $x = 27$

B $x = 37$

C $x = 59$

D $x = 69$

4 What is the missing number in this function table?

x	*y*
3	9
6	12
10	16
14	?

A 19

B 20

C 28

D 42

5 How can you simplify the following expression?

$$3z + 4 - 2z + 3$$

A $5z + 7$

B $5z + 1$

C $z + 7$

D $8z^2$

6 Which expression means three times a number minus 2?

A $3 - 2x$

B $2x + 3$

C 1

D $3x - 2$

7 Which equation has the same solution as $8 + x = 14$?

A $8 \times 8 + x = 14 \times 8$

B $8 \div 8 + x = 14 \div 8$

C $8 - 8 + x = 14 - 8$

D $8 + x = 14 - 8$

8 There are 7 girls and 2 boys that have speaking roles in the school play. Last year, there were more parts, but the ratio of girls to boys was the same. Which could have been the ratio of girls to boys?

A 12 to 7

B 14 to 4

C 21 to 5

D 25 to 8

9 What is the value of n in the following equation?

$$5n - 8 = 22$$

A $n = 3\frac{1}{5}$

B $n = 4\frac{2}{5}$

C $n = 5\frac{3}{5}$

D $n = 6$

10 Which equation can you use to express the relationship between the length of the side of a square and the perimeter of the square? Use P for the perimeter and s for the length of a side.

A $P = 4s$

B $P = s \div 4$

C $P = s^2$

D $P = s + 4$

11 Sharon bought 3 pounds of shrimp for $21.60. Last week she bought 5 pounds of shrimp at the same unit price. How much money did Sharon spend last week?

A $ 7.20

B $36.00

C $43.20

D $57.60

12 What is the value of j in the following equation?

$$j \div 4 = 16$$

A $j = 4$

B $j = 20$

C $j = 48$

D $j = 64$

13 Which is **NOT** one of the ordered pairs for triangle *HJK*?

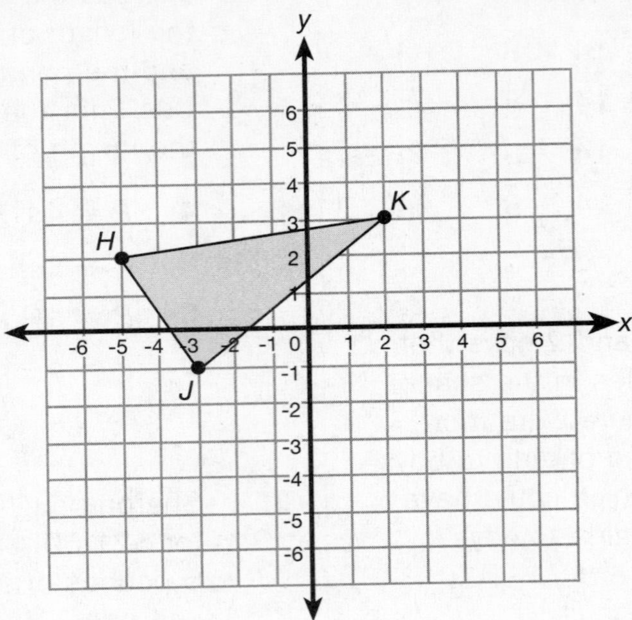

A (−5, 2)

B (−3, −1)

C (3, 2)

D (2, 3)

14 Which could be represented by the equation $8h + 5$?

A \$8 per hour plus a \$5 fee

B \$5 per hour plus a \$8 fee

C \$13 per hour

D \$8 for the first hour and \$5 for the next hour

15 A plane is traveling at 350 miles per hour. How many miles has the plane traveled after $4\frac{1}{4}$ hours?

A 1,400 miles

B $1{,}487\frac{1}{2}$ miles

C 1,575 miles

D $1{,}662\frac{1}{2}$ miles

OPEN-ENDED ITEM

16 The function table shows the relationship between the length of a side of a regular pentagon and its perimeter.

Length of Side (in cm)	Perimeter (in cm)
1	5
2	10
3	15
4	20

What rule represents the function?

____

Graph the function.

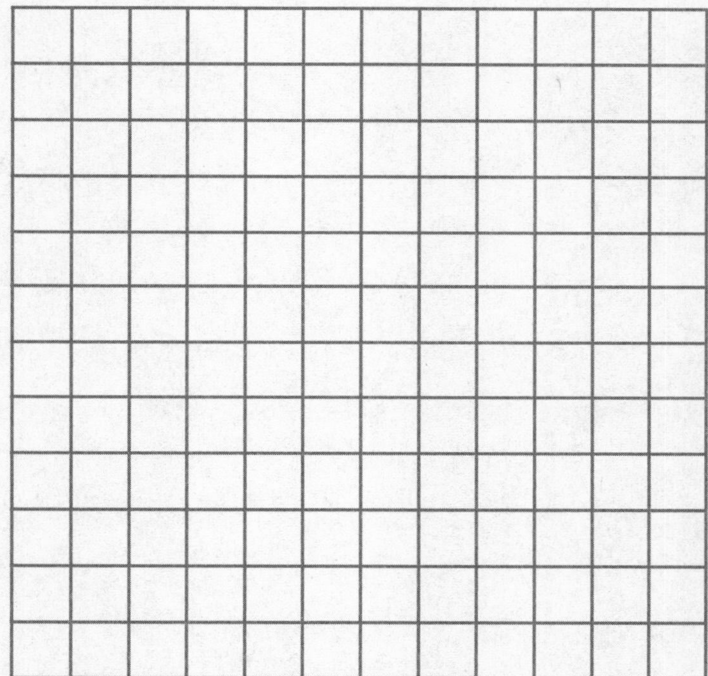

If the lengths of the sides are 9 centimeters, what is the perimeter? __________

Explain how you found your answer.

____

____

____

____

CHAPTER 3 Measurement

23 Convert Measures

GLCEs: M.UN.06.01

Getting the Idea

There are two measurement systems, the customary system and the metric system. The customary system is used in the United States, while the metric system is used in most of the rest of the world. This lesson will convert units of measurement within each system. This lesson will also include conversions of time, which has one system.

To convert a larger unit to a smaller unit, multiply. To convert a smaller unit to a larger unit, divide.

Length

Customary units of length include **inches (in.), feet (ft), yards (yd)**, and **miles (mi)**. Metric units of length include **millimeters (mm), centimeters (cm), meters (m)**, and **kilometers (km)**. The table below shows the conversions for both systems of length.

Customary Units of Length		
1 foot (ft)	=	12 inches (in.)
1 yard (yd)	=	3 feet
1 yard	=	36 inches
1 mile (mi)	=	5,280 feet
	=	1,760 yards
Metric Units of Length		
1 centimeter (cm)	=	10 millimeters (mm)
1 meter (m)	=	100 centimeters
1 meter	=	1000 millimeters
1 kilometer (km)	=	1000 meters

EXAMPLE 1

Nancy jogged 8 miles. How many yards did she run?

STRATEGY **Multiply to convert a larger unit to a smaller unit.**

STEP 1 Write the relationship between miles and yards.

1 mile = 1,760 yards

STEP 2 Multiply the number of miles by 1,760 to find the number of yards.

1,760 × 8 = 14,080

SOLUTION **Nancy ran 14,080 yards.**

Weight and Mass

Weight is the gravitational force on an object, while mass is a property of the object that, in part, determines its weight. Weight is often measured in customary units, such as **ounces (oz)**, **pounds (lb)**, and **tons (T)**. Mass is often measured in metric units, such as **milligrams (mg)**, **grams (g)**, **kilograms (kg)**, and **metric tons.** The table opposite shows the conversions among units of weight and mass.

Customary Units of Weight		
1 pound (lb)	=	16 ounces (oz)
1 ton (t)	=	2000 pounds
Metric Units of Mass		
1 gram (g)	=	1000 milligrams (mg)
1 kilogram (kg)	=	1000 grams
1 metric ton (t)	=	1000 kilograms

EXAMPLE 2

A book has a mass of 678 grams. How many kilograms are equal to 678 grams?

STRATEGY **Divide to convert a smaller unit to a larger unit.**

STEP 1 Write the relationship between kilograms and grams.

1 kilogram = 1,000 grams

STEP 2 Divide the number of grams by 1,000 to find the number of kilograms.

678 ÷ 1,000 = 0.678

SOLUTION **The book has a mass of 0.678 kilogram.**

Capacity

Customary units of capacity include **fluid ounces (fl oz), cups (c), pints (pt), quarts (qt)**, and **gallons (gal)**. Metric units of capacity include **milliliters (mL)** and **liters (L)**.

The table below shows the conversions among units of capacity.

Customary Units of Capacity		
1 cup (c)	=	8 fluid ounces (fl oz)
1 pint (pt)	=	2 cups
1 quart (g)	=	2 pints
1 gallon (gal)	=	4 quarts
Metric Units of Capacity		
1 liter (L)	=	1000 milliliters (mL)

EXAMPLE 3

A fish bowl has a capacity of 192 fluid ounces. How many quarts is that?

STRATEGY **Divide to convert a smaller unit to a larger unit.**

STEP 1 Write the relationship between quarts and fluid ounces.

1 quart = 2 pints
= 4 cups
= 32 fluid ounces

STEP 2 Divide the number of fluid ounces by 32 to find the number of quarts.

$192 \div 32 = 6$

SOLUTION **The fish bowl has a capacity of 6 quarts.**

Units of Area

Area is measured in **square units**. A square unit is a square with a measure of 1 unit, such as a square inch or a square centimeter shown opposite.

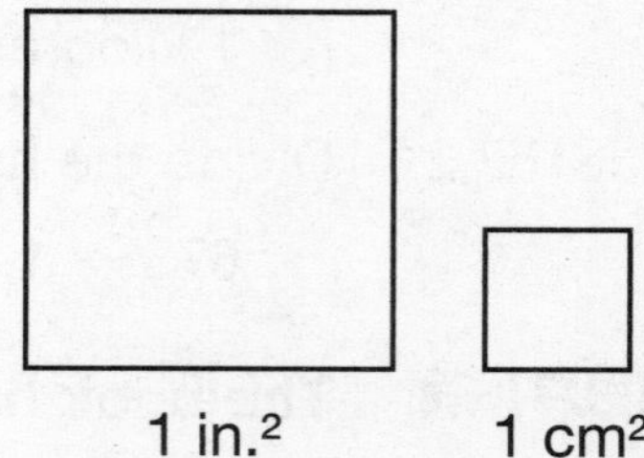

The table opposite shows conversions of customary units of area.

Customary Units of Area		
1 ft^2	=	144 $in.^2$
1 yd^2	=	9 ft^2
Metric Units of Area		
1 cm^2	=	100 mm^2
1 m^2	=	10000 cm^2

EXAMPLE 4

Nick's backyard is rectangular and is 90 feet long by 60 feet wide. How many square yards is Nick's backyard?

STRATEGY **Find the area in square feet. Then convert to square yards.**

STEP 1 Find the area of the backyard.

The formula for the area of a rectangle is $A = lw$.

90 ft $\times$ 60 ft = 5,400 ft^2

STEP 2 Write the relationship between square yards and square feet.

1 square yard = 9 square feet

STEP 3 Divide the number of square feet by 9.

5,400 $ft^2 \div 9 = 600$ yd^2

SOLUTION **Nick's backyard has an area of 600 yd^2.**

COACHED EXAMPLE

At her last checkup, Mocha, a chocolate Labrador puppy, weighed 19 pounds 12 ounces. How many ounces is that?

THINKING IT THROUGH

Write the relationship between pounds and ounces: 1 pound = ______ ounces

Multiply to convert a ____________ unit to a ____________ unit.

Multiply the pounds by ______.

Multiply: ________________________

What do you need to do with the 12 ounces? ____________

Compute: ________________________

So, Mocha weighs ______ ounces.

Lesson Practice

Choose the correct answer.

1. How many grams are equal to 2.35 kilograms?

A 23.5 g

B 235 g

C 2,350 g

D 23,500 g

2. The ceiling in Mrs. Abrams's class is 12 feet 4 inches high. How many inches high is it?

A 124 in.

B 136 in.

C 140 in.

D 148 in.

3. Which measures of capacity are equivalent?

A 8 quarts and 2 gallons

B 32 fluid ounces and 2 cups

C 64 fluid ounces and 4 quarts

D 16 pints and 1 gallon

4. A bottle of water has a capacity of 750 milliliters. Which is an equivalent measure in liters?

A 0.75 L

B 7.5 L

C 75 L

D 7,500 L

5. Which number makes this sentence true?

450 cm = ______ m

A 0.45 **C** 45

B 4.5 **D** 4,500

6. Kim weighed 102 ounces when she was born. What was Kim's weight in pounds and ounces?

A 5 pounds 2 ounces

B 6 pounds 6 ounces

C 8 pounds 6 ounces

D 10 pounds 2 ounces

7. Before arriving at a bridge, drivers see this sign.

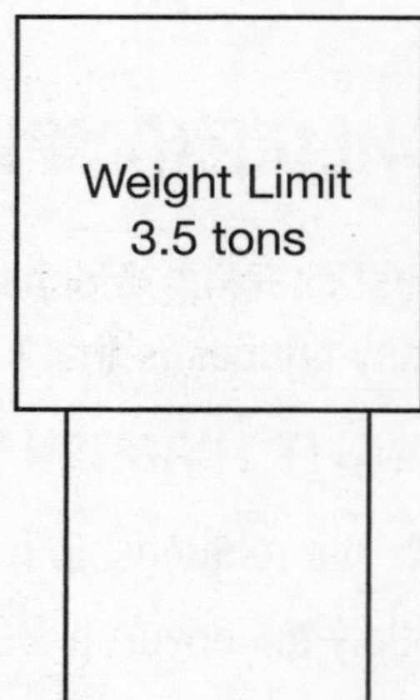

What is the weight limit in pounds?

A 350 lb **C** 3,500 lb

B 700 lb **D** 7,000 lb

8. How many square meters are equal to 70,000 square centimeters?

A 7 sq m

B 70 sq m

C 700 sq m

D 7,000 sq m

OPEN-ENDED ITEM

9. In his workouts, Willie sprints 200 yards a total of 10 times. Then he jogs 1,500 yards before working out with weights.

How many feet does Willie sprint or jog in his workouts?

____

How many more feet does Willie need to jog or sprint to run a total of 2 miles?

____

Explain how you found your answers.

____

____

____

____

____

____

24 Volume

GLCEs: M.TE.06.03

Getting the Idea

Volume is the measure of the inside region of a **solid figure**, which is measured in **cubic units**. A cubic unit can be any unit such as a cubic inch (in.^{3}) or a cubic centimeter (cm^3), both shown opposite.

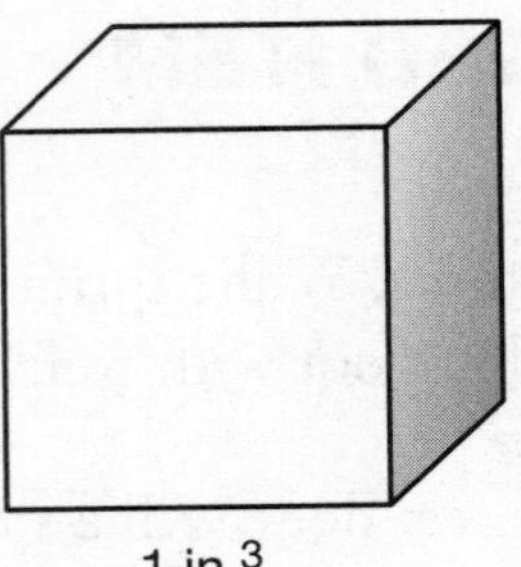

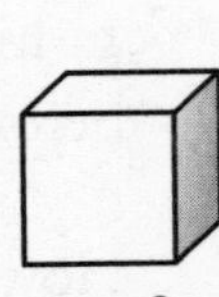

To find volume of a **rectangular prism** or a **cube**, you can count the number of cubes that would fit inside the figure.

EXAMPLE 1

What is the volume of this rectangular prism?

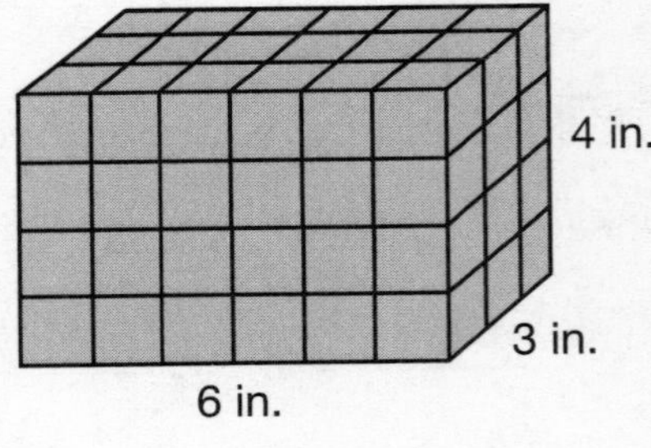

STRATEGY **Count the number of cubes by layer.**

STEP 1 Find the number of cubes on the bottom layer.

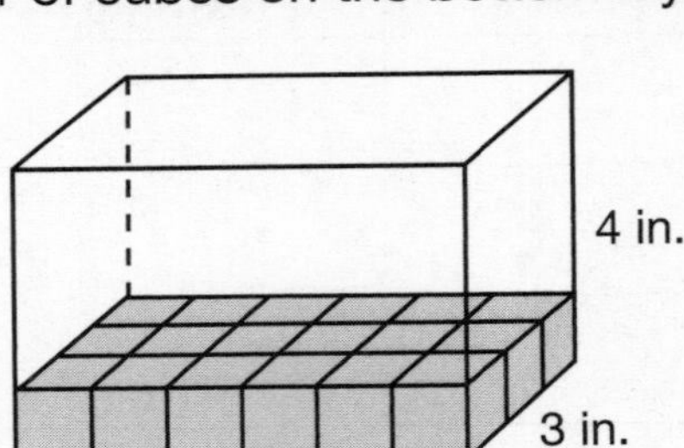

There are 3 rows and 6 columns of cubes: $3 \times 6 = 18$.

There are 18 cubes in the bottom layer.

STEP 2 Multiply the number of cubes on the bottom layer by the number of layers.

There are 4 layers.

$18 \times 4 = 72$

SOLUTION **The volume of the rectangular prism is 72 cubic inches.**

You can also use this formula to find the volume of a rectangular prism:
$V = lwh$ or Volume = length × width × height.

EXAMPLE 2

What is the volume of this fish tank?

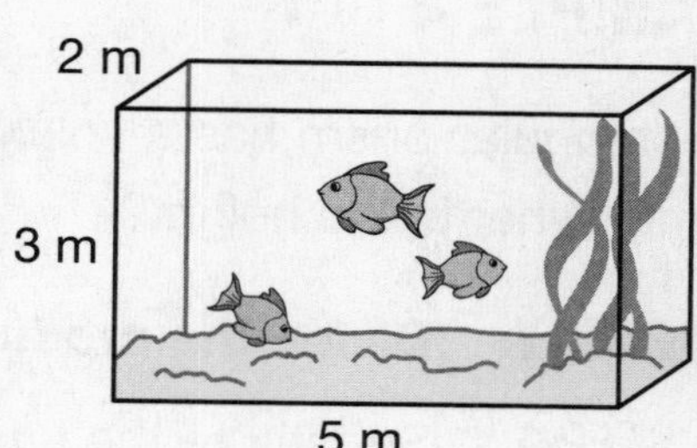

STRATEGY **Use the formula for finding the volume of a rectangular prism.**

STEP 1 Substitute the values into the formula.

$V = 5 \text{ m} \times 2 \text{ m} \times 3 \text{ m}$

STEP 2 Multiply.

$V = 5 \text{ m} \times 2 \text{ m} \times 3 \text{ m}$

$V = 30 \text{ m}^3$

SOLUTION **The fish tank has a volume of 30 cubic meters or 30 m^3.**

A cube is a rectangular prism with 6 square **faces**. To find the volume of a cube you can multiply the length of a **side** by itself three times, or $V = s^3$.

EXAMPLE 3

What is the volume of this cube?

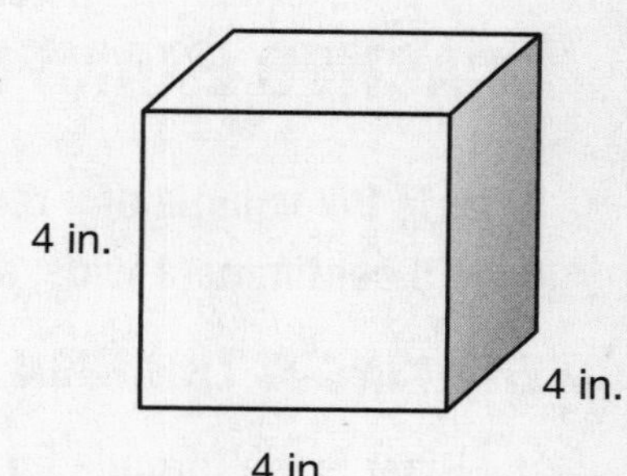

STRATEGY **Use the formula for finding the volume of a cube.**

STEP 1 Substitute the values into the formula.

$V = 4 \text{ in.} \times 4 \text{ in.} \times 4 \text{ in.}$

STEP 2 Multiply.

$V = 4 \text{ in.} \times 4 \text{ in.} \times 4 \text{ in.}$

$V = 64 \text{ in.}^3$

SOLUTION **The volume of the cube is 64 in.^3.**

You can reverse the formula for the volume of a rectangular prism to find a dimension if you are given the volume and two of the dimensions. You can do this by dividing the volume by the product of the two known dimensions.

EXAMPLE 4

A rectangular prism has a volume of 280 cm^3. It has a length of 8 cm and a width of 7 cm^2. What is the height?

STRATEGY **Divide the product by the the product of the two known dimensions.**

STEP 1 Substitute the known values into the formula for volume.

$V = lwh$

$V = 8 \text{ cm} \times 7 \text{ cm} \times h$

STEP 2 Find the product of the two known dimensions.

$8 \text{ cm} \times 7 \text{ cm} = 56 \text{ cm}^2$

STEP 3 Divide the volume by the product of the two known dimensions.

$280 \text{ cm}^3 \div 56 \text{ cm}^2 = 5 \text{ cm}$

SOLUTION **The height is 5 cm.**

COACHED EXAMPLE

What is the volume of a rectangular prism that is 7 centimeters long, 5 centimeters wide, and 6 centimeters high?

6 cm
5 cm
7 cm

THINKING IT THROUGH

What is the formula for the volume of a rectangular prism?

____

Substitute the values into the formula. ________________________

Multiply. ________________________

The volume of the rectangular prism is ______ cubic centimeters.

Lesson Practice

Choose the correct answer.

1. A cube measures 5 centimeters on each side.

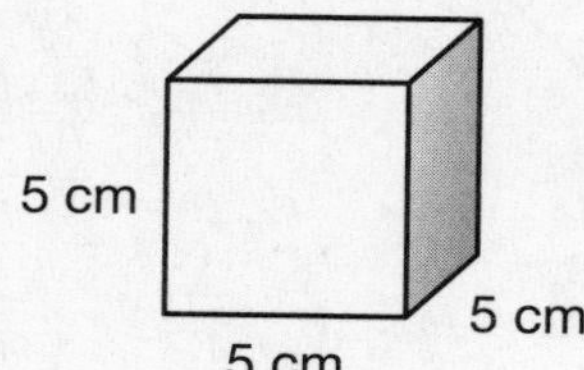

What is the volume of the number cube?

A 15 cm^3 C 75 cm^3

B 25 cm^3 D 125 cm^3

2. What is the volume of this rectangular prism?

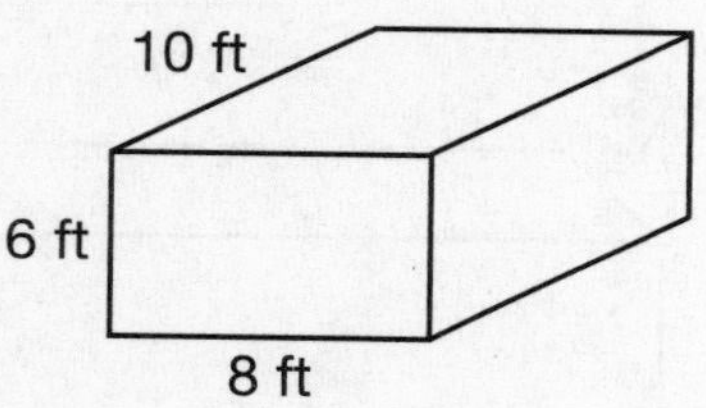

A 188 ft^3

B 240 ft^3

C 480 ft^3

D 960 ft^3

3. A rectangular prism has a length of 12 meters, a width of 9 meters, and a height of 10 meters. What is the volume of the rectangular prism?

A $1{,}080 \text{ m}^3$

B $1{,}260 \text{ m}^3$

C $1{,}800 \text{ m}^3$

D $2{,}160 \text{ m}^3$

4. Which rectangular prism has the *greatest* volume?

A

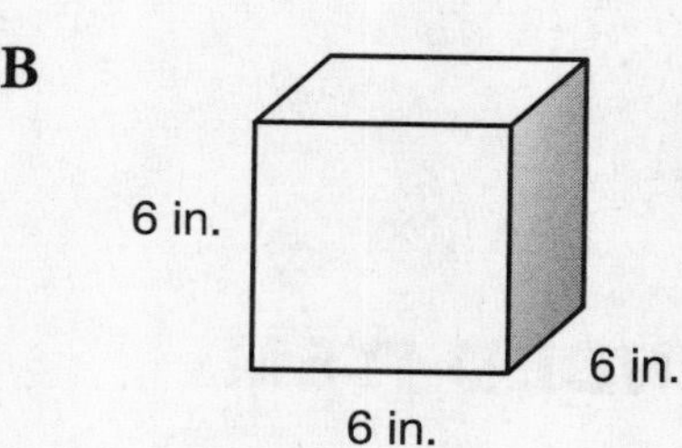

B

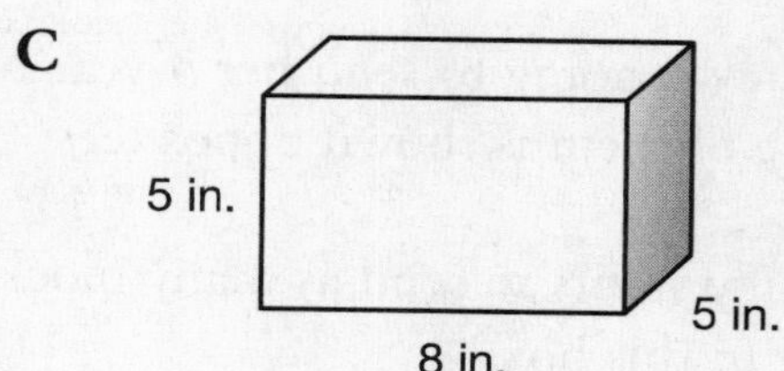

C

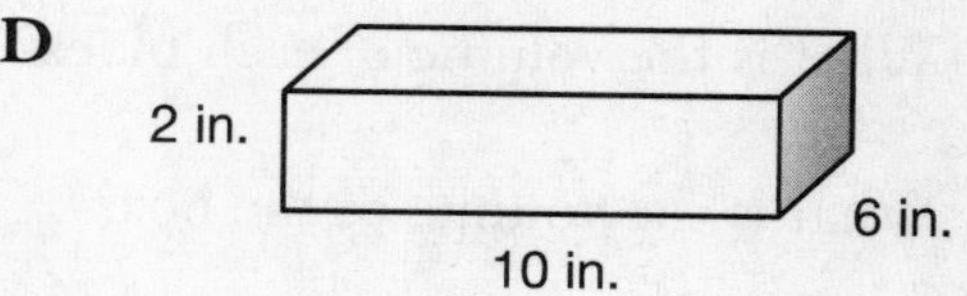

D

2 in.

6 in.

10 in.

5. A rectangular prism has a volume of 150 cm^3. The length is 10 cm, and the height is 3 cm. What is the width?

A 5 cm

B 15 cm

C 50 cm

D 120 cm

6. What is the volume of this swimming pool?

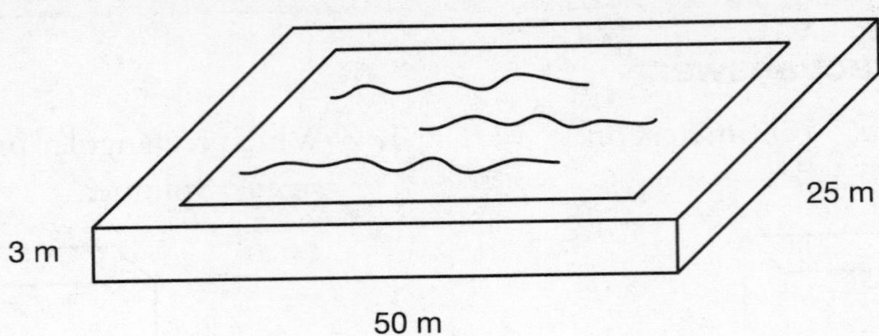

A 375 m^3

B 1,475 m^3

C 2,950 m^3

D 3,750 m^3

OPEN-ENDED ITEM

7. Marcy is going to send her 3-year-old cousin building blocks. One of them is shown opposite.

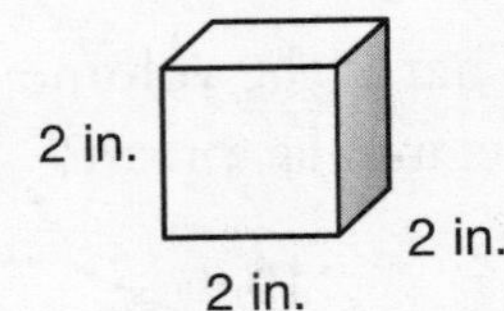

Marcy wants to send as many blocks as she can put in this box.

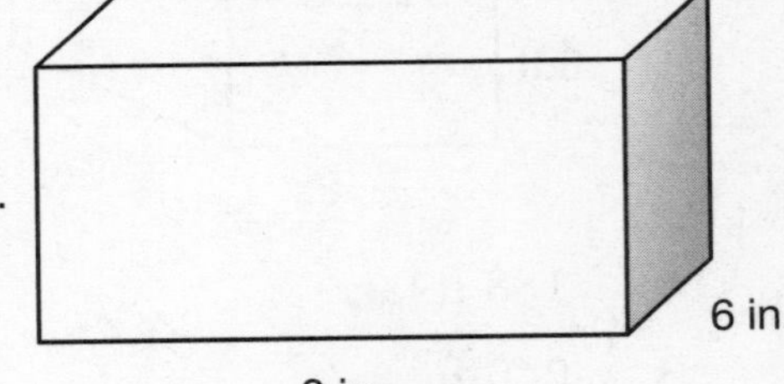

What is the volume of each block? ______________

What is the volume of the box? ______________

How many blocks can Marcy put in this box? ______________

Explain how you found your answer.

____

____

____

____

____

____

Lesson

25 Surface Area

GLCEs: M.TE.06.03

Getting the Idea

Surface area is the total area of the surfaces of a solid figure. Like area, surface area is measured in square units.

You can use a **net** to help you find the surface area of a rectangular prism. A net is a two-dimensional pattern that can be folded to form a solid figure. A rectangular prism has 6 faces, so a net of a rectangular prism would show 6 faces.

EXAMPLE 1

What is the surface area of this rectangular prism?

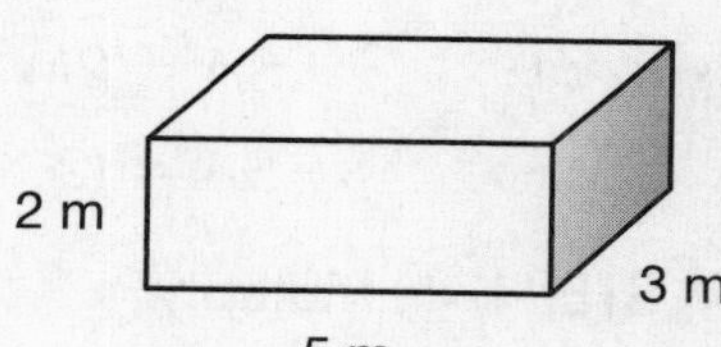

STRATEGY **Draw a net to show each face. Then find the area of each of the faces.**

STEP 1 Draw the net showing the dimensions of the rectangular prism.

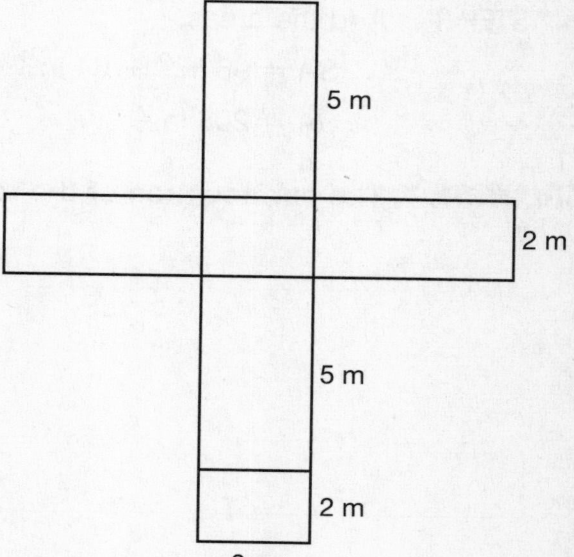

STEP 2 Find the area of each of the faces.

$A = 3 \times 5 = 15 \text{ m}^2$

$A = 3 \times 2 = 6 \text{ m}^2$

$A = 5 \times 2 = 10 \text{ m}^2$

$A = 3 \times 5 = 15 \text{ m}^2$

$A = 3 \times 2 = 6 \text{ m}^2$

$A = 5 \times 2 = 10 \text{ m}^2$

STEP 3 Add the areas of the faces.

$15 \text{ m}^2 + 15 \text{ m}^2 + 6 \text{ m}^2 + 6 \text{ m}^2$
$+ 10 \text{ m}^2 + 10 \text{ m}^2 = 62 \text{ m}^2$

SOLUTION **The surface area of the rectangular prism is 62 m^2.**

You may have noticed that each face has an opposite **congruent** face. A rectangular prism will have at most three different-sized faces. So you can use this formula to find the surface area of a rectangular prism: $SA = 2lw + 2lh + 2wh$.

EXAMPLE 2

What is the surface area of this rectangular prism?

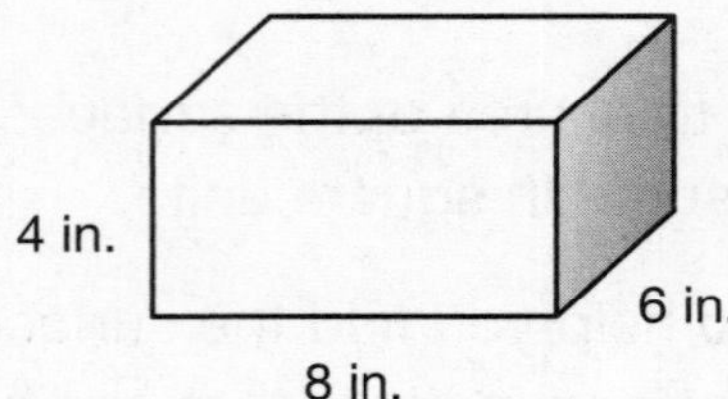

STRATEGY **Use the formula for finding the surface area of a rectangular prism.**

STEP 1 Substitute the values into the formula.

The length is 8 in., the width is 6 in., and the height is 4 in.

$SA = 2lw + 2lh + 2wh$

$SA = (2 \times 8 \text{ in.} \times 6 \text{ in.}) + (2 \times 8 \text{ in.} \times 4 \text{ in.}) + (2 \times 6 \text{ in.} \times 4 \text{ in.})$

STEP 2 Multiply.

$SA = (2 \times 8 \text{ in.} \times 6 \text{ in.}) + (2 \times 8 \text{ in.} \times 4 \text{ in.}) + (2 \times 6 \text{ in.} \times 4 \text{ in.})$

$SA = 96 \text{ in.}^2 + 64 \text{ in.}^2 + 48 \text{ in.}^2$

STEP 3 Add the areas.

$SA = 96 \text{ in.}^2 + 64 \text{ in.}^2 + 48 \text{ in.}^2$

$SA = 208 \text{ in.}^2$

SOLUTION **The surface area of the rectangular prism is 208 in.^{2}.**

To find the surface area of a cube, you can use the formula $SA = 6e^2$, where e is the length of an **edge**.

EXAMPLE 3

What is the surface area of this cube?

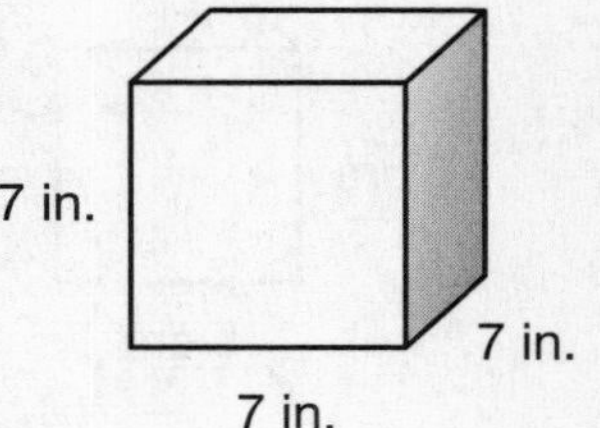

STRATEGY **Use the formula for finding the surface area of a cube.**

STEP 1 Substitute the values into the formula.

$SA = 6 \times 7 \text{ in.} \times 7 \text{ in.}$

STEP 2 Multiply.

$SA = 6 \times 7 \text{ in.} \times 7 \text{ in.}$

$SA = 294 \text{ in.}^2$

SOLUTION **The surface area of the cube is 294 in.^{2}.**

COACHED EXAMPLE

What is the surface area of a rectangular prism that is 9 centimeters long, 7 centimeters wide, and 6 centimeters high?

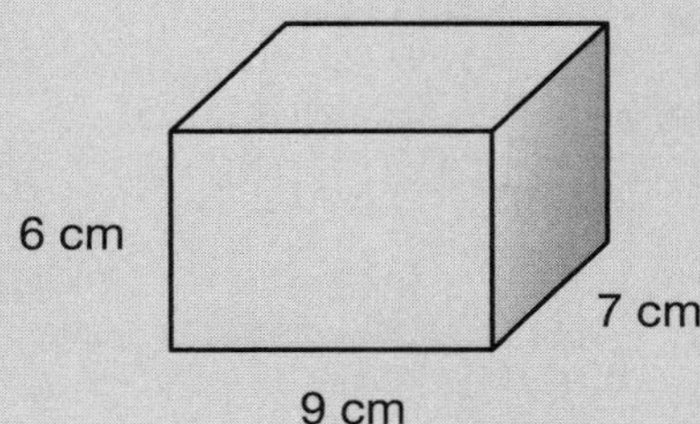

THINKING IT THROUGH

The formula for the surface area of a rectangular prism is $SA = 2lw + 2lh + 2wh$.

Substitute the values of the rectangular prism into the formula.

(2 × ______ × ______) + (2 × ______ × ______) + (2 × ______ × ______)

Multiply to find the area of each of the faces.

Add to find the surface area.

So, the surface area of the rectangular prism is ______________________.

Lesson Practice

Choose the correct answer.

1. What is the surface area of this cube?

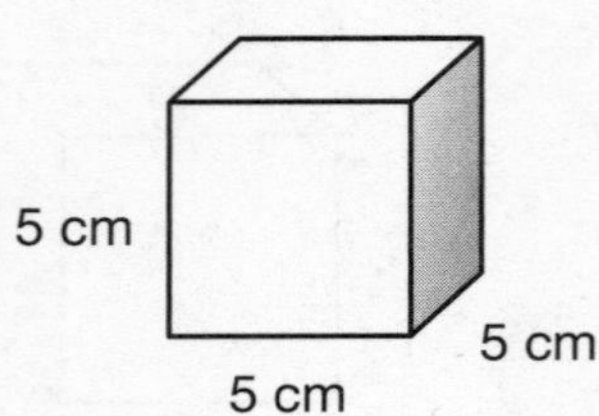

A 25 cm^2

B 30 cm^2

C 125 cm^2

D 150 cm^2

2. What is the surface area of this rectangular prism?

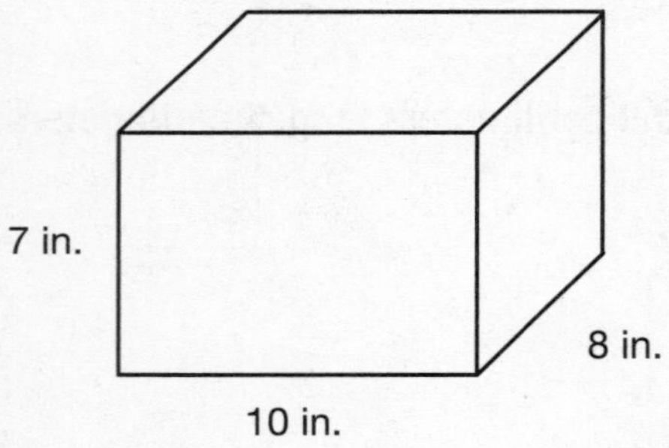

A 206 $in.^2$

B 280 $in.^2$

C 412 $in.^2$

D 560 $in.^2$

3. Steve's basement is 15 feet long, 12 feet wide, and the ceilings are 9 feet high. He is going to paint the walls and the ceiling, but not the floor. What is the surface area that he will need to paint?

A 423 ft^2

B 666 ft^2

C 846 ft^2

D 1,620 ft^2

4. Which rectangular prism has the *greatest* surface area?

A

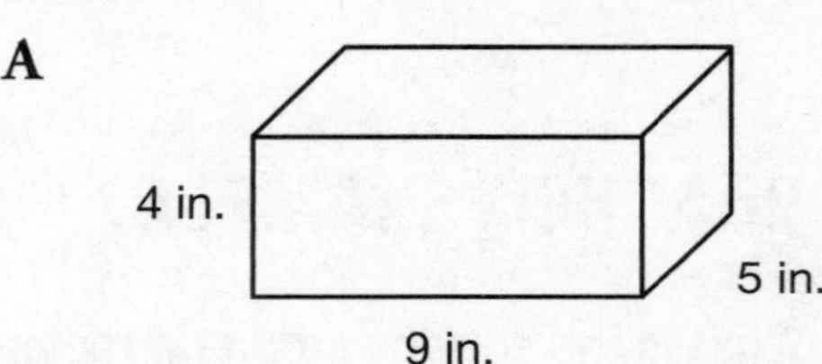

B

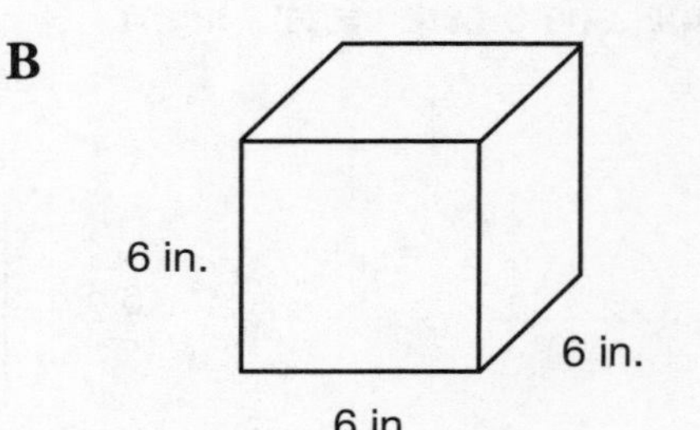

C

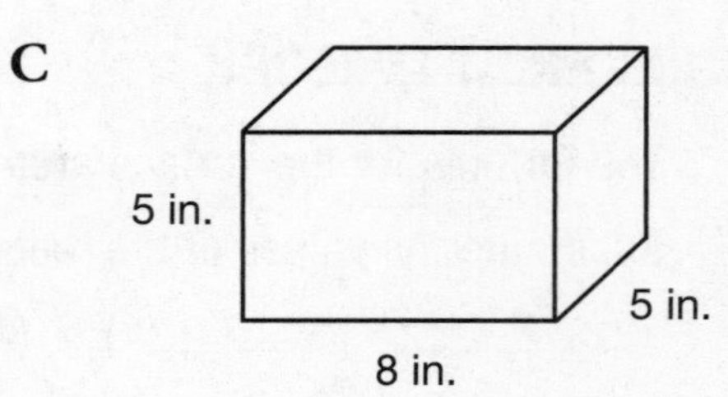

D

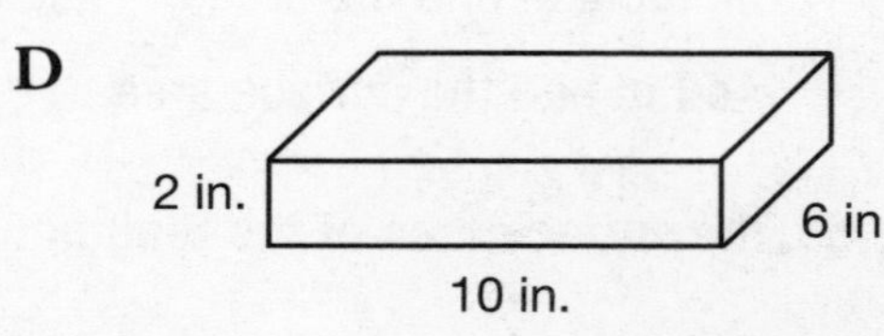

5. What is the surface area of this rectangular prism?

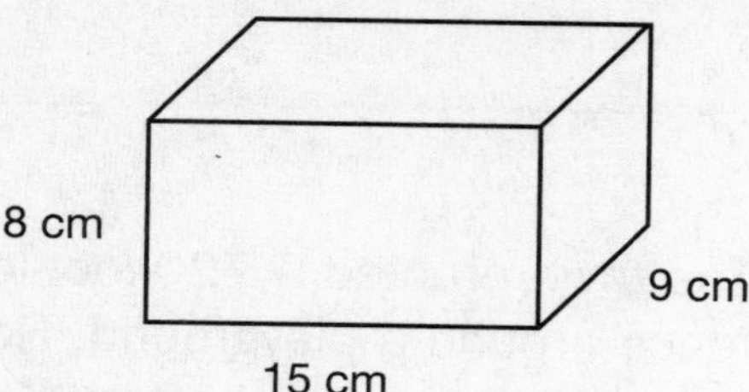

A 327 cm^2

B 540 cm^2

C 634 cm^2

D 654 cm^2

6. Sue is painting a door that is 80 inches tall, 36 inches wide, and 2 inches thick. Sue will not paint the bottom of the door. What is the surface area of the door that Sue will paint?

A $3{,}344 \text{ in.}^2$

B $6{,}064 \text{ in.}^2$

C $6{,}152 \text{ in.}^2$

D $6{,}224 \text{ in.}^2$

OPEN-ENDED ITEM

7. Katie is going to paint the walls and the ceiling of her bedroom. Her bedroom is rectangular and is 14 feet long, 12 feet wide, and the ceilings are 8 feet high. She has two windows that are each 5 feet long by 4 feet wide.

What is the total surface area that Katie will paint? ____________________

Explain how you found your answer.

____

____

____

____

____

____

3 MEAP Review

Choose the correct answer.

1 Rick has to fill a 2-gallon pot with water. He only has a 1-pint measuring cup. How many times will Rick have to fill the pot with water from the pint measuring cup?

A 4

B 8

C 12

D 16

Use this cube to answer questions 2 and 3.

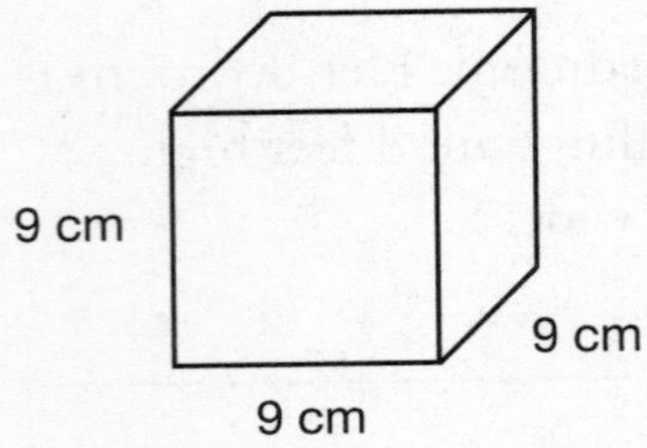

2 What is the volume of the cube?

A 27 cm^3

B 243 cm^3

C 486 cm^3

D 729 cm^3

3 What is the surface area of the cube?

A 81 cm^2

B 243 cm^2

C 486 cm^2

D 729 cm^2

4 The town erected a 720-foot-long fence around a playground. How many yards long is the fence?

A 60 yards

B 240 yards

C 2,160 yards

D 8,640 yards

5 What number makes this sentence true?

27.2 m = _____ km

A 0.0272

B 0.272

C 2.72

D 27,200

6 Patti's dog plays in a pen that is 12 feet long and 6 feet wide. What is the area of the pen in square yards?

A 8 yd^2

B 24 yd^2

C 36 yd^2

D 72 yd^2

Use the rectangular prism to answer questions 7 and 8.

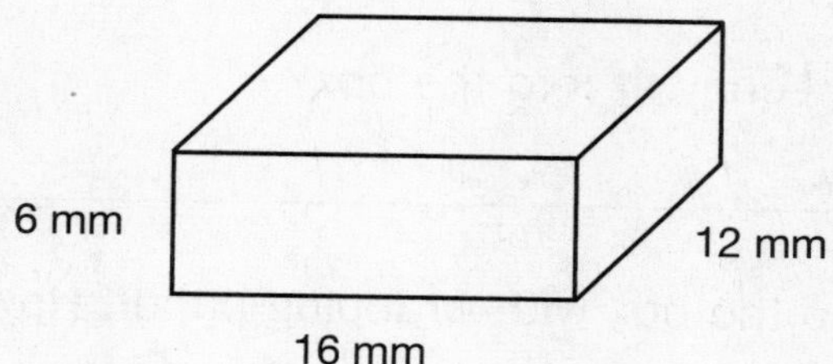

7 What is the volume of the rectangular prism?

A 360 mm^3

B 720 mm^3

C 1,152 mm^3

D 2,304 mm^3

8 What is the surface area of the rectangular prism?

A 360 mm^2

B 720 mm^2

C 1,152 mm^2

D 2,304 mm^2

OPEN-ENDED ITEM

9 Lenny is going to pack as many 3-inch-long cubes as he can into this box.

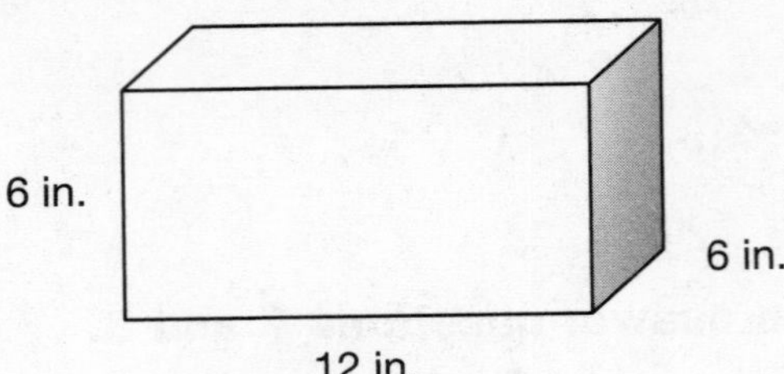

How many cubes can Lenny fit into the box?

____

Lenny is going to wrap the box with wrapping paper. How much wrapping paper will he need?

____

Explain how you found your answers.

____

____

____

____

____

____

CHAPTER

4 Geometry

26 Lines and Angles

GLCEs: G.GS.06.01

Getting the Idea

A **line** is a set of points that form a straight path that goes in opposite directions without end. A **ray** is part of a line that has one endpoint and goes without end in one direction. A **line segment** is part of a line that has two endpoints.

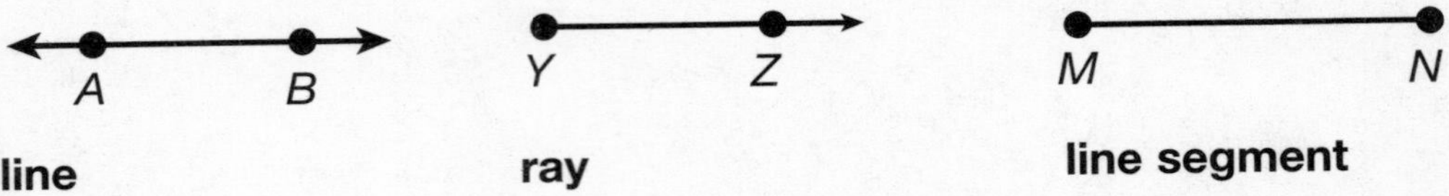

You can read the name of a line or a line segment in either direction. The line above can be read as line *AB* ($\overleftrightarrow{AB}$) or line *BA* ($\overleftrightarrow{BA}$) and the line segment can be read as line segment *MN* ($\overline{MN}$) or line segment *NM* ($\overline{NM}$). A ray is read with the endpoint first, so the ray is read ray *YZ* ($\overrightarrow{YZ}$).

Pairs of lines can be classified as **parallel lines, intersecting lines**, or **perpendicular lines.** Parallel lines or parallel line segments never meet and remain the same distance apart. Intersecting lines cross and intersecting line segments meet or cross. Perpendicular lines and perpendicular line segments intersect and form **right angles**.

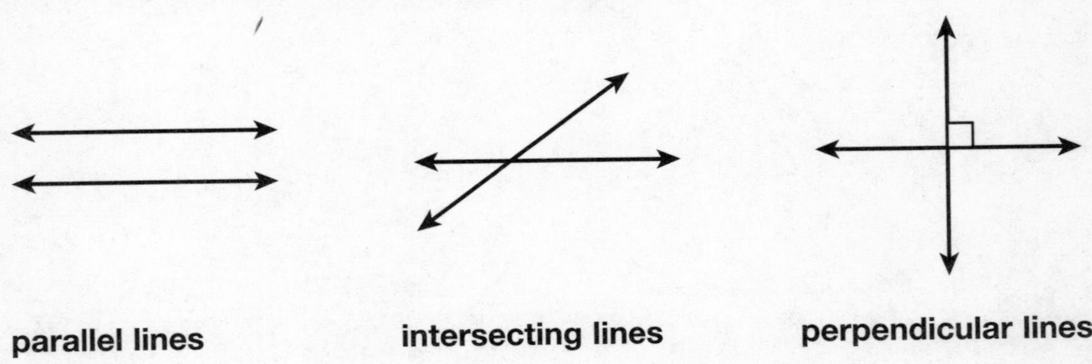

EXAMPLE 1

Are lines *l* and *n* parallel, intersecting, or perpendicular?

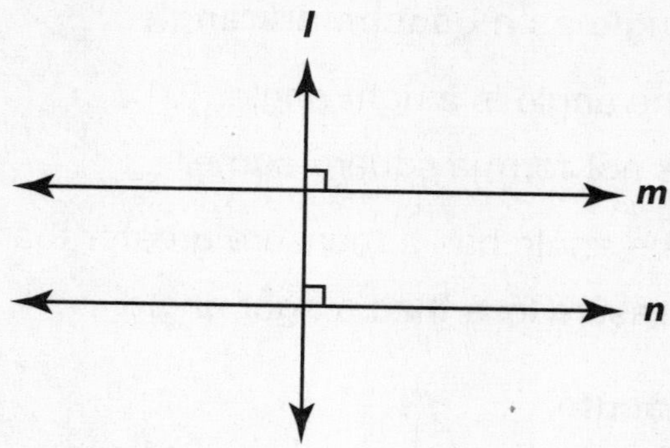

STRATEGY **Use the process of elimination to determine the relationship.**

STEP 1 Parallel lines never meet and remain the same distance apart.

Line *l* and line *n* meet.

Lines *l* and *n* are not parallel because they intersect.

STEP 2 Intersecting lines that meet at a right angle are perpendicular.

Lines *l* and *n* appear to meet at a right angle.

Lines *l* and *n* are perpendicular.

SOLUTION **Lines *l* and n are intersecting and perpendicular.**

All lines that are perpendicular also intersect.

An **angle** is formed by two rays that share a **vertex**. Angles are measured in **degrees** (°) and can be classified as **acute angles, right angles, obtuse angles**, or **straight angles** by their angles measures.

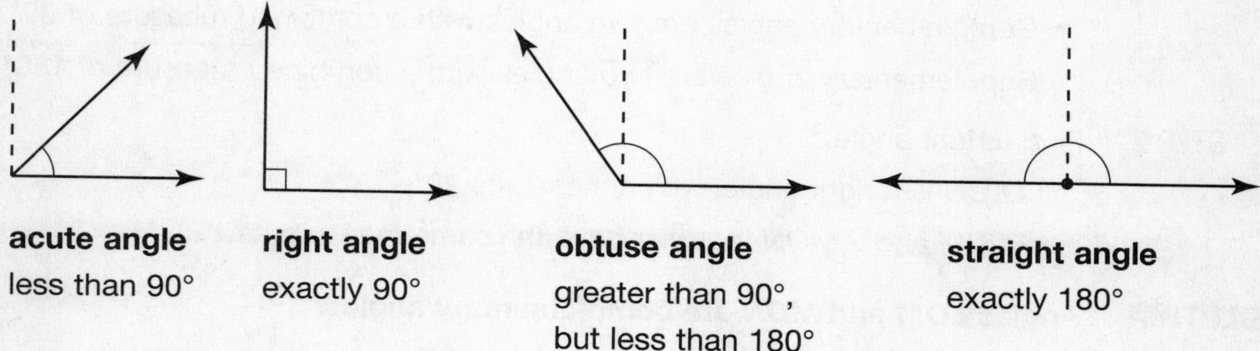

acute angle
less than 90°

right angle
exactly 90°

obtuse angle
greater than 90°, but less than 180°

straight angle
exactly 180°

EXAMPLE 2

How can this angle be classified?

STRATEGY **Use a right angle as a benchmark angle.**

STEP 1 Determine if the angle is a right angle.

No. It does not form a square corner.

STEP 2 Determine if the angle has a measure greater than or less than a right angle.

It has a measure less than a right angle.

SOLUTION **The angle is acute.**

Pairs of angles can be classified as **complementary angles** or **supplementary angles**. Two angles that have a combined measure of 90° are complementary angles. Two angles that have a combined measure of 180° are supplementary angles.

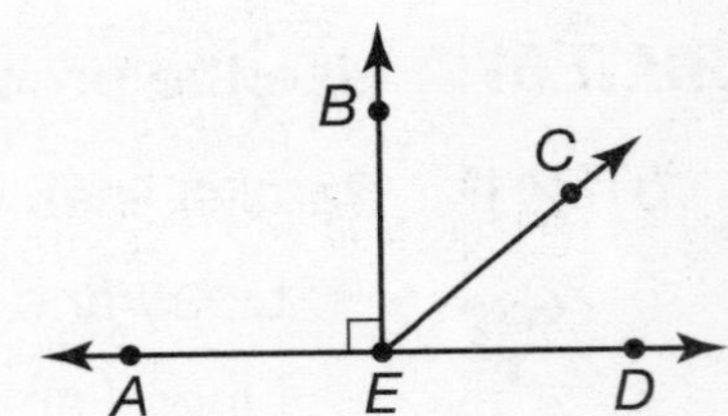

Angles *DEC* and *BEC* are complementary angles.

Angles *AEC* and *DEC* are supplementary angles.

EXAMPLE 3

Are angles *LOM* and *MON* complementary angles, supplementary angles, or neither?

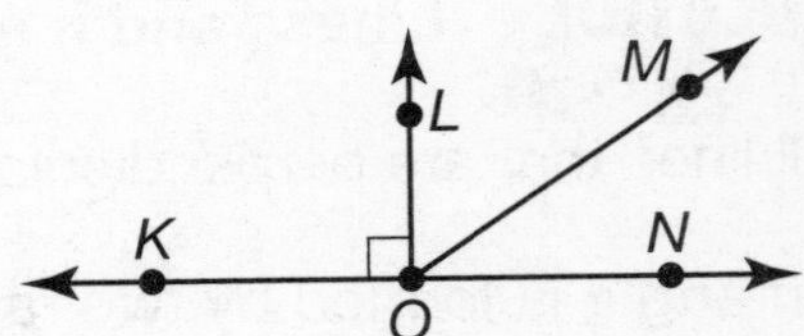

STRATEGY **Use the properties of right angles and straight angles to classify a pair of angles.**

STEP 1 Determine the properties of complementary and supplementary angles.

Complementary angles are two angles with a combined measure of 90°.

Supplementary angles are two angles with a combined measure of 180°.

STEP 2 Find a right angle.

$\angle LON$ is a right angle, which measures 90°.

$\angle LOM$ and $\angle MON$ together have the same measure as $\angle LON$.

SOLUTION **Angles *LOM* and *MON* are complementary angles.**

Adjacent angles have the same vertex and a common side, but have no interior points in common. In the previous diagram, ∠*LOM* and *MON* are adjacent angles.

Vertical angles are two nonadjacent angles formed by intersecting lines. Vertical angles are congruent.

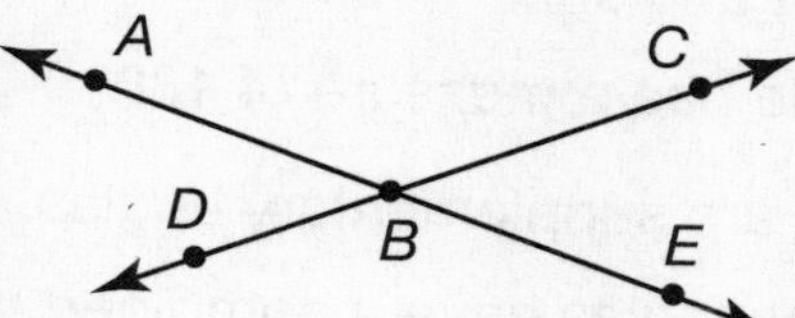

∠*ABD* and ∠*CBE* are vertical angles. ∠*ABD* and ∠*ABC* are not vertical angles.

A line that cuts through a pair of lines is called a **transversal**. When parallel lines are cut by a transversal, the **corresponding** and **alternate interior angles** are congruent.

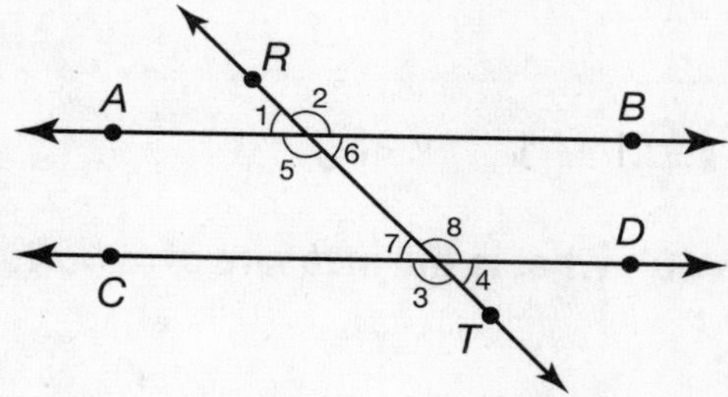

$\overleftrightarrow{AB}$ and $\overleftrightarrow{CD}$ are cut by $\overleftrightarrow{RT}$, which is a transversal. Angles 5, 6, 7, and 8 are interior angles because they lie between $\overleftrightarrow{AB}$ and $\overleftrightarrow{CD}$. Angles 5 and 8 and angles 6 and 7 are alternate interior angles.

Corresponding angles are two angles in corresponding positions, formed by a transversal crossing two lines. Corresponding angles are congruent.

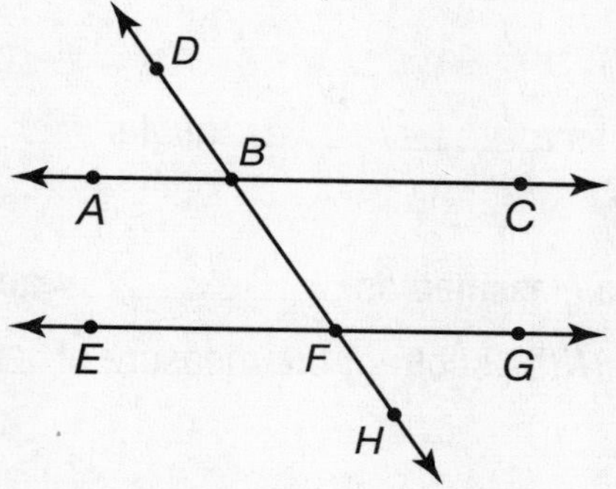

Angles *ABD* and *EFB* are corresponding angles. Angles *CBD* and *GFB* are corresponding angles. The letter *m* before an angle represents the measure of an angle.

EXAMPLE 4

In the previous diagram if ∠*EFB* has a measure of 45°, what is the measure of ∠*GFB*?

STRATEGY **Use the properties of angles to find the angle measure.**

STEP 1 ∠*EFG* is a straight angle.

A straight angle has a measure of 180°.

STEP 2 ∠*EFB* and ∠*GFB* are supplementary angles.

Supplementary angles have a combined measure of 180°.

STEP 3 Subtract the *m* ∠*EFB* from 180°.

$180° - 45° = 135°$

SOLUTION **The *m* ∠*GFB* is 135°.**

COACHED EXAMPLE

If the measure of ∠*PQR* is 50°, what is the measure of ∠*NQR*?

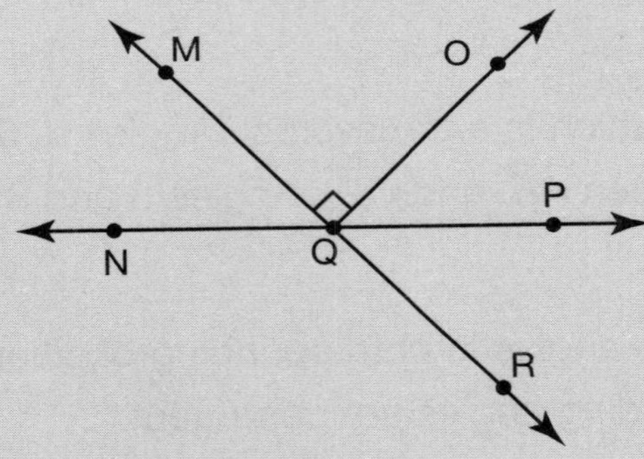

THINKING IT THROUGH

∠*NQP* can be classified as a ____________ angle.

∠*NQP* has a measure of ______°.

∠*PQR* and ∠*NQR* can be classified as ____________ angles.

To find the measure of ∠*NQR*, subtract the measure of ∠*PQR* from ______°.

Subtract. ____________

So, the measure of ∠*NQR* is ______°.

Lesson Practice

Choose the correct answer.

1. Which *best* describes the relationship between $\overline{AB}$ and $\overline{CD}$?

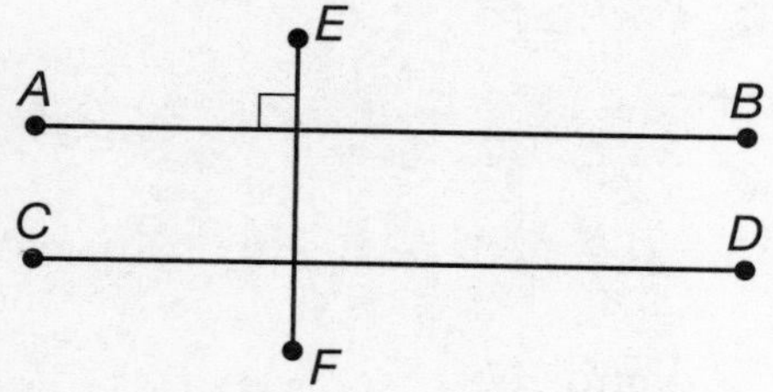

A perpendicular line segments
B perpendicular lines
C parallel line segments
D parallel lines

Use this set of angles to answer questions 2 and 3.

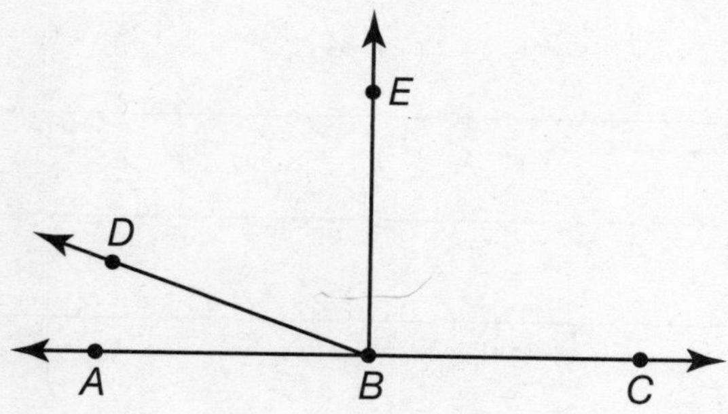

2. Which pair of angles are complementary angles?

A $\angle ABD$ and $\angle DBE$
B $\angle ABD$ and $\angle CBE$
C $\angle DBE$ and $\angle CBE$
D $\angle ABD$ and $\angle ABE$

3. If the measure of $\angle ABD$ is 25°, what is the measure of $\angle DBC$?

A 25°
B 65°
C 90°
D 155°

Use the diagram to answer questions 4 and 5.

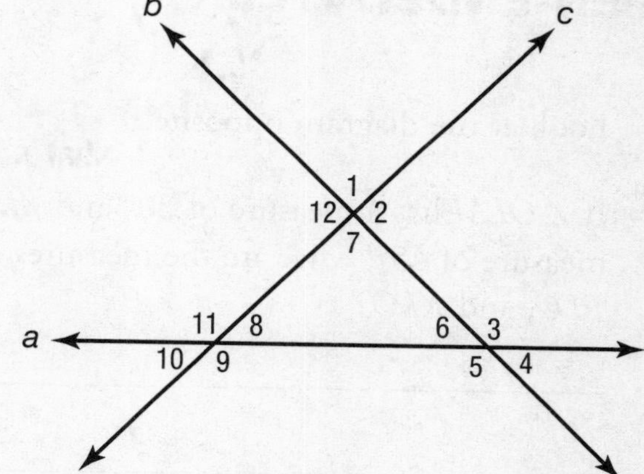

4. Which pair of angles are alternate interior angles?

A angles 6 and 7
B angles 6 and 8
C angles 3 and 11
D angles 6 and 9

5. If the measure of $\angle 9$ is 135°, which other angle has a measure of 135°?

A $\angle 5$ **C** $\angle 7$
B $\angle 6$ **D** $\angle 8$

6. Which pair of angles are vertical angles?

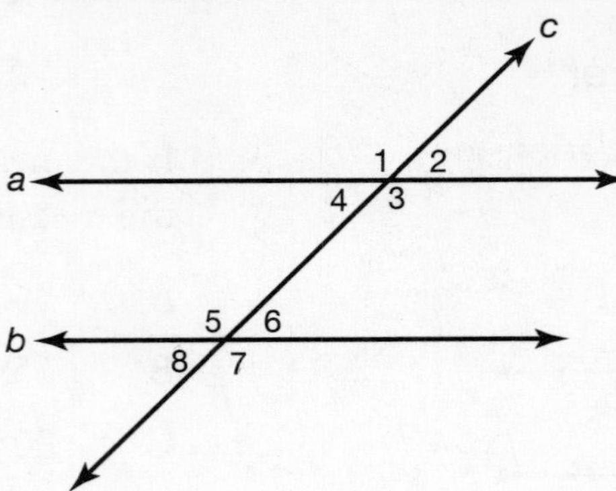

A $\angle 1$ and $\angle 2$

B $\angle 3$ and $\angle 6$

C $\angle 4$ and $\angle 6$

D $\angle 5$ and $\angle 7$

OPEN-ENDED ITEM

7. Look at the diagram opposite.

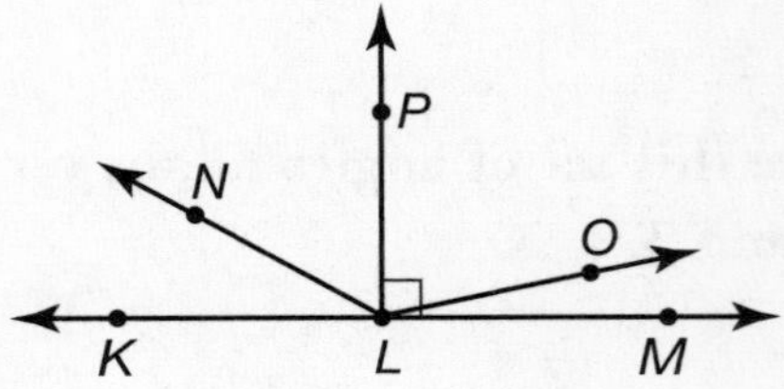

If $\angle OLM$ has a measure of 20° and $\angle NLK$ has a measure of 45°, what are the measures of angles *PLN*, *PLO*, and *KLO*?

Explain your answers.

Lesson

27 Triangles

GLCEs: G.GS.06.01

Getting the Idea

Triangles are **polygons** with 3 **sides** and 3 **vertices.** Triangles can be classified by the number of equal sides.

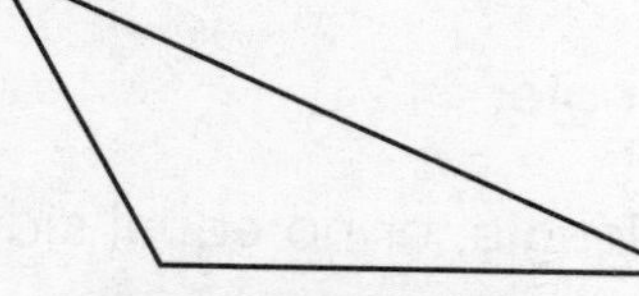

scalene triangle
No sides or angles are equal.

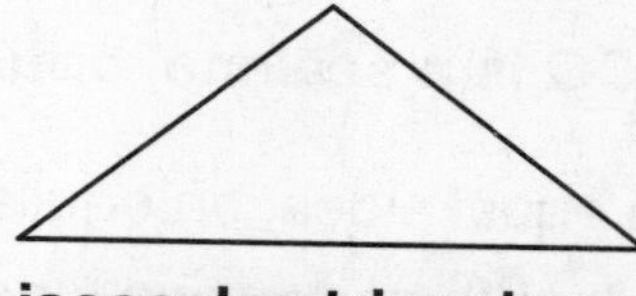

isosceles triangle
At least 2 sides or angles are equal.

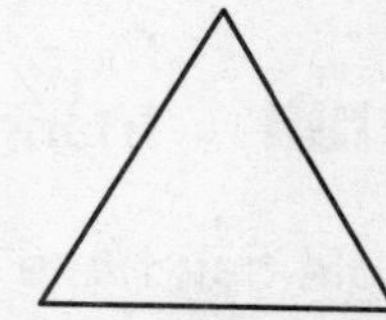

equilateral triangle
3 sides and angles are equal.

A triangle can also be classified by the measure of its greatest angle.

acute triangle
All 3 angles are less than 90°.

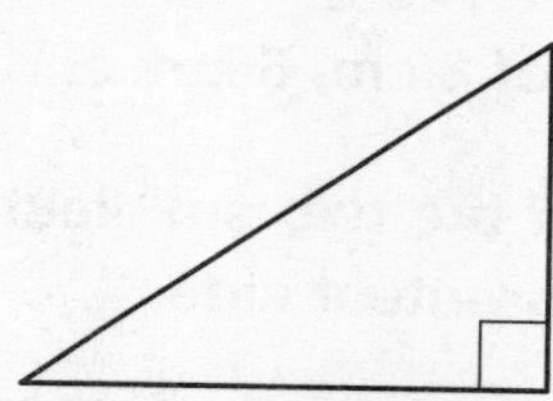

right triangle
One angle is a right angle.

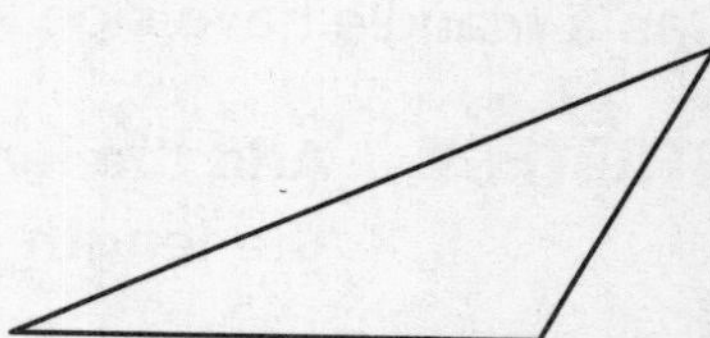

obtuse triangle
One angle is an obtuse angle.

EXAMPLE 1

How can you classify triangle *ADC*?

STRATEGY **Classify by the number of equal sides. Then classify by its greatest angle measure.**

STEP 1 Determine if there are any equal sides. Use a ruler if necessary.

None of the sides are equal. The triangle is scalene.

STEP 2 Determine if the triangle has a right angle or an obtuse angle.

$\angle ADC$ is obtuse. The triangle is obtuse.

SOLUTION **Triangle *ADC* is a scalene, obtuse triangle.**

A triangle can have three equal sides, an equilateral triangle, or no equal sides, a scalene triangle. In any case, the length of any two sides of a triangle is greater than or equal to the length of the third side.

EXAMPLE 2

Can a triangle have side lengths of 8 cm, 6 cm, and 3 cm?

STRATEGY **Add the lengths of the two smallest sides. Then compare that sum to the length of the greatest side.**

STEP 1 Add the lengths of the two smallest sides.

$6 \text{ cm} + 3 \text{ cm} = 9 \text{ cm}$

STEP 2 Compare the sum of the lengths of the smaller sides to the length of the greatest side.

$9 \text{ cm} > 8 \text{ cm}$

SOLUTION **Since the sum of the lengths of the smaller sides is greater than the length of the greatest side, a triangle can have dimensions of 8 cm, 6 cm, and 3 cm.**

Here is the triangle that is formed.

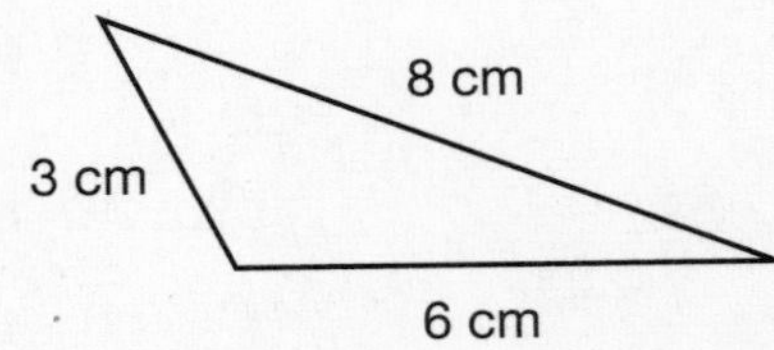

The sum of the measures of the interior angles of any triangle is 180°.

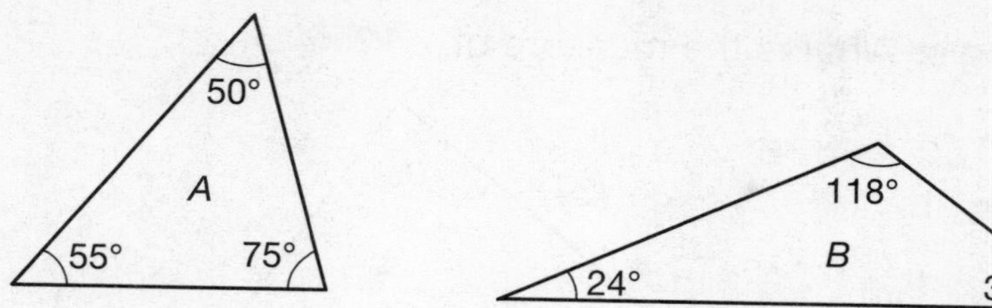

The sum of the measures of the angles in triangle *A* is 180° since 55° + 75° + 50° = 180° as do the angles in triangle *B* since 24° + 38° + 118° = 180°.

EXAMPLE 3

What is the missing angle measure in this triangle?

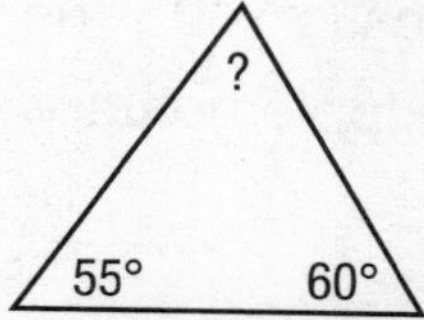

STRATEGY **Subtract the sum of the known angles from 180°.**

STEP 1 Add the measures of the two known angles.

55° + 60° = 115°

STEP 2 Subtract the sum of the known angles from 180°.

180° − 115° = 65°

SOLUTION **The missing angle has a measure of 65°.**

You can use what you know about triangles to find the measures of the **exterior angles** of a triangle. An exterior angle is an angle formed between one side of a polygon and the extension of an adjacent side. To find the measure of an exterior angle of a triangle, add the measures of the sum of the two **remote interior angles**. A remote interior angle of a triangle is an interior angle that is not adjacent to a given exterior angle. The sum of the exterior angles of any **convex polygon** is 360°.

EXAMPLE 4

Angle 1 is an exterior angle. What is the measure of $\angle 1$?

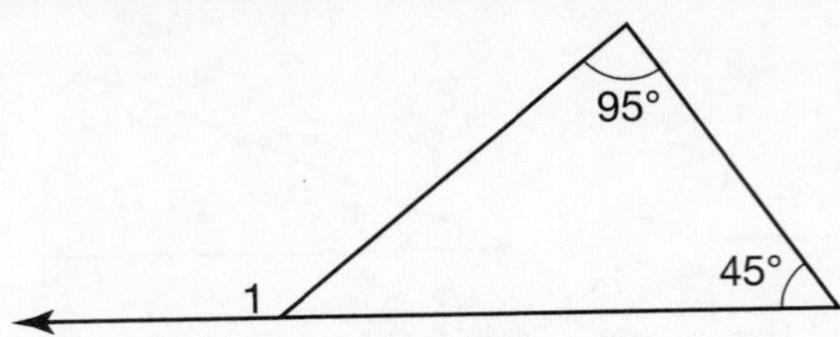

STRATEGY **Add the two known interior angles.**

$95° + 45° = 140°$

SOLUTION **The measure of $\angle 1$ is 140°.**

You could have found the measure by finding the measure of the third interior angle. Since the sum of the two known interior angles is 140°, the third interior angle has a measure of 40°. Angle 1 and the 40° angle are supplementary angles, so the measure of $\angle 1$ is 140°.

COACHED EXAMPLE

What is the measure of $\angle P$?

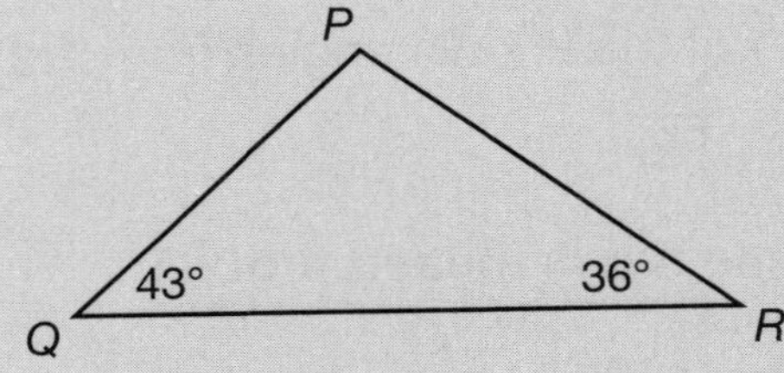

THINKING IT THROUGH

The sum of the measures of the interior angles of any triangle is ______°.

To find the measure of an unknown angle, ______________ the sum of the two known angle measures from ______ degrees.

Add the two known angles measures: $43° + 36° =$ ______°

Subtract. ______________

So, $\angle P$ has a measure of ______°.

Lesson Practice

Choose the correct answer.

1. How can this triangle be classified?

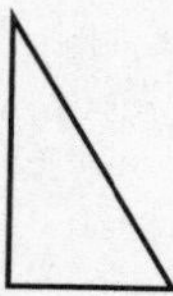

A scalene, right

B scalene, obtuse

C isosceles, right

D isosceles, obtuse

2. One of the angle measures of an isosceles triangle is 74°. Which **CANNOT** be one of the other angle measures?

A 32°

B 53°

C 74°

D 106°

3. Which set of side lengths can form a triangle?

A 7 in., 6 in., 15 in.

B 8 in., 8 in., 20 in.

C 8 in., 12 in., 16 in.

D 9 in., 15 in., 25 in.

4. What is the measure of angle *C*?

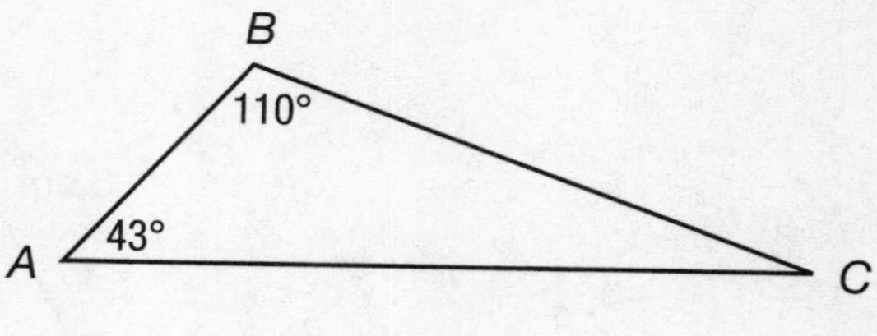

A 27°

B 37°

C 47°

D 153°

5. Which could be the angle measures of an isosceles, obtuse triangle?

A 50°, 65°, 65°

B 50°, 50°, 100°

C 45°, 45°, 90°

D 70°, 10°, 100°

6. What is the measure of $\angle G$?

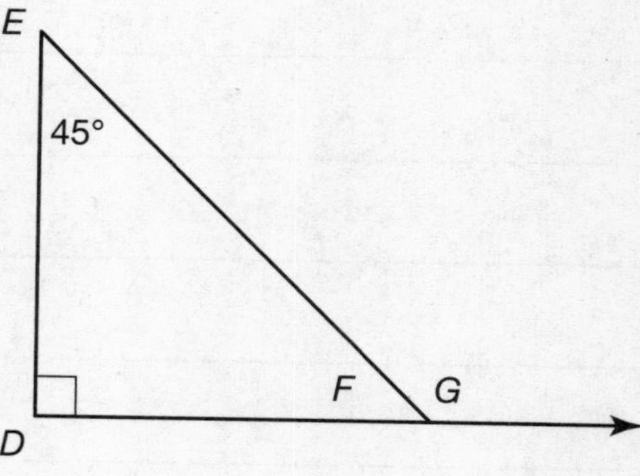

A 45°

B 90°

C 135°

D 145°

OPEN-ENDED ITEM

7. Look at the triangle below.

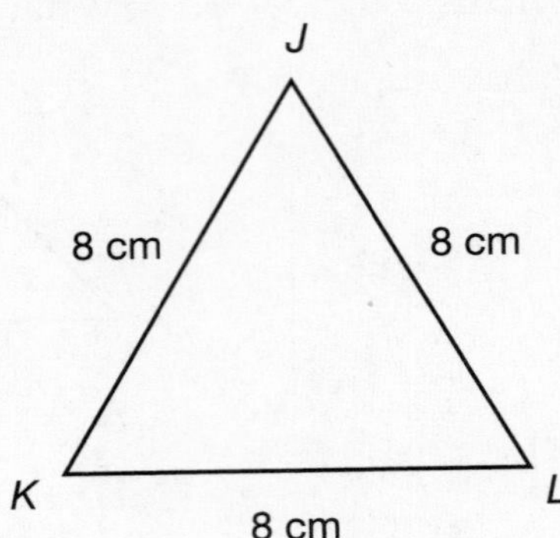

Classify the triangle as *acute*, *right*, or *obtuse* and *scalene*, *isosceles*, or *equilateral*.

____

What are the angle measures of each of the angles?

____

What is the sum of the exterior angles of the triangle?

____

Explain your answers.

____

____

____

____

____

____

Lesson

28 Congruent Polygons

GLCEs: G.GS.06.02

Getting the Idea

Congruent polygons have the same size and the same shape. That means that the corresponding sides of the polygons are congruent and the corresponding angles of the polygons are congruent.

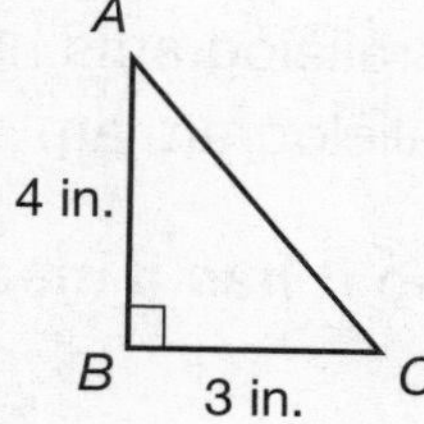

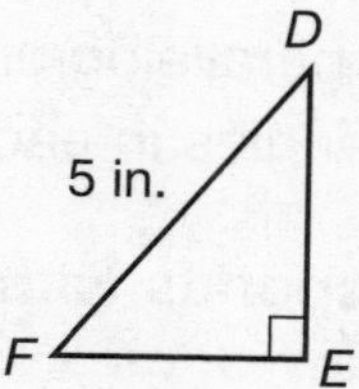

Triangles *ABC* and *DEF* are congruent because each has the same size and the same shape. It does not matter that $\triangle DEF$ has been flipped. The symbol $\cong$ means congruent. There is enough information given to find all of the unknown side lengths.

$\overline{AB} \cong \overline{DE}$, so $\overline{DE}$ has a length of 4 inches.

$\overline{BC} \cong \overline{EF}$, so $\overline{EF}$ has a length of 3 inches.

$\overline{AC} \cong DF \cong$, so $\overline{AC}$ has a length of 5 inches.

EXAMPLE 1

Figures *GHIJ* and *KLMN* are congruent. What is the $m\ \angle N$?

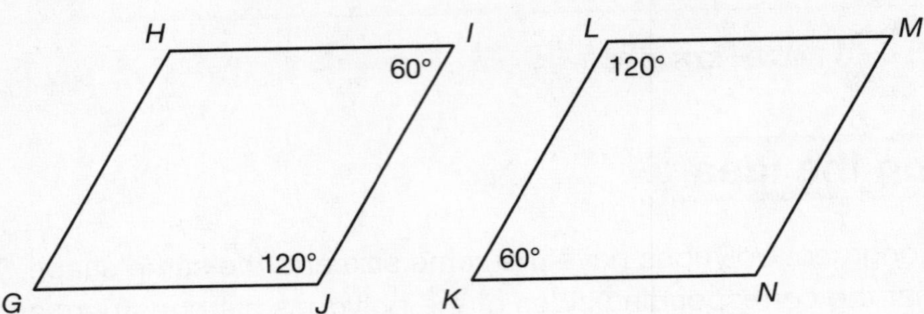

STRATEGY **Compare the corresponding sides.**

The figures are parallelograms. Parallelograms have two pairs of congruent angles, so the angles in each parallelogram are either 60° or 120°.

SOLUTION **Angle *N* corresponds with ∠*J*, so it has a measure of 120°.**

COACHED EXAMPLE

Are these trapezoids congruent?

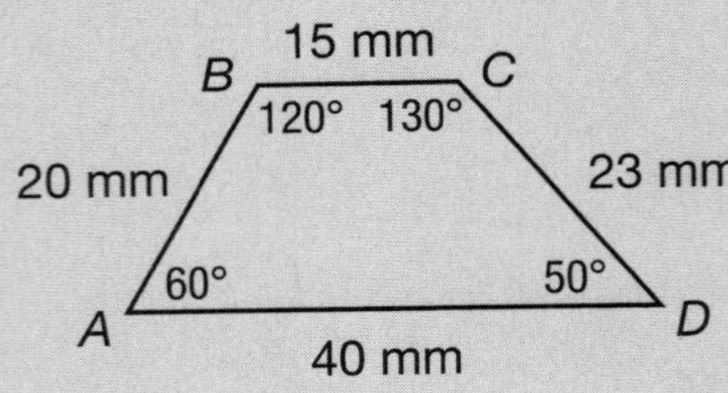

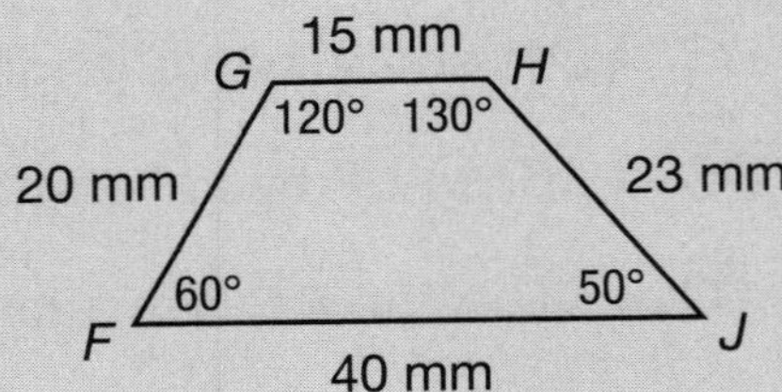

THINKING IT THROUGH

Do the trapezoids have the same shape? ______

Are the corresponding sides congruent? ______

Are the corresponding angles congruent? ______

So, the figures ______ congruent.

Lesson Practice

Choose the correct answer.

1. Which sentence is **NOT** true?

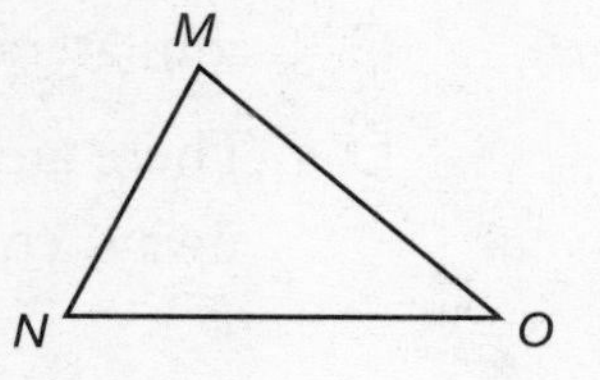

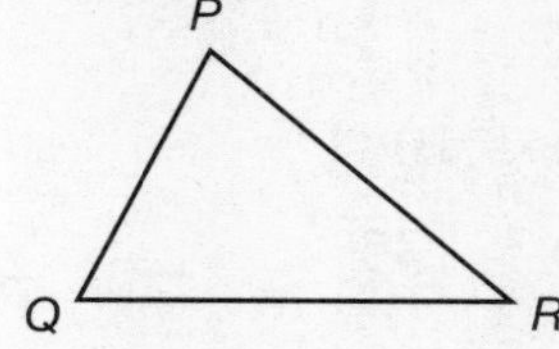

A $m\angle M = m\angle P$

B $m\angle O = m\angle Q$

C $\overline{MN} \cong \overline{PQ}$

D $\overline{NO} \cong \overline{QR}$

2. Which pair of polygons is congruent to each other?

A

C

B

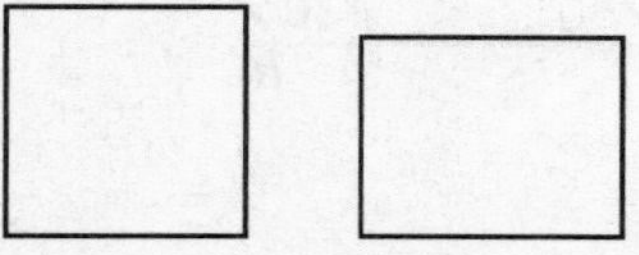

D

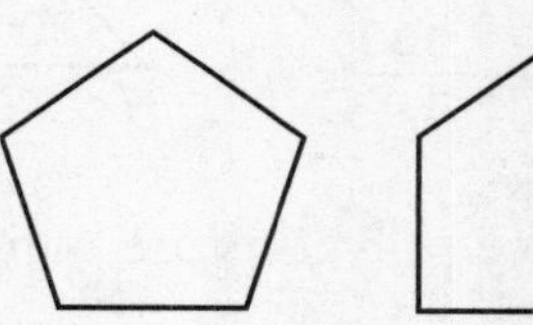

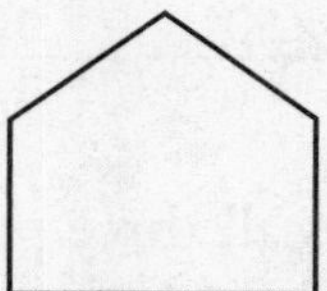

3. Which sentence about these triangles is true?

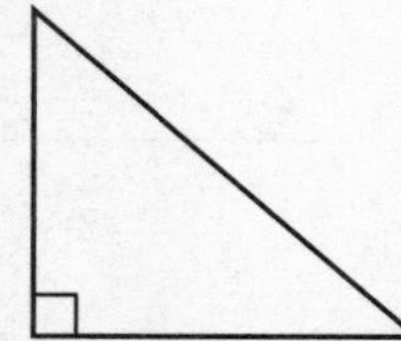

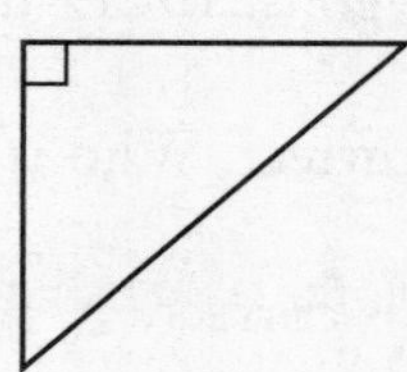

A They are congruent.

B They are not congruent because they have different shapes.

C They are not congruent because they have different sizes.

D They are not congruent because they have different positions.

4. Three of the angle measures of a quadrilateral that Teri drew are 58°, 95°, and 72°. Scott drew a congruent quadrilateral to Teri's. Which is one of the angle measures of Scott's quadrilateral?

A 32° **C** 108°

B 85° **D** 135°

5. Which polygons are always congruent to each other?

A rectangles

B squares

C equilateral triangles

D There are no polygons that are always congruent to each other.

OPEN-ENDED ITEM

6. Look at the polygons below.

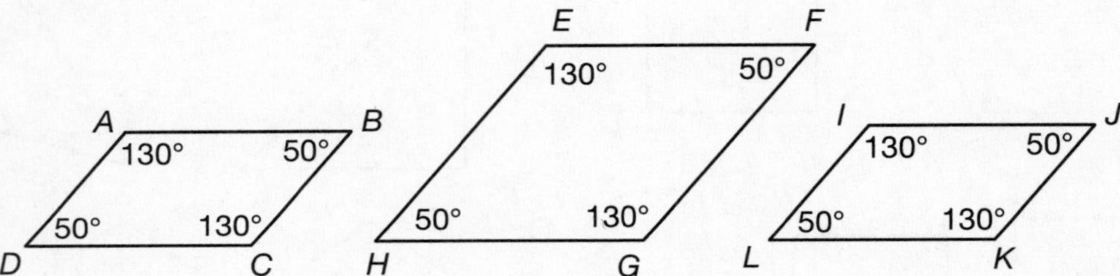

Paige says all three polygons are congruent.

Tom says that only polygons *ABCD* and *IJKL* are congruent.

Mindy said that only polygons *ABCD* and *EFGH* are congruent.

One of these students is correct. Who is correct? ___________

Explain why your choice is correct.

____

____

____

____

Lesson

29 Transformations

GLCEs: G.TR.06.03, G.TR.06.04

Getting the Idea

Transformations change the position of figures. A transformation does not change the size or shape of a figure, so the transformed figure, the **image**, is congruent to the original figure, the **pre-image**. A transformation can be a **translation**, **reflection**, or **rotation**.

A translation moves a figure along a line.

A reflection produces a mirror image of a figure.

A rotation turns a figure around a point. This rotation is a $\frac{1}{4}$ (90°) clockwise turn.

EXAMPLE 1

Describe the transformation of pentagon *A* to pentagon *B*. If it was a rotation, explain how many degrees it was rotated.

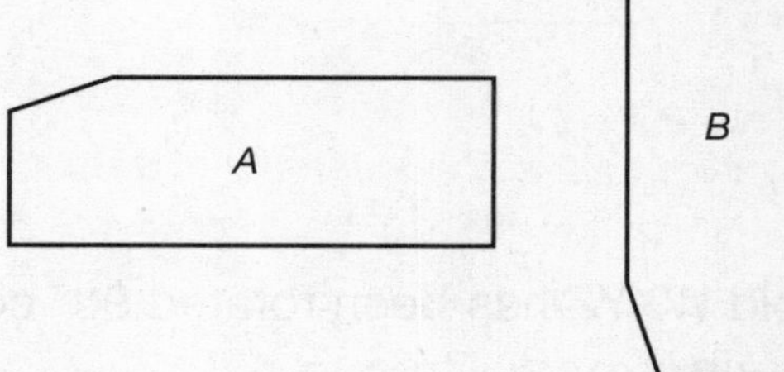

STRATEGY **Use the definitions of transformations to determine the transformation.**

STEP 1 Determine the transformation.

Figure *B* was not moved along a line from figure A. It is not a translation.
Figure *B* is not a mirror image of figure A. It is not a reflection.
Figure *B* was turned on a point, so it is a rotation.

STEP 2 Determine the rotation. Turn the book until figure *A* matches figure *B*.

SOLUTION **Figure *B* was rotated 90° counterclockwise.**

You can represent transformations on a coordinate grid. As shown, the pre-image, trapezoid *ABCD*, has been translated 6 units right and 4 units down to form the image, trapezoid *A′B′C′D′*. The image of a transformation can be written by using the same letters and adding a ′ after each letter.

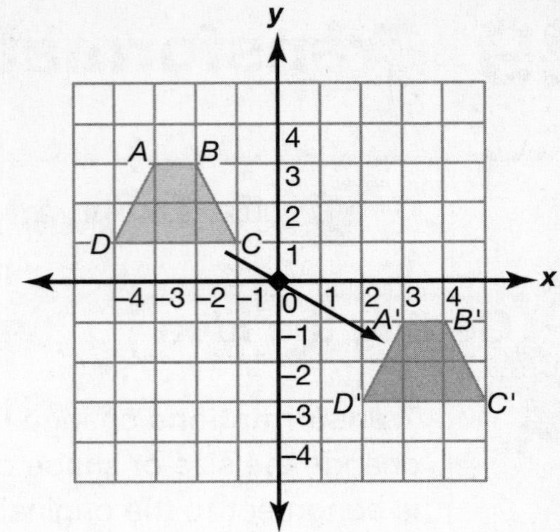

Triangle *ABC* has been reflected across the *y*-axis to form triangle *A′B′C′*. As you can see, the *y*-coordinates of the image remain the same, but the *x*-coordinates are opposites.

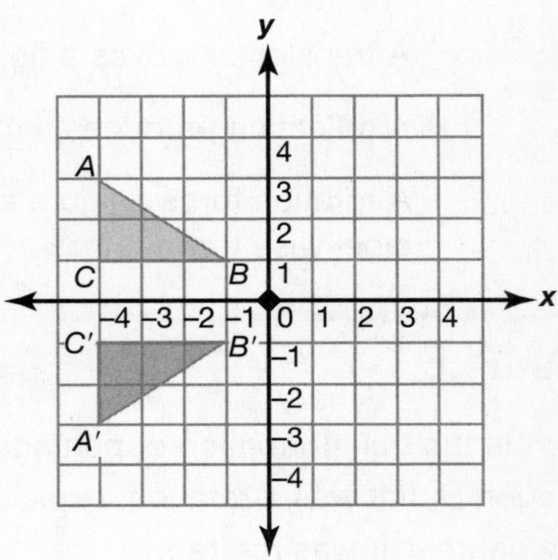

Trapezoid *WXYZ* has been rotated 90° counterclockwise about the origin to form trapezoid *W′X′Y′Z′*.

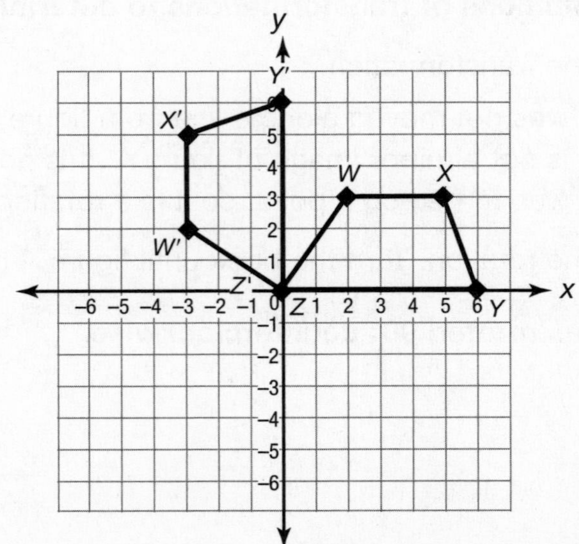

EXAMPLE 2

Describe the transformation of trapezoid *DEFG* to form trapezoid *D′E′F′G′*.

STRATEGY **Use the definitions of transformations.**

STEP 1 Determine the transformation.

Trapezoid *D′E′F′G′* is a mirror image of trapezoid *DEFG*. It is a reflection.

STEP 2 Describe the reflection.

The *x*-coordinates are different, the y-coordinates are the same, so the trapezoid was reflected across the *y*-axis.

SOLUTION **Trapezoid *DEFG* was reflected across the *y*-axis.**

Figures can be moved using a combination of transformations.

EXAMPLE 3

Which combinations of transformations has moved rectangle *HIJK*?

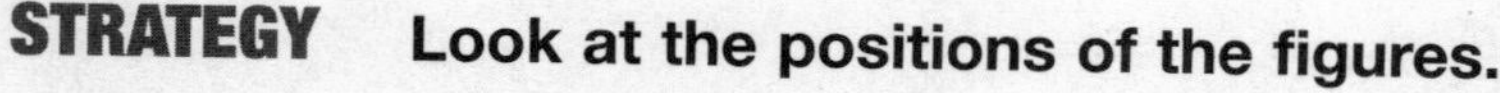

STRATEGY **Look at the positions of the figures.**

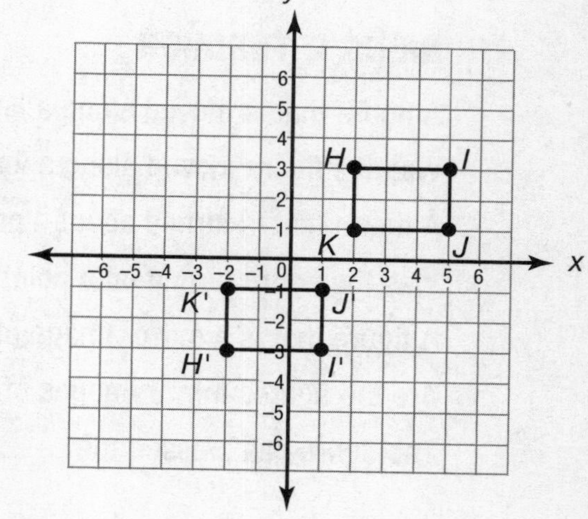

STEP 1 See if the rectangle was reflected across the *x*-axis.

One of the transformations is a reflection.

STEP 2 The image has not been turned, but moved along a line.

The ordered pairs of the image are (−1, −3), (2, −3), (2, −1), (−1, −1), so all of the *x*-coordinates are 3 less than after the reflection.

The second transformation is a translation.

SOLUTION **Rectangle *HIJK* was reflected across the *x*-axis and then translated 3 units left.**

COACHED EXAMPLE

How was the triangle transformed?

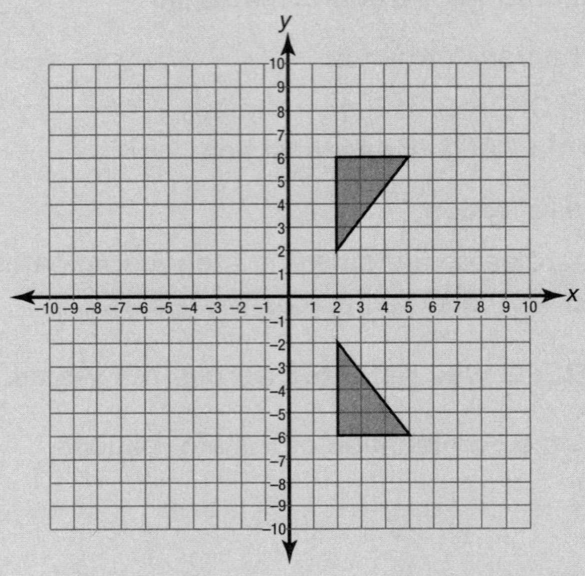

THINKING IT THROUGH

A figure that is moved along a line is a ____________________________.

Was the figure moved along a line? ____________

A figure that is turned about a point is a ____________________________.

Was the figure turned on a point? ____________

A figure that is a mirror image of another is a ____________________________.

Are the figures mirror images of each other? ______

The figure has crossed the ______ -axis.

So, the transformation is a ____________________________.

Lesson Practice

Choose the correct answer.

1. Which *best* describes the transformation of figure *A* to figure *B*?

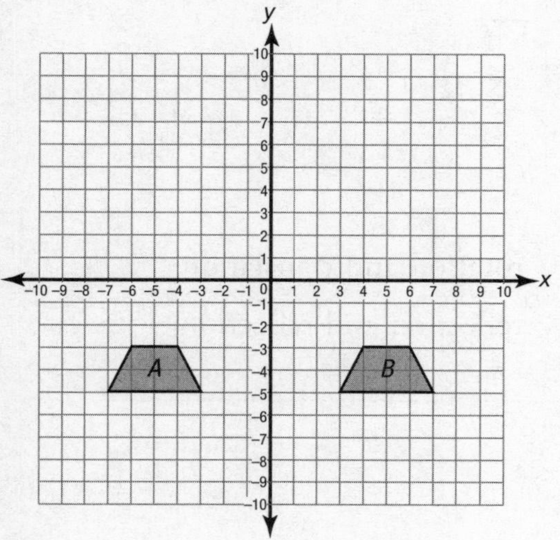

A reflection across the *x*-axis

B reflection across the *y*-axis

C rotation 90° clockwise about the origin

D rotation 180° about the origin

2. Which shows the rhombus after a 90° clockwise rotation?

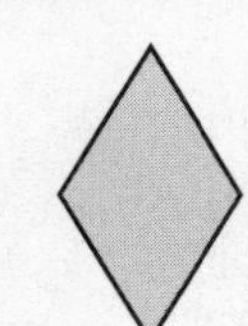

A

C

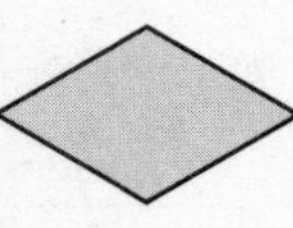

B

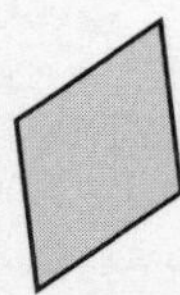

D

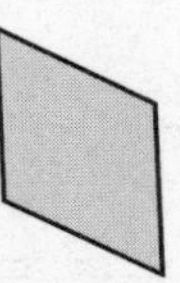

3. Which *best* describes the transformation of triangle *JKL* to triangle *J′K′L′*?

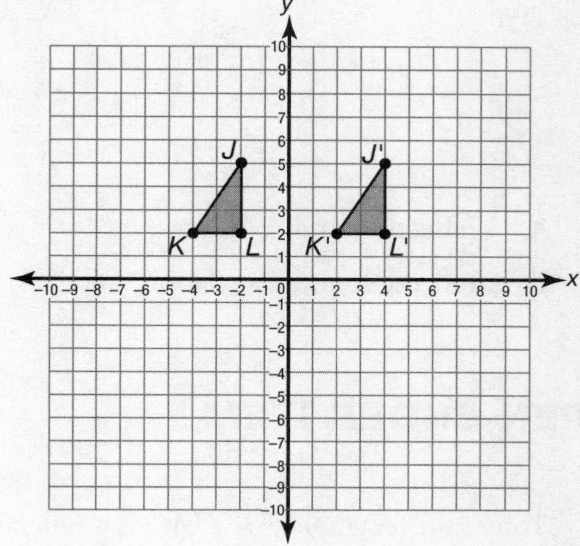

A translation

B rotation 90° about the origin

C reflection across the *y*-axis

D reflection across the *x*-axis

4. Which two transformations were used to transform trapezoid *S* to trapezoid *T*?

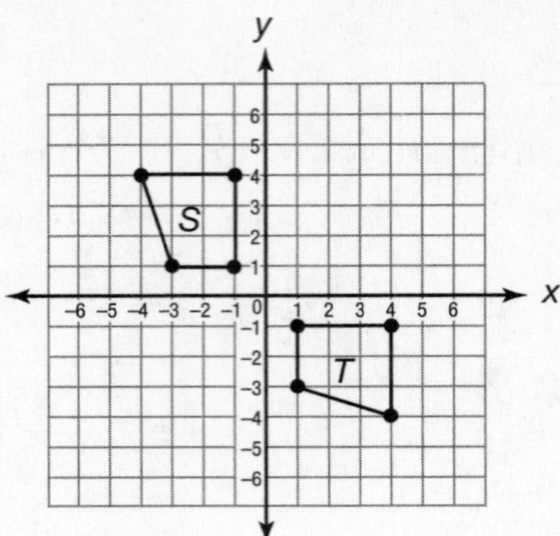

A reflection and rotation

B reflection and translation

C rotation and translation

D reflection and reflection

OPEN-ENDED ITEM

5. Tony said rectangle *J′K′L′M′* is a reflection of *JKLM* because it has crossed the *x*-axis. Sylvia said that *J′K′L′M′* is a rotation of *JKLM*.

Who is correct: Tony, Sylvia, both, or neither? ___________

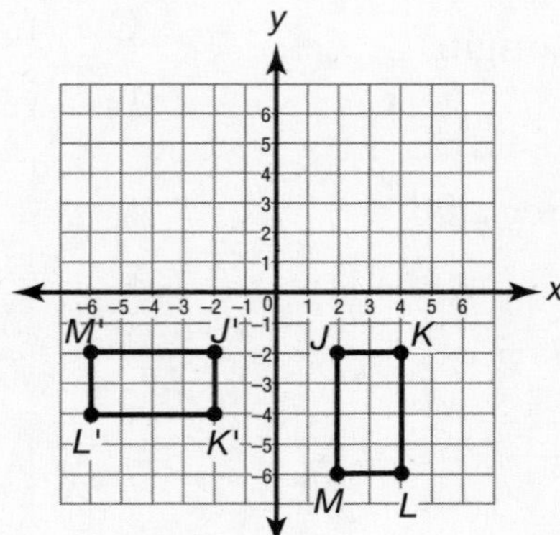

Explain why your choice is correct.

____

____

____

____

CHAPTER

MEAP Review

Choose the correct answer.

1 Which set of dimensions could form a triangle?

A 9 cm, 7 cm, 15 cm

B 12 cm, 8 cm, 22 cm

C 15 cm, 12 cm, 30 cm

D 16 cm, 5 cm, 24 cm

2 Which *best* describes the transformation of figure *A* to figure *B*?

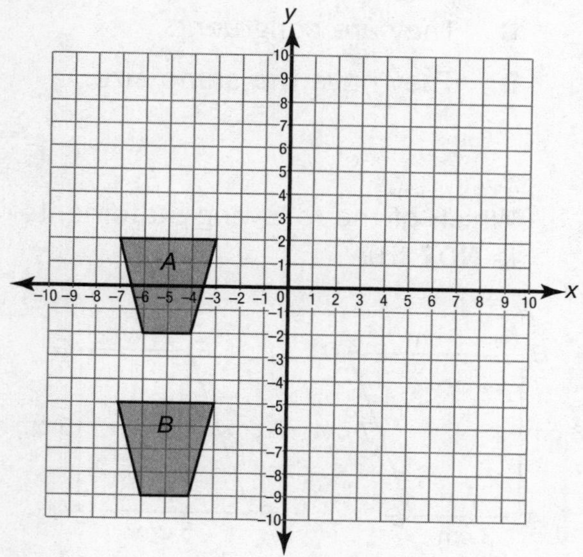

A reflection across the *x*-axis

B reflection across the *y*-axis

C rotation

D translation

3 Which figure is congruent to this figure?

A

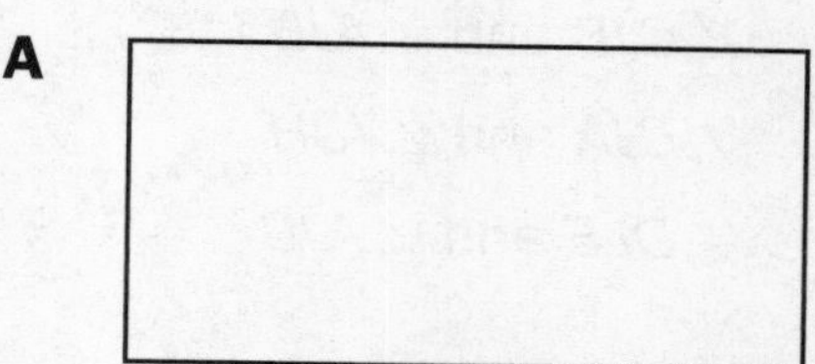

B

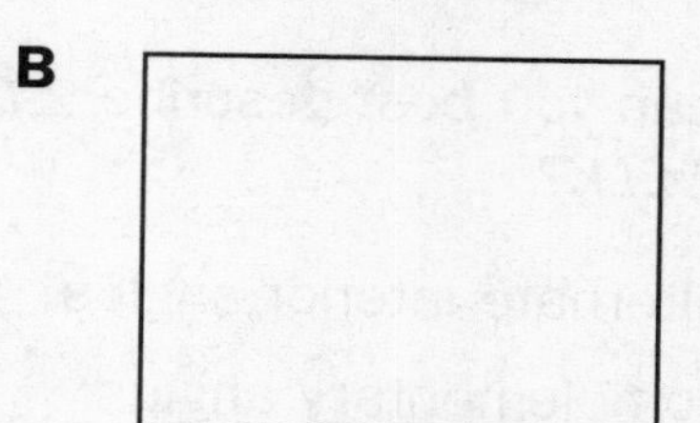

C

D

Use the diagram for questions 4–6.

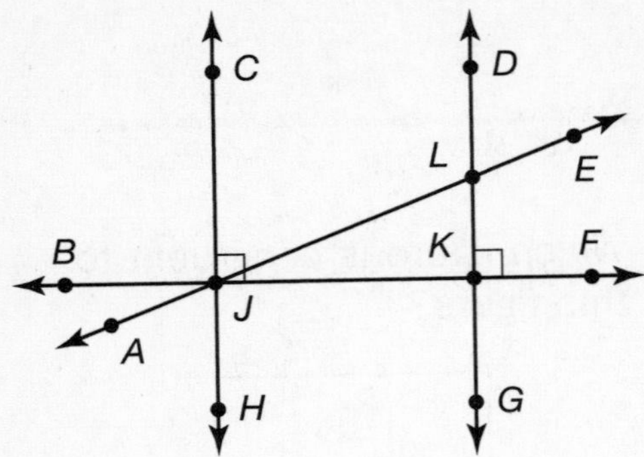

4 Which pair of angles are supplementary angles?

A $\angle AJH$ and $\angle AJB$

B $\angle CJB$ and $\angle AJB$

C $\angle CJA$ and $\angle AJH$

D $\angle DLE$ and $\angle AJB$

5 How can you *best* describe $\angle DLJ$ and $\angle ELK$?

A alternate interior angles

B complementary angles

C corresponding angles

D vertical angles

6 If $\angle JLK$ has a measure of 60°, what is the measure of *ELK*?

A 30°

B 45°

C 120°

D 135°

7 What is the measure of $\angle 1$?

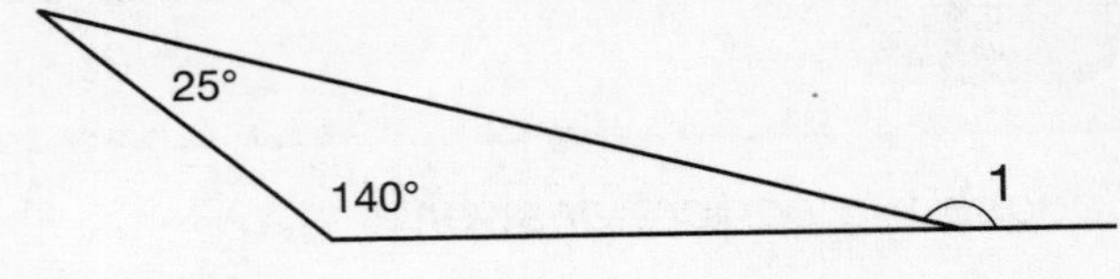

A 15°

B 40°

C 140°

D 165°

8 Which is **NOT** true about transformations of less than 360° of figures?

A They have the same position.

B They have the same shape.

C They are congruent.

D They have the same size.

9 Which of the following statements is **NOT** true?

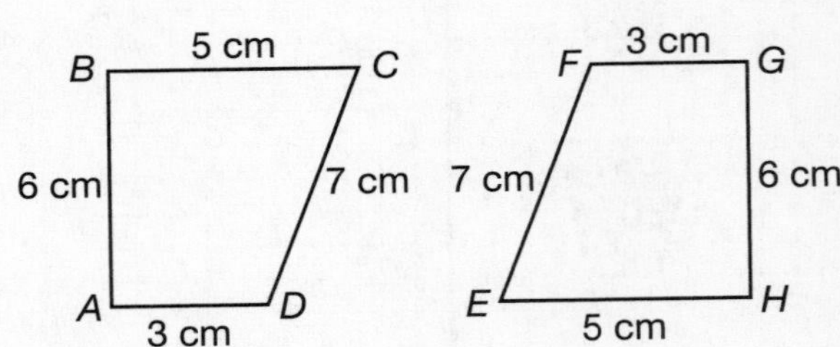

A $ABCD \cong EFGH$

B $\overline{AB} \cong \overline{GH}$

C $\angle C = \angle G$

D $\overline{BC} \cong \overline{EH}$

OPEN-ENDED ITEM

10 Look at the diagram of rectangle *EFGH.*

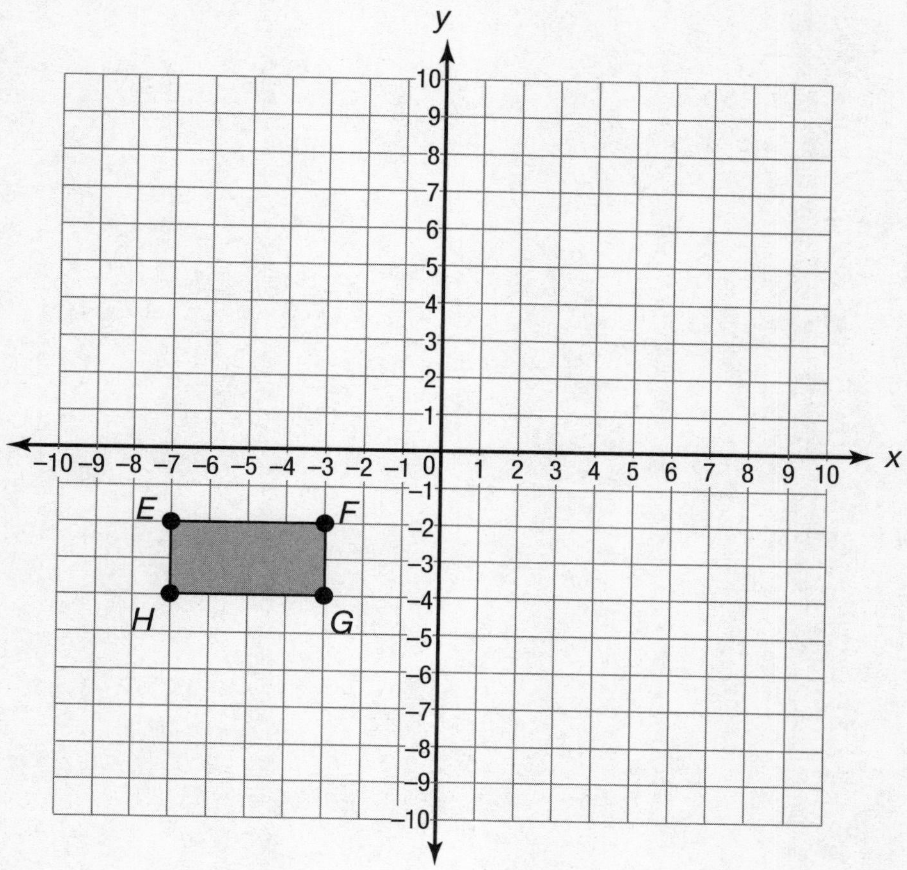

Translate rectangle *EFGH* 4 units to the right and 2 units down. Label *E′F′G′H′* on the grid.

CHAPTER

Data and Probability

30 Probability of Simple Events

GLCEs: D.PR.06.01, D.PR.06.02

Getting the Idea

Probability measures the chance of an event happening. The probability, P, of an event, A, is

$$P(\text{A}) = \frac{\{\text{number of } \textbf{favorable outcomes}\}}{\{\text{number of } \textbf{possible outcomes}\}}$$

The number of possible outcomes must have the same chance of occurring. For example, a number cube has 6 faces, so there are 6 possible outcomes when you toss a number cube. When you spin a spinner, each spinner section must be equal.

Probability can be expressed as a fraction in simplest form, a decimal between 0 and 1, and as a percent from 0% to 100%. An event that is **certain** has a probability of 1 or 100%. An event that is **impossible** has a probability of 0. An event that is **equally likely** to happen or not to happen has a probability of $\frac{1}{2}$, 0.5, or 50%.

EXAMPLE 1

What is the probability of the spinner landing on an odd number? Write the probability as a fraction in simplest form.

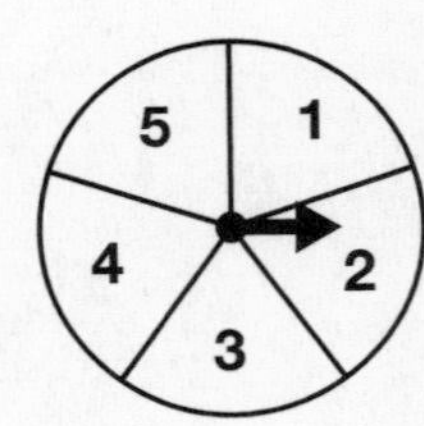

STRATEGY **Write a ratio of the number of favorable outcomes to the number of possible outcomes.**

STEP 1 Find the number of possible outcomes.

The spinner is divided into 5 equal sections, so there are 5 possible outcomes.

STEP 2 Find the number of favorable outcomes.

The numbers 1, 3, and 5 are odd numbers, so there are 3 favorable outcomes.

SOLUTION **The probability of spinning an odd number is $\frac{3}{5}$.**

As a decimal, the probability of the spinner landing on an odd number is 0.6, and as a percent, it is 60%.

The probability of the spinner landing on an even number is $\frac{2}{5}$. Since $\frac{2}{5} + \frac{3}{5} = 1$, it is certain that you would spin an even number or an odd number. It is impossible that you would spin a number greater than 5.

Probability will not always be an exact measure of what will happen. **Experimental probability** measures the probability of what has already happened. For example, suppose you tossed a number cube, with faces numbered 1–6, 20 times and recorded these results.

Numbers Tossed

Number	Times Tossed	Probability
1	4	$\frac{4}{20}$
2	2	$\frac{2}{20}$
3	5	$\frac{5}{20}$
4	3	$\frac{3}{20}$
5	4	$\frac{4}{20}$
6	2	$\frac{2}{20}$

The **theoretical probability** for tossing each number is $\frac{1}{6}$. However, none of the experimental probabilities for the numbers were equal to $\frac{1}{6}$. For example, the experimental probability of tossing a 5 in this **trial** is $\frac{4}{20}$ or $\frac{1}{5}$. If you were to conduct another trial, you would most likely get different results.

When conducting an experiment, it is necessary that all possible outcomes have an equal chance of occurring. For example, if you were to pick a card from a pile of cards, you would need to pick one **at random**, which in this case would be without looking.

EXAMPLE 2

Ms. Thomas asked each of her 16 students to name their favorite flavor of ice cream. Of those students, 6 said vanilla, 5 said chocolate, 3 said strawberry, and 2 said chocolate chip mint. If Ms. Thomas were to pick one student at random, what is the probability, written as a percent, that she would pick someone who likes chocolate chip mint the best?

STRATEGY **Write a ratio.**

STEP 1 Find the number of possible outcomes.

Each of the 16 students is a possible outcome.

STEP 2 Find the number of favorable outcomes.

The 2 students who liked chocolate chip mint are the favorable outcomes.

STEP 3 Convert the probability to a percent.

The probability is $\frac{2}{16}$ or $\frac{1}{8}$ as a fraction, which is equal to 12.5%.

SOLUTION **The probability of Ms. Thomas picking, at random, a student who likes chocolate chip mint ice cream the best is 12.5%.**

COACHED EXAMPLE

What is the probability, written as a decimal, of the spinner landing on X or Y?

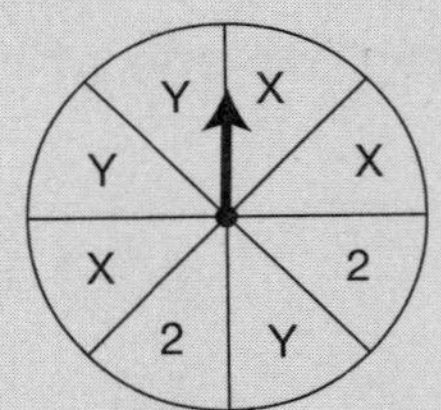

THINKING IT THROUGH

What are the possible outcomes? ____________

What are the favorable outcomes? ____________

What is the probability written as a fraction and as a decimal? ____________

So, the probability of the spinner landing on X or Y is ____________.

Lesson Practice

Choose the correct answer.

1. What is the $P(2)$?

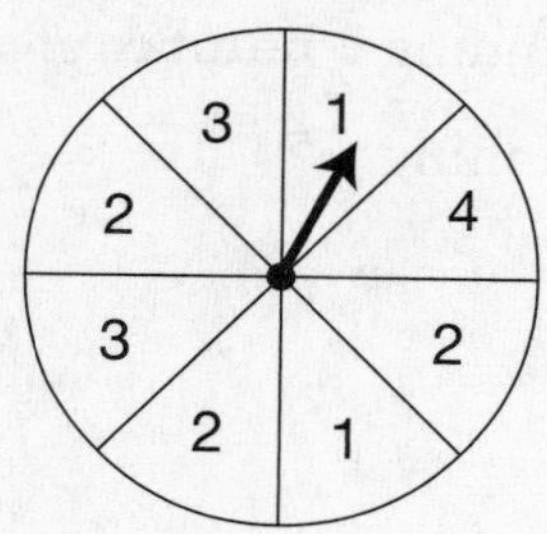

A 0.125

B 0.25

C 0.375

D 0.5

2. What is the probability of tossing a number greater than 4 on a number cube with faces numbered 1–6?

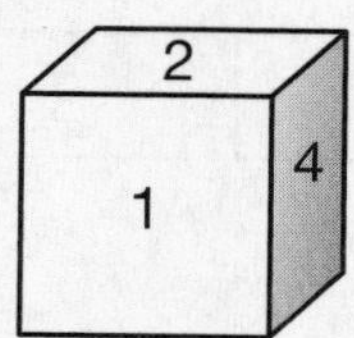

A $\frac{1}{6}$

B $\frac{1}{3}$

C $\frac{1}{2}$

D $\frac{2}{3}$

3. Sophie is conducting an experiment. If she picks one sock at random, what is P (white sock)?

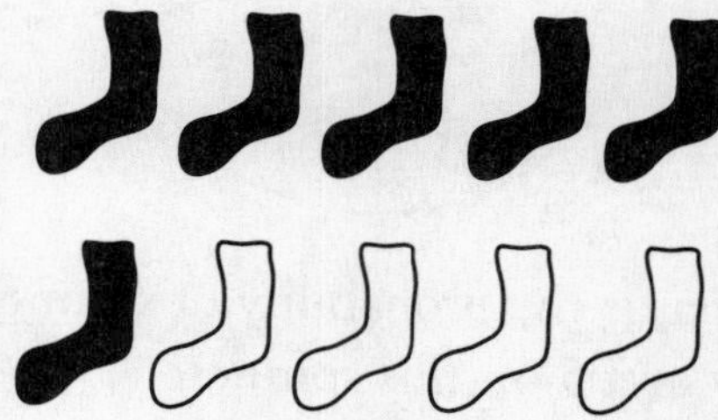

A 40%

B 50%

C 60%

D $66\frac{2}{3}$%

4. The table displays the number of times each student has won the weekly spelling bee in Ms. Cho's class.

Spelling Bees Won	
Student	**Bees Won**
Earl	6
Jamie	4
Carlos	5
Katie	3

What is the probability that Jamie will win the next spelling bee?

A $\frac{2}{9}$

B $\frac{1}{4}$

C $\frac{5}{18}$

D $\frac{1}{3}$

Use the spinner to answer questions 5 and 6.

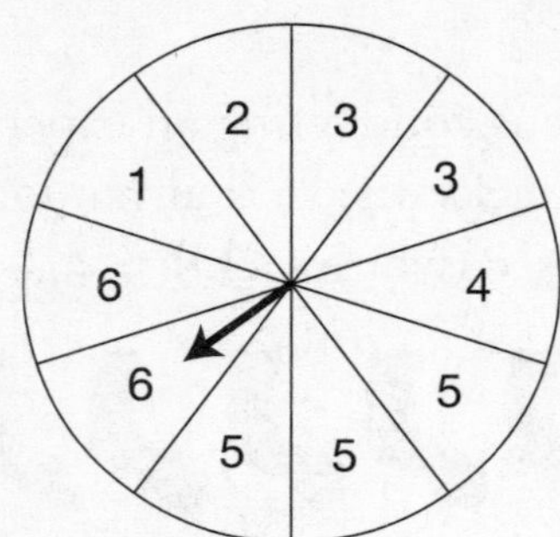

5. What is the probability of spinning a 3 or a 5 on this spinner?

A	20%	**C**	40%
B	30%	**D**	50%

6. Using the spinner, which event is impossible?

A spinning a prime number

B spinning a number less than 7

C spinning a number greater than 1

D spinning a 7

OPEN-ENDED ITEM

7. Virginia has written the letters to her name on index cards

V	I	R	G	I	N	I	A

Virginia is going to pick one of the cards at random.

What are the possible outcomes? ______________________

How many possible outcomes are there? ___________

What is *P*(vowel)? Write your answer as a decimal. ___________

Explain how you determined your answer.

____

____

____

____

31 Probability of Compound Events

GLCEs: D.PR.06.02

Getting the Idea

You can find the probability of two events occurring. The first step in finding the probability of a **compound event** is to find the number of possible outcomes. A **tree diagram** can be used to find the number of possible outcomes for two or more events. For example, you can use a tree diagram to show the number of possible outcomes for tossing two coins.

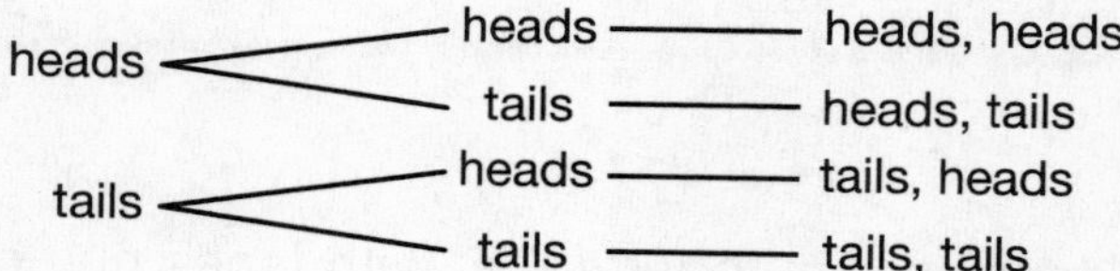

As you can see, there are 4 possible outcomes. There are two ways to have 1 heads and 1 tails.

You can also use the **Fundamental Counting Principle** to find the number of possible outcomes. The Fundamental Counting Principle states that the number of possible outcomes is the product of the number of possible outcomes for each event.

Event # 1		**Event # 2**		
2 possible outcomes	×	2 possible outcomes	=	4 possible outcomes

EXAMPLE 1

An ice cream shop offers 3 flavors of ice cream, which can be put in a cup or a cone. How many possible ways can you order 1 flavor of ice cream in 1 container?

STRATEGY **Use the Fundamental Counting Principle.**

STEP 1 Find the number of possible outcomes for the flavors of ice cream.

There are 3 flavors, so there are 3 possible outcomes.

STEP 2 Find the number of possible outcomes for the containers.

There are 2 types of containers, so there are 2 possible outcomes.

STEP 3 Multiply the number of possible outcomes for each event.

$3 \times 2 = 6$

SOLUTION There are 6 possible ways to order 1 flavor of ice cream in 1 container.

To find the probability of a compound event, you can multiply the probability of each event occurring. For example, the probability of tossing heads on 2 coins can be found this way:

Coin 1: probability of tossing heads $= \frac{1}{2}$

Coin 2: probability of tossing heads $= \frac{1}{2}$

The possibility of tossing heads on 2 coins $= \frac{1}{2} \times \frac{1}{2} = \frac{1}{4}$.

EXAMPLE 2

What is the probability of tossing a number cube, with faces numbered 1–6, and spinning this spinner and getting a 3 on both?

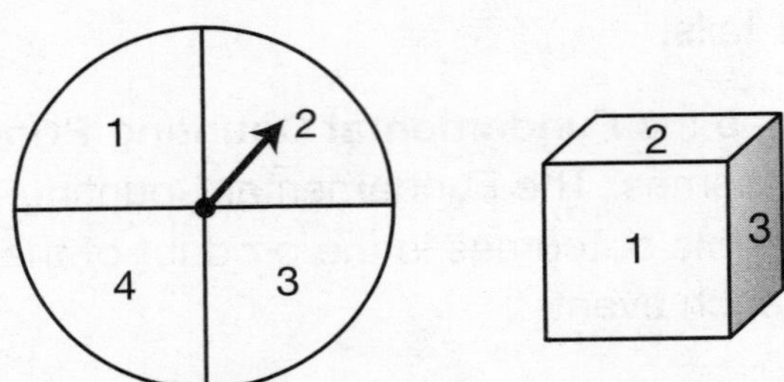

STRATEGY Find the probability of each event and multiply.

STEP 1 Find the probability of spinning a 3 on the spinner.

The probability is $\frac{1}{4}$.

STEP 2 Find the probability of tossing a 3 on the number cube.

The probability is $\frac{1}{6}$.

STEP 3 Multiply.

$\frac{1}{4} \times \frac{1}{6} = \frac{1}{24}$

SOLUTION The probability of spinning a 3 and tossing a 3 is $\frac{1}{24}$.

Sometimes, finding the probability of a compound event will require making a tree diagram or an organized list.

EXAMPLE 3

What is the probability of tossing two number cubes, each with faces numbered 1–6, and getting a sum of 6?

STRATEGY **Find the number of possible outcomes. Then make an organized list.**

STEP 1 Find the number of possible outcomes for tossing two number cubes.

Each number cube has 6 possible outcomes.

$6 \times 6 = 36$. There are 36 possible outcomes.

STEP 2 Make an organized list to find all the sums that can be made.

$1 + 1;\ 1 + 2;\ 1 + 3;\ 1 + 4;\ 1 + 5;\ 1 + 6$

$2 + 1;\ 2 + 2;\ 2 + 3;\ 2 + 4;\ 2 + 5;\ 2 + 6$

$3 + 1;\ 3 + 2;\ 3 + 3;\ 3 + 4;\ 3 + 5;\ 3 + 6$

$4 + 1;\ 4 + 2;\ 4 + 3;\ 4 + 4;\ 4 + 5;\ 4 + 6$

$5 + 1;\ 5 + 2;\ 5 + 3;\ 5 + 4;\ 5 + 5;\ 5 + 6$

$6 + 1;\ 6 + 2;\ 6 + 3;\ 6 + 4;\ 6 + 5;\ 6 + 6$

STEP 3 Count the number of ways to toss a 6.

There are five ways to toss a sum of 6 with two number cubes.

SOLUTION **The probability of tossing a 6 is $\frac{5}{36}$.**

COACHED EXAMPLE

Devin is going to spin each spinner one time. What is the probability that she will spin an even number on both spinners?

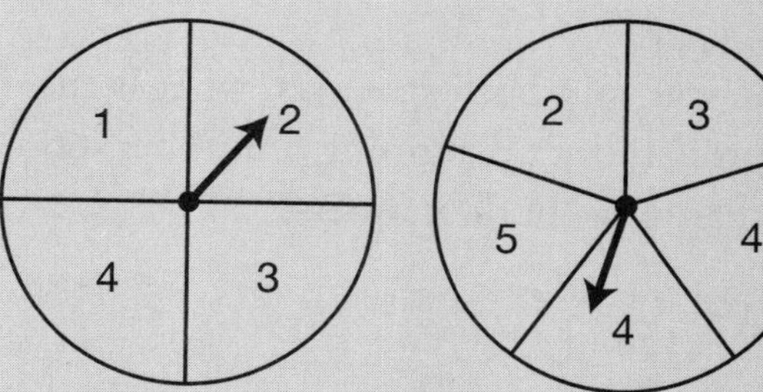

THINKING IT THROUGH

The probability of spinning an even number on the spinner on the left is ______.

The probability of spinning an even number on the spinner on the right is ______.

Multiply. ______ × ______ = ______

So, the probability that Devin will spin an even number on both spinners is ______.

Lesson Practice

Choose the correct answer.

Use the spinners to answer questions 1–4.

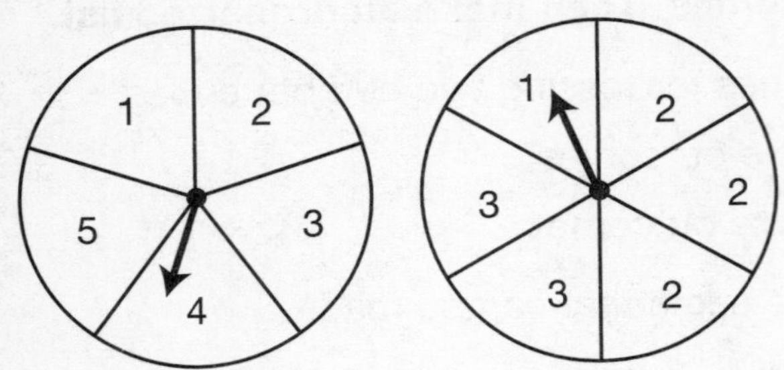

1. If you spin both spinners, how many possible outcomes are there?

   A 11
   B 22
   C 30
   D 36

2. If you spin both spinners, what is the probability of spinning a 2 on both spinners?

   A $\frac{1}{10}$
   B $\frac{1}{8}$
   C $\frac{1}{5}$
   D $\frac{1}{2}$

3. If you spin both spinners, what is the probability of spinning a number less than 4 on both spinners?

   A $\frac{3}{20}$
   B $\frac{1}{5}$
   C $\frac{3}{10}$
   D $\frac{3}{5}$

4. If you spin both spinners and add the numbers that the spinners land on, what is the probability that the sum will be 5?

   A $\frac{1}{10}$
   B $\frac{1}{6}$
   C $\frac{1}{5}$
   D $\frac{1}{4}$

5. Maria has 4 red pencils and 2 blue pencils. She picks one pencil at random and returns it. Then she picks a second pencil at random. What is the probability that she picked a red pencil and a blue pencil?

   A $\frac{1}{12}$
   B $\frac{1}{9}$
   C $\frac{1}{6}$
   D $\frac{2}{9}$

6. A pizzeria offers the following lunch specials of one slice of pizza with one topping and a drink for $1.99.

Toppings	Drinks
Extra Cheese	Soda
Sausage	Fruit Drink
Pepperoni	Juice
Mushroom	
Broccoli	

   Donna asks the owner to pick a slice and a drink at random. What is the probability that Donna received a meat topping (sausage or pepperoni) and a soda?

   A $\frac{2}{15}$
   B $\frac{1}{8}$
   C $\frac{1}{5}$
   D $\frac{4}{15}$

7. What is the probability of tossing a sum of 7 with two number cubes, with faces numbered 1–6?

A $\frac{5}{36}$

B $\frac{1}{6}$

C $\frac{7}{36}$

D $\frac{2}{9}$

8. For a vacation, Carrie brought 4 DVDs that can be classified as comedies and 3 DVDs that can be classified as dramas. Carrie picked a DVD at random, watched it, and returned it. Then she picked another DVD at random. What is the probability that both DVDs were dramas? (HINT: She may have watched the same DVD twice.)

A $\frac{9}{49}$

B $\frac{12}{49}$

C $\frac{16}{49}$

D $\frac{3}{7}$

OPEN-ENDED ITEM

9. Carl is going to toss a number cube, with faces numbered 1–6, and spin this spinner.

How many possible outcomes are there? __________

What is the probability of getting an even number on both the spinner and the number cube? __________

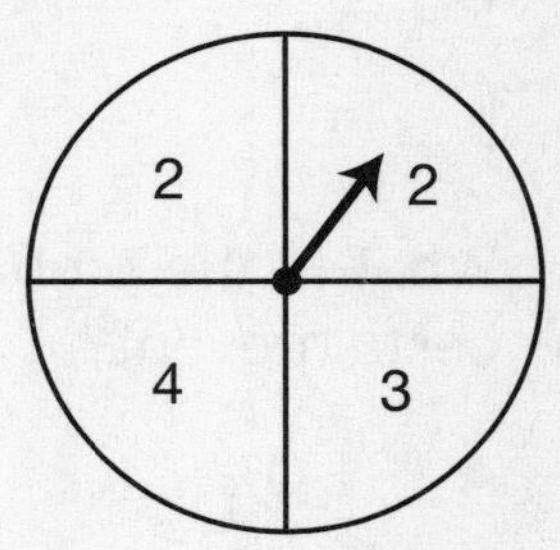

What is the probability that the sum of the spinner and the number cube will be 8 or greater? __________

Explain how you found your answer.

___

___

___

___

___

___

MEAP Review

Choose the correct answer.

1 Sheila is going to spin this spinner.

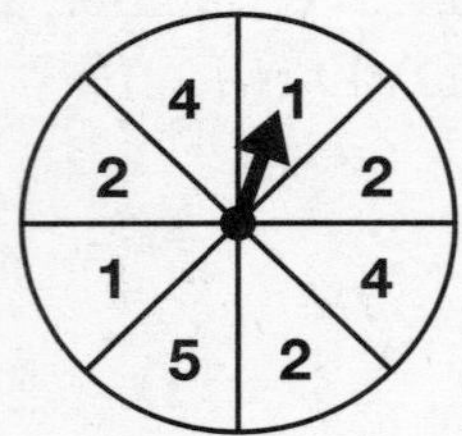

What is the probability that Sheila will spin a 4?

A $\frac{1}{8}$

B $\frac{1}{4}$

C $\frac{3}{8}$

D $\frac{1}{2}$

2 What is the probability of a certain event?

A 0%

B 25%

C 50%

D 100%

3 What is the probability of tossing two number cubes, each with faces labeled 1–6, and getting a sum of 9?

A $\frac{1}{9}$

B $\frac{5}{36}$

C $\frac{1}{6}$

D $\frac{7}{36}$

4 Gina has 6 tops and 4 pairs of pants to choose from for her outfit today. How many possible outfits can Gina wear?

A 10

B 12

C 20

D 24

5 Through December, Keri had won 7 spelling bees. All of the other students had won a combined 3 spelling bees. What is the experimental probability that Keri will win the next spelling bee?

A 30% **B** 50%

C 70% **D** 100%

6 Willie has 5 hip hop CDs and 3 jazz CDs. He plays one CD, puts it back, and then plays another CD. What is the probability that both CDs he played were hip hop?

A $\frac{15}{64}$ **B** $\frac{25}{64}$

C $\frac{3}{8}$ **D** $\frac{5}{8}$

7 Rosa is going to spin these two spinners one time and multiply the numbers. What is the probability that the product of the numbers will be *less than* 20?

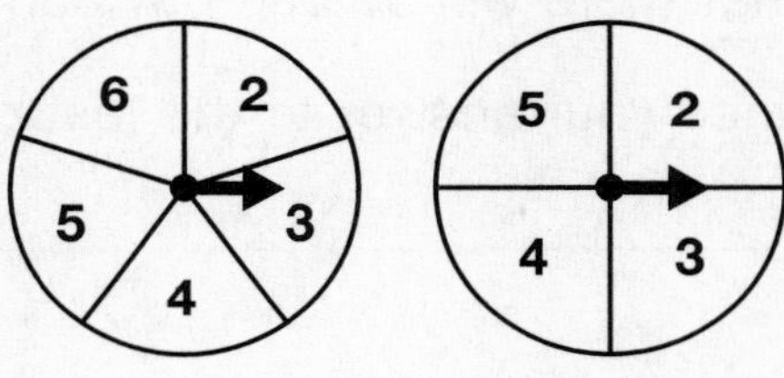

A 0.5 **B** 0.6

C 0.65 **D** 0.75

8 Maureen has cards with these figures on them. Which two events are equally likely?

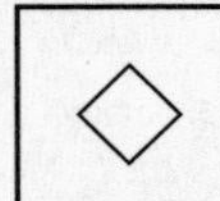 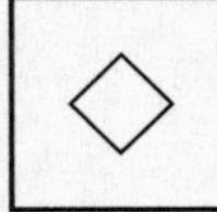 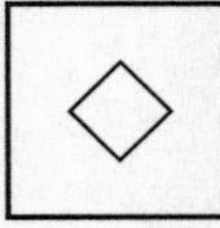 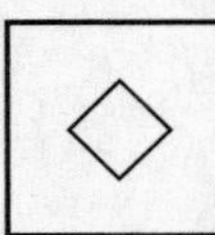 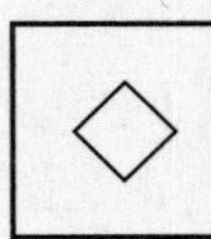

A Picking a diamond or not picking a diamond

B Picking a star or picking a heart

C Picking a heart or picking a diamond

D Picking a star or picking a diamond

OPEN-ENDED ITEM

9 The table displays the number of students that have an opportunity to be soloists at the Spring Concert Jubilee.

Potential Soloists			
Sixth Grade		**Seventh Grade**	
Boys	**Girls**	**Boys**	**Girls**
1	3	3	2

The chorus director, Ms. Finn, will pick one sixth-grade student and one seventh-grade student at random.

What is the probability that each will be a boy? ___________

What is the probability that each will be a girl? ___________

What is the probability that there will be one boy and one girl chosen? ______

Explain how you determined your answer to the last question.

____

____

____

____

____

____

Focus on MEAP
Supporting On-Grade Level GLCEs,
Mathematics, Grade 6

POSTTEST

Name:

PART 1

DIRECTIONS

This test has four parts. You may **NOT** use a calculator on this part. You may use open space in this practice test for scratch paper.

There is one type of item on this test: multiple choice.

1. Multiple-choice items will require you to choose the best answer from among four answer choices. For these items, use only a No. 2 pencil to mark your answer on your **Answer Sheet**. If you erase an answer, be sure to erase it completely. If you skip an item, be sure to mark the answer to the next item in the correct place on your **Answer Sheet**.

Sample Multiple-Choice Item:

Kelly asked 80 students about their favorite kind of movies. Thirty-five percent said comedy. How many people out of 80 said comedy?

A 25

B 26

C 27

D 28

For this sample item, the correct answer is **D**.

GO ON TO THE NEXT PAGE

You will be timed to finish Part 1 of this test.

1. Once you have reached the word **STOP** in the practice test, do **NOT** go on to the next page.
2. If you finish early, you may check your work in Part 1 of the test **ONLY**. Do **NOT** look at items in other parts of the test.

WAIT. DO NOT GO ON UNTIL TOLD TO DO SO.

POSTTEST

1 A stack of newspapers is $8\frac{7}{16}$ inches high. Mr. Forman adds a second stack that is $6\frac{3}{4}$ inches high. If he places the second stack atop the first stack, how high is the stack?

A $14\frac{1}{2}$ inches

B $15\frac{3}{16}$ inches

C $15\frac{1}{4}$ inches

D $15\frac{5}{16}$ inches

2 What is $\frac{5}{8} \times \frac{4}{9}$?

A $\frac{5}{18}$

B $\frac{1}{4}$

C $\frac{1}{3}$

D $\frac{9}{17}$

3 What is $2\frac{1}{5} \div 4\frac{2}{3}$?

A $\frac{15}{154}$

B $\frac{33}{70}$

C $2\frac{4}{33}$

D $10\frac{4}{15}$

4 Barbara, Kirsten, and Ling live west to east on the same road in the order listed. Kirsten lives $2\frac{3}{4}$ miles from Barbara and $4\frac{3}{10}$ miles from Ling. How much closer does Kirsten live to Barbara than to Ling?

A $1\frac{9}{20}$ miles

B $1\frac{1}{2}$ miles

C $1\frac{11}{20}$ miles

D $1\frac{3}{5}$ miles

5 What is $4\frac{1}{5} \times 2\frac{2}{3}$?

A $8\frac{2}{15}$

B $8\frac{13}{15}$

C $10\frac{2}{3}$

D $11\frac{1}{5}$

6 The SpaceFright rollercoaster can seat 72 people at one time. It runs 266 times each week. If every seat is taken in a week, how many people can ride the SpaceFright?

A 2,394

B 18,152

C 18,752

D 19,152

STOP. DO NOT GO ON UNTIL TOLD TO DO SO.

PART 2

DIRECTIONS

You will now begin Part 2 of this test. You may use a calculator on this part of the test, and you may use open space in this practice test for scratch paper.

If you finish early, you may check your work for Part 2 **ONLY**.

Do **NOT** look at items in other parts of this test.

You will be timed to finish Part 2 of this test.

POSTTEST

WAIT. DO NOT GO ON UNTIL TOLD TO DO SO.

POSTTEST

7 What is the rule of this function table?

x	y
12	2
30	5
42	7
72	12

A $y = x - 10$

B $y = 6x$

C $y = x \div 6$

D $y = x - 60$

8 Which number makes this sentence true?

27.5 g = ______ mg

A 2,750

B 27,500

C 275,000

D 2,750,000

9 Some of the fastest men in the world can run a mile in 4 minutes. How many miles per hour are they averaging for a 4-minute run?

A 4 miles per hour

B 12 miles per hour

C 15 miles per hour

D 20 miles per hour

10 Tina bought a magazine for $3.95 and a book for $18.65. She paid 5% tax on both items. How much money did Tina spend, including the tax?

A $23.73

B $25.99

C $27.60

D $33.90

11 The equation $7h = \$24.50$ represents the time and the cost that Brett rented a bicycle. The variable h represents the hours. How many hours did Brett rent a bicycle?

A 3

B 3.25

C 3.5

D 3.75

12 Which ratio is equal to 9 to 24?

A 6 to 16

B 12 to 27

C 15 to 48

D 18 to 42

GO ON TO THE NEXT PAGE

13 Which point is located at $(-3, -4)$?

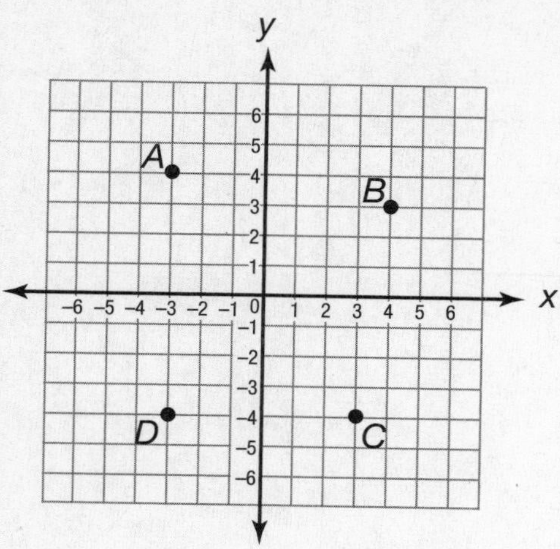

A *A*

B *B*

C *C*

D *D*

14 Rachel brought two CDs for a car trip. The first CD plays music for 52.93 minutes. The second CD plays music for 73.6 minutes. How many minutes of music does Rachel have on the two CDs together?

A 125.99

B 126.53

C 135.99

D 136.53

15 Of the 280 students at Jefferson Middle School, 65% are bused. How many students are bused?

A 182

B 195

C 204

D 210

16 Which is an expression?

A $x = 3$

B $2 + 2x = 4$

C $2(3 \times 5x) = 30x$

D $\frac{9x + 7}{5}$

17 Which fraction and decimal are equivalent?

A 0.525 and $\frac{11}{20}$

B 0.6875 and $\frac{11}{16}$

C 0.72 and $\frac{37}{50}$

D 0.84 and $\frac{17}{20}$

GO ON TO THE NEXT PAGE

18 Which *best* describes this transformation?

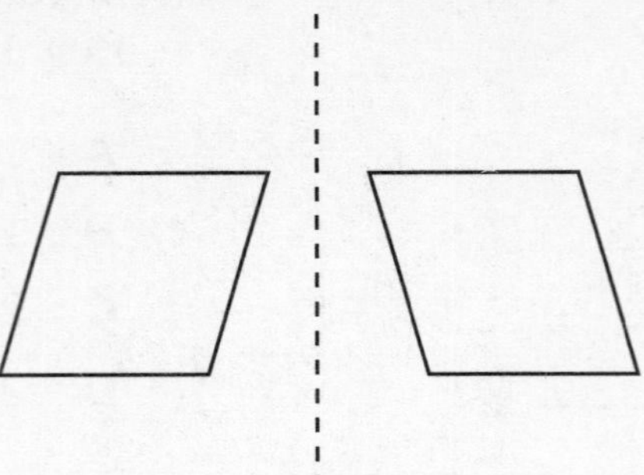

A reflection

B rotation of 90°

C rotation of 180°

D translation

19 Which figure is congruent to this figure?

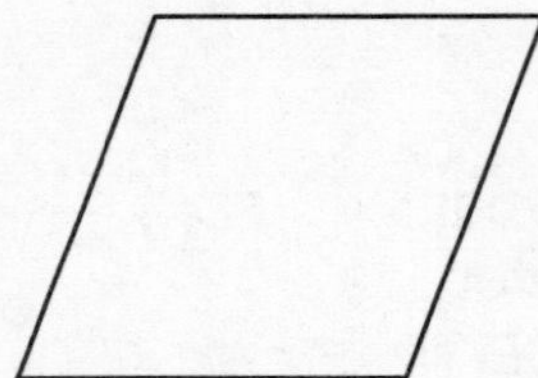

A

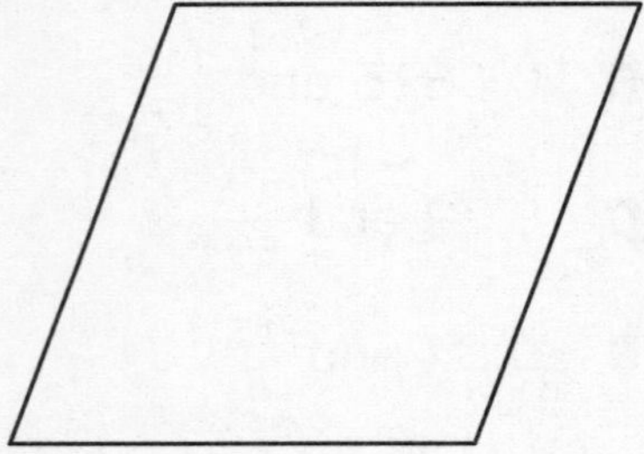

B

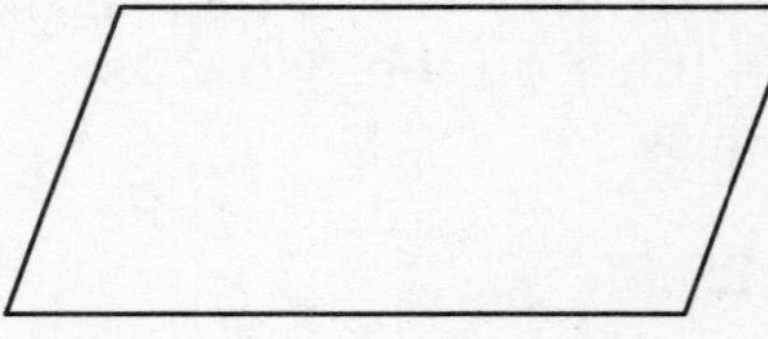

C

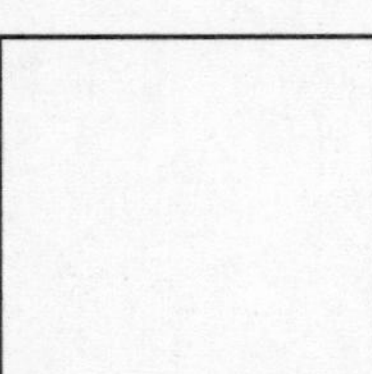

D

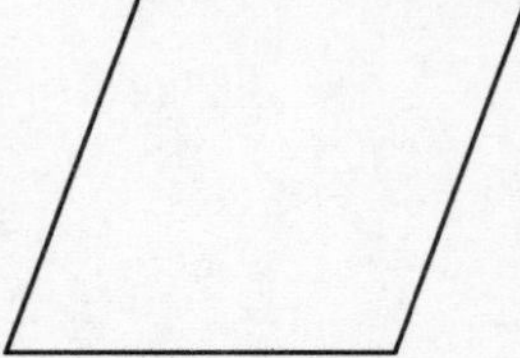

GO ON TO THE NEXT PAGE

20 Which sentence is true?

A $|-4| > 4$

B $|3| < -3$

C $|5| = |-5|$

D $|-3| > 3$

21 Mrs. Higgins runs an office of 38 staff people, who are all paid the same weekly amount. She pays out $26,795 each week to the staff. Which is the *best* estimate for the amount of money that each employee earns each week?

A $ 700

B $ 800

C $ 900

D $1,000

22 Which expression shows four more than five times a number?

A $4m + 5$

B $4m - 5$

C $5m + 4$

D $5m - 4$

23 Which proves that -3.2 is a rational number?

A $-3 + -0.2$

B $|-3.2|$

C -3.20

D $-\frac{16}{5}$

24 Which has the same solution as $6x - 4 = 14$?

A $3x - 4 = 7$

B $12x - 8 = 28$

C $2x - 1 = 11$

D $9x - 4 = 21$

25 Darla is going to spin these two spinners.

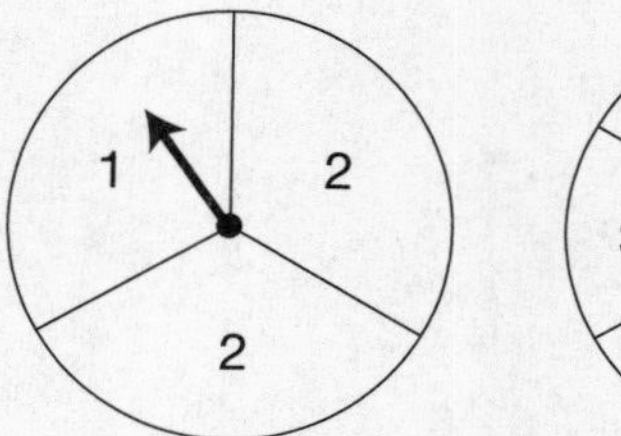

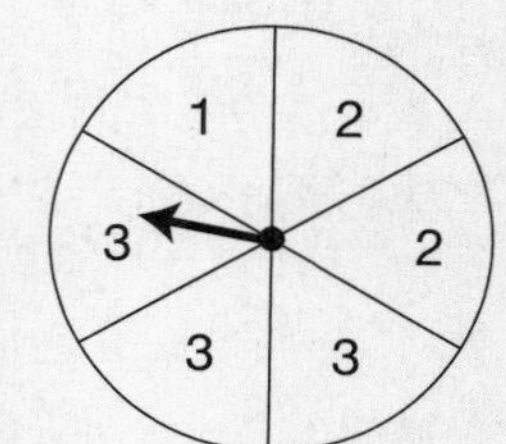

What is the probability that Darla will spin a number greater than 1 on both spinners?

A $\frac{1}{2}$

B $\frac{5}{9}$

C $\frac{2}{3}$

D $\frac{5}{6}$

STOP. DO NOT GO ON UNTIL TOLD TO DO SO.

PART 3

DIRECTIONS

You will now begin Part 3 of this test. You may use a calculator on this part of the test, and you may use open space in this practice test for scratch paper.

If you finish early, you may check your work for Part 3 **ONLY**.

Do **NOT** look at items in other parts of this test.

You will be timed to finish Part 3 of this test.

WAIT. DO NOT GO ON UNTIL TOLD TO DO SO.

POSTTEST

26 Zweiben's All-You-Can-Eat Buffet charges $4.50 per pound. If the Bigger family purchases 4.5 pounds of food, how much will they be charged?

A $18.00

B $19.25

C $20.25

D $22.50

27 An acre is a measure of area that is equivalent to 43,560 ft^2. What is the measure of an acre in square yards?

A 4,840 yd^2

B 14,520 yd^2

C 130,680 yd^2

D 392,040 yd^2

28 If $-\frac{3}{8}$ is placed on this number line, between which two letters will it be placed?

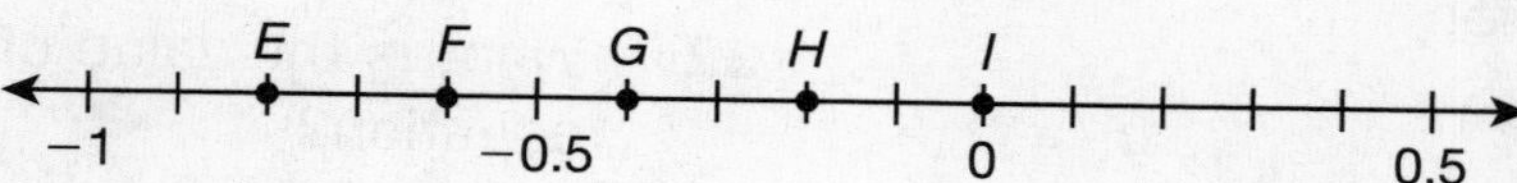

A *E* and *F*

B *F* and *G*

C *G* and *H*

D *H* and *I*

GO ON TO THE NEXT PAGE

29 The bill at lunch was $37.40. If Lisa leaves an 18% tip, how much money does she give the waitress for a tip?

A $ 2.99
B $ 6.73
C $40.39
D $44.13

30 Dallas was planning on jogging 5.25 miles this morning. When Dallas had finished 0.75 of his run, he felt his hamstring tighten, causing him to stop. How far did Dallas run before he stopped?

A 3.8275 miles
B 3.8375 miles
C 3.8475 miles
D 3.9375 miles

31 The graph shows the distance and the time that a car traveled. How many miles per hour did the car travel?

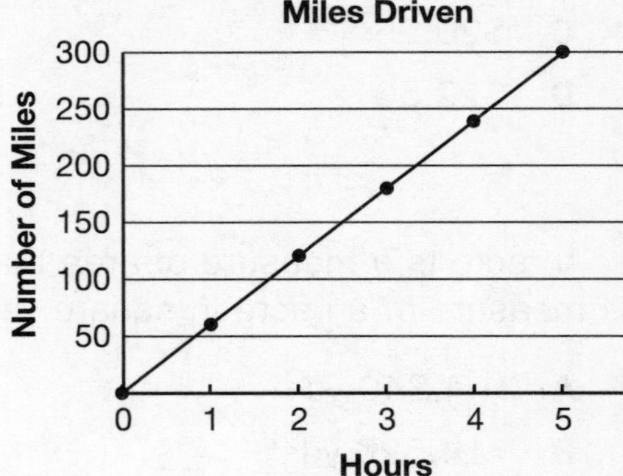

A 50
B 55
C 60
D 65

32 What is the value of n in this equation?

$$25n = 800$$

A $n = 2$
B $n = 4$
C $n = 16$
D $n = 32$

33 What is 28% of 375?

A 90
B 105
C 115
D 125

GO ON TO THE NEXT PAGE

34 The Backwards Society is sponsoring a $\frac{3}{4}$-mile backward run. There will be water stops each $\frac{1}{8}$ mile. If W represents the number of water stops, which can be used to represent the situation?

A $W = \frac{3}{4} \div \frac{1}{8}$

B $W = \frac{1}{8} \div \frac{3}{4}$

C $W = \frac{3}{4} \times \frac{1}{8}$

D $W = \frac{3}{4} + \frac{1}{8}$

35 When Curtis lifts weights, he does reps with 125 pounds. How many reps must he do to lift a total of 1 ton?

A 4

B 8

C 12

D 16

36 Which two numbers have a sum of 0?

A $-\frac{3}{5} + \frac{3}{5}$

B $-\frac{2}{3} + -\frac{2}{3}$

C $-1\frac{1}{4} + \frac{4}{5}$

D $-2 + -2$

37 What is the location of point J?

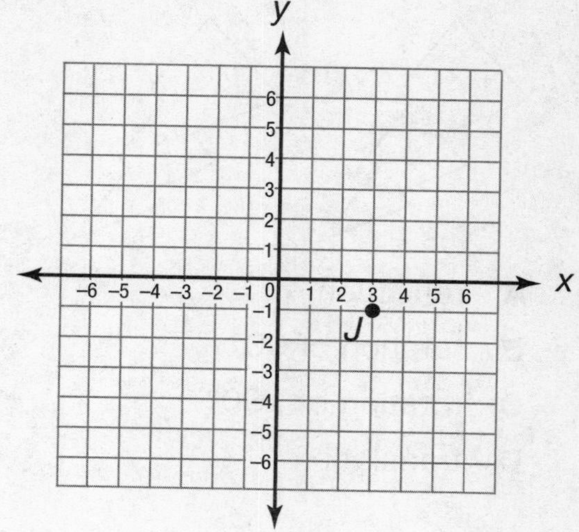

A (3, −1)

B (3, 1)

C (−1, 3)

D (−1, 3)

38 There are 2,736 members of an organization that has 38 branches. Each branch of the organization has the same number of people in it. How many people are in each branch?

A 62

B 67

C 72

D 76

GO ON TO THE NEXT PAGE

POSTTEST

POSTTEST

39 How was figure *A* transformed into figure *B*?

A reflection

B rotation of 90°

C rotation of 180°

D translation

40 Nora is going to spin this spinner. Which event is impossible?

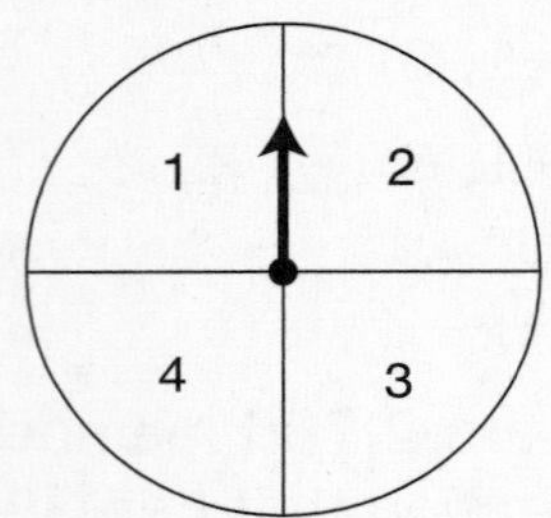

A spinning a number greater than 3

B spinning a number less than 1

C spinning an odd number

D spinning a composite number

41 Which number completes this proportion?

$$\frac{10}{15} = \frac{18}{\square}$$

A 23

B 25

C 27

D 30

42 The tallest student in Ms. Fox's class is 178 centimeters tall. How many millimeters tall is that student?

A 17.8

B 1,780

C 17,800

D 178,000

43 Mickey is playing a board game. He is going to toss the two number cubes, each with faces numbered 1–6. If he tosses a 9 or greater he will win the game. What is the probability that Mickey will win?

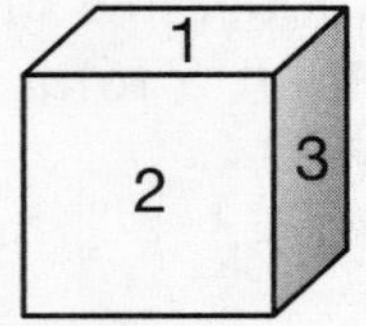

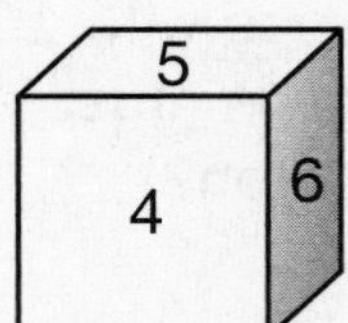

A $\frac{5}{18}$

B $\frac{1}{3}$

C $\frac{3}{7}$

D $\frac{4}{9}$

STOP. DO NOT GO ON UNTIL TOLD TO DO SO.

PART 4

DIRECTIONS

You will now begin Part 4 of this test. You may use a calculator on this part of the test, and you may use open space in this practice test for scratch paper.

If you finish early, you may check your work for Part 4 **ONLY**.

Do **NOT** look at items in other parts of this test.

You will be timed to finish Part 4 of this test.

WAIT. DO NOT GO ON UNTIL TOLD TO DO SO.

44 In the 2004 Presidential Election, John F. Kerry received 1,445,014 votes, and George W. Bush received 1,346,695 votes in Michigan. Which is the *best* estimate of how many more votes Kerry received than Bush in Michigan?

A 90,000

B 98,000

C 99,000

D 100,000

45 Carl can type 62 words per minute. If he types at that rate for $4\frac{1}{2}$ minutes, how many words will he type?

A 248

B 264

C 279

D 295

46 A computer is on sale at 20% off. It originally cost $750. What is the sale price of the computer?

A $600

B $625

C $730

D $900

47 Charlene is 18 years older than her brother Brent. The equation $c - 18 = 34$ represents the situation. If c represents Charlene, how many years old is she?

A 16 years old

B 26 years old

C 42 years old

D 52 years old

48 Frankie weighs p pounds. He weighs 12 more pounds than Nikki. Which of the following expresses Nikki's weight?

A $12 + p$

B $p - 12$

C $p \div 12$

D $12 - p$

49 Which has the same solution as $\frac{3}{4} \div \frac{2}{5}$?

A $\frac{3}{4} \times 2\frac{1}{2}$

B $1\frac{1}{4} \times \frac{2}{5}$

C $1\frac{1}{4} \times 2\frac{1}{2}$

D $\frac{2}{5} \div \frac{3}{4}$

GO ON TO THE NEXT PAGE

50 A survey was taken of 350 likely voters. Of those surveyed, 38% were unsure of where they stand on the issue of renaming the town. How many people of those surveyed were unsure of where they stand on the issue?

A 114 **B** 126

C 133 **D** 152

51 Last weekend, Michele spent $3\frac{3}{4}$ hours writing a book report and $2\frac{3}{4}$ hours doing her math homework. How many hours did she spend either writing a book report or doing her math homework?

A $5\frac{1}{4}$ hours **B** $5\frac{1}{2}$ hours

C $6\frac{1}{4}$ hours **D** $6\frac{1}{2}$ hours

52 Which *best* explains how figure *C* was transformed into figure *D*?

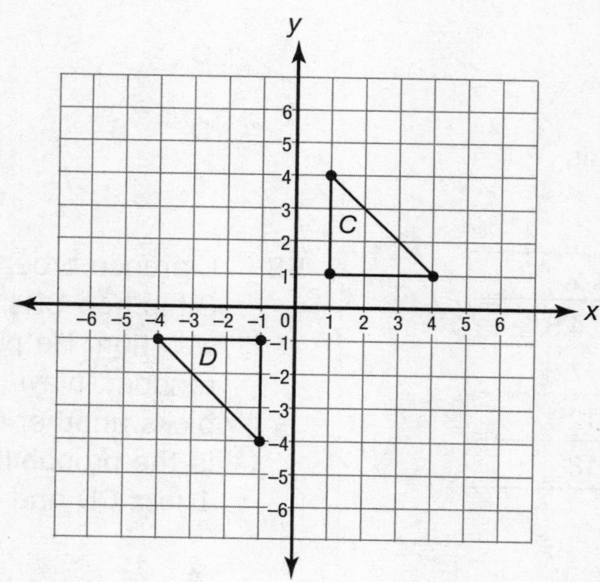

A rotation of 90° about the origin and a translation

B reflection across the *y*-axis and a translation

C rotation of 90° about the origin and a reflection across the *x*-axis

D rotation of 90° about the origin and a reflection across the *y*-axis

GO ON TO THE NEXT PAGE

POSTTEST

53 Ollie earned $613.20 last week. If he earns $16.80 per hour, how many hours did he work last week?

A 31.1 hours

B 31.6 hours

C 36.5 hours

D 37.1 hours

54 Which is 0.32 written as a fraction in simplest form?

A $\frac{8}{25}$

B $\frac{13}{40}$

C $\frac{7}{20}$

D $\frac{3}{8}$

55 What is the rule of this function table?

x	y
3	4.5
5	7.5
8	12
12	18

A $y = x + 1.5$

B $y = 1.5x$

C $y = 2x - 6$

D $y = x + 6$

56 Dr. Snyder makes house calls. She charges $125 per hour plus a $75 fee for making the house call. Which equation represents the amount of money that Dr. Snyder makes for a house call?

A $C = 125h - 75$

B $C = 75h + 125$

C $C = 200$

D $C = 125h + 75$

57 Which number is an integer but is neither positive nor negative?

A $-2\frac{1}{4}$

B -1

C 0

D 3

58 Clarence brought 5 jazz CDs and 3 hip hop CDs with him on vacation. He picks one CD at random, plays it, returns it, and picks another CD at random. What is the probability that he will play 1 jazz CD and 1 hip hop CD?

A $\frac{15}{64}$

B $\frac{25}{64}$

C $\frac{1}{2}$

D $\frac{5}{8}$

GO ON TO THE NEXT PAGE

59 A wading pool has an area of 120 square meters. What is the area in square centimeters?

A 1,200 cm^2

B 12,000 cm^2

C 120,000 cm^2

D 1,200,000 cm^2

60 In July a theater that can seat 2,792 people had a performance each night and was sold out each time. Which is the *best* estimate of the number of people who attended a performance in July?

A 60,000

B 70,000

C 80,000

D 90,000

61 Which explains how the letter p can be transformed into the letter d?

A rotation of 90°

B rotation of 180°

C translation

D reflection

62 What is the location of point K?

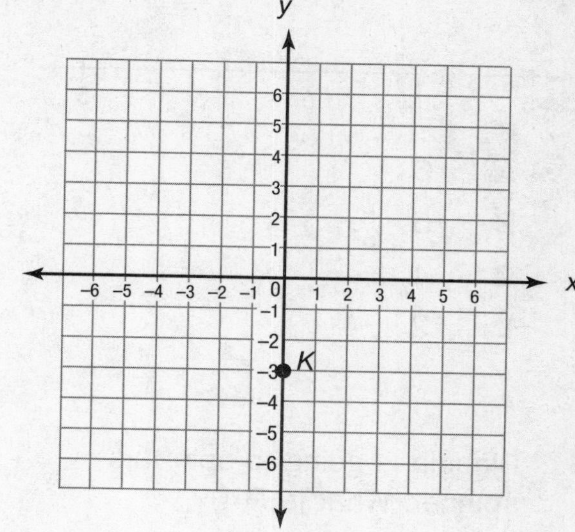

A (0, −3)

B (0, 3)

C (3, 0)

D (−3, 0)

63 Terrance is a large tipper. He gives a tip of 22% if he believes he received superior service and 18% for average service. At Moe's, his bill came to \$17.50 and he received superior service. How much of a tip did Terrance leave?

A \$3.15

B \$3.50

C \$3.85

D \$4.20

GO ON TO THE NEXT PAGE

POSTTEST

64 What is the location of point L on the number line?

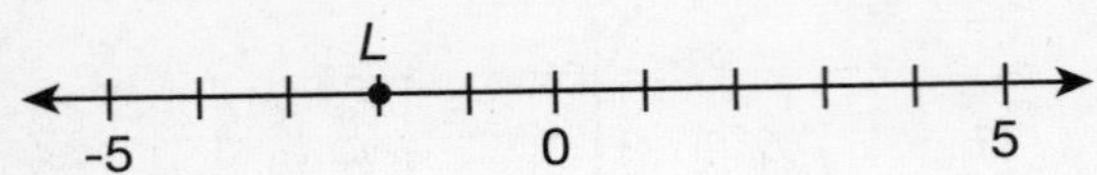

A -6

B -5

C -4

D -2

65 Claudia is going to spin this spinner. What is $P(4)$?

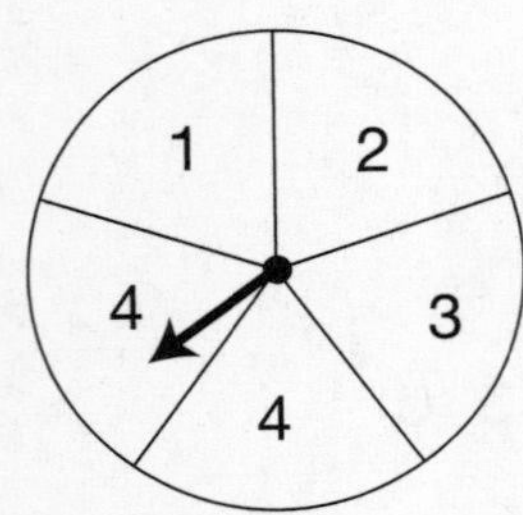

A 20%

B 30%

C 40%

D 50%

66 Which list orders the numbers from *greatest* to *least*?

A $\frac{4}{5}$, 0.85, -0.9, $-\frac{7}{8}$

B 0.85, $\frac{4}{5}$, $-\frac{7}{8}$, -0.9

C 0.85, $\frac{4}{5}$, -0.9, $-\frac{7}{8}$

D -0.9, $-\frac{7}{8}$, 0.85, $\frac{4}{5}$

67 What is the value of g in this equation?

$$9g = 126$$

A $g = 12$

B $g = 14$

C $g = 16$

D $g = 18$

68 Marvin has 18 daily customers and 12 Sunday-only customers on his paper route. George has the same ratio of daily to Sunday-only customers. If George has 45 daily customers, how many Sunday-only customers does he have?

A 24

B 27

C 30

D 36

69 Which makes this sentence true?

81 in. = ______

A 6 ft 9 in.

B 8 ft 1 in.

C 9 ft

D 10 ft 1 in.

GO ON TO THE NEXT PAGE

POSTTEST

70 Which pair of figures is congruent?

A

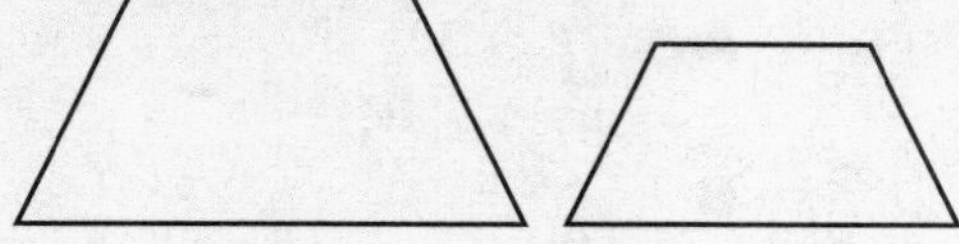

B

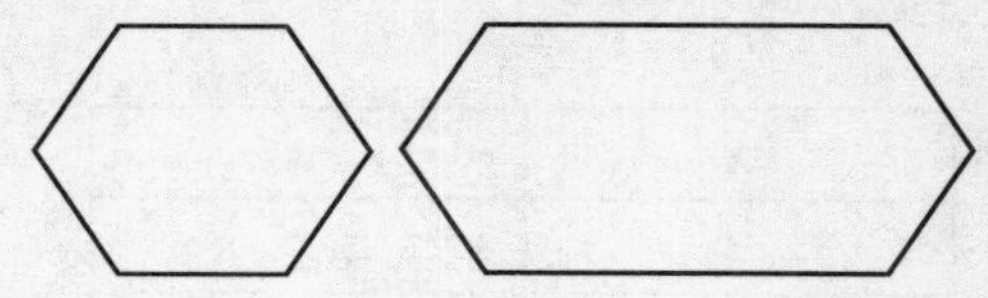

C

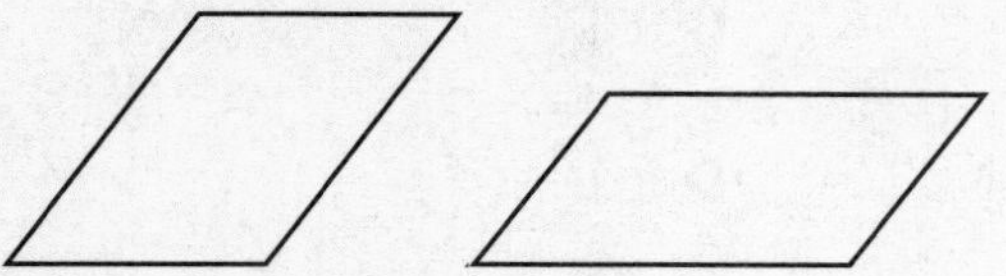

D

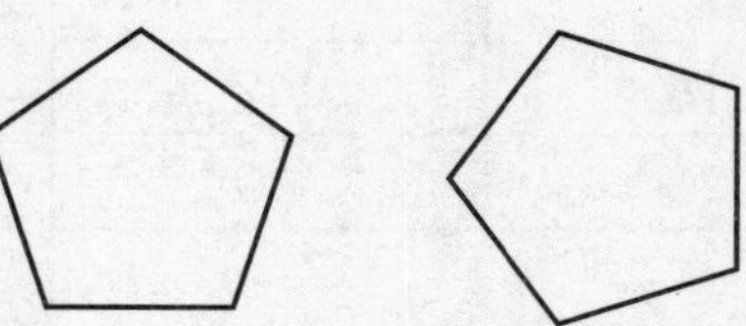

71 Which equation has the same solution as $2x + 5 = 9$?

A $5x + 5 = 12$

B $2x + 8 = 12$

C $2x - 2 = 12$

D $x + 4 = 8$

72 Real Flakes costs $3.52 for a 1-pound box. The 40-ounce box costs the same unit rate as the 1-pound box. How much money does the 40-ounce box cost?

A $ 8.80

B $10.56

C $14.08

D $140.80

73 Emily lives $1\frac{3}{5}$ miles from school and $3\frac{1}{2}$ miles from Uncle Quentin's home. How much closer does Emily live to school than to Uncle Quentin's?

A $1\frac{1}{10}$ miles

B $1\frac{9}{10}$ miles

C $2\frac{1}{10}$ miles

D $2\frac{9}{10}$ miles

GO ON TO THE NEXT PAGE

74 What is the missing number in this function table?

x	*y*
9	2
12	5
18	?
26	19

A 6

B 8

C 11

D 13

75 What is 64% of 350?

A 224

B 231

C 238

D 245

76 In 2000, the population of Detroit was 951,270. In 1950, the population of Detroit had 898,298 more people than in 2000. Which is the *best* estimate for the population of Detroit in 1950?

A 1,800,000

B 1,850,000

C 1,900,000

D 2,000,000

77 What is $\frac{7}{10} \div \frac{3}{8}$?

A $\frac{1}{4}$

B $\frac{21}{80}$

C $1\frac{3}{4}$

D $1\frac{13}{15}$

78 Tim bought a book for $18.75 and a CD for $14.89. He paid with a $50 bill. How much change did Tim receive?

A $16.36

B $16.46

C $17.36

D $83.64

79 Leida is going to spin this spinner and toss a number cube with faces labeled 1–6.

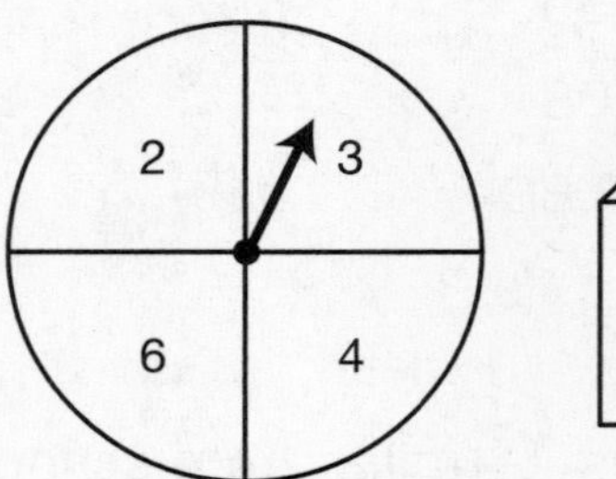

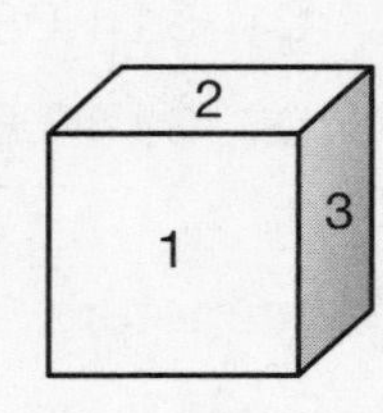

What is the probability that she will spin a product of 12?

A $\frac{1}{24}$

B $\frac{1}{12}$

C $\frac{1}{6}$

D $\frac{1}{4}$

STOP.

Glossary

absolute value The distance from 0 on a number line. **(Lesson 12)**

acute angle An angle that has a measure less than 90°. **(Lesson 26)**

acute triangle A triangle with 3 acute angles. **(Lesson 27)**

addend A number to be added. **(Lesson 1)**

adjacent angles Angles that have the same vertex and a common side. **(Lesson 26)**

alternate interior angle Two nonadjacent angles formed by a transversal that are on opposite sides of the transversal and between the two lines crossed by the transversal. **(Lesson 26)**

angle A figure formed by two rays with the same endpoint. **(Lesson 26)**

area The number of square units needed to cover a region or figure. **(Lesson 23)**

at random To choose in such a way that each member of a set has an equal chance of being chosen. **(Lesson 30)**

centimeter (cm) A metric unit of length; 100 centimeters = 1 meter. **(Lesson 23)**

certain An event that must happen. **(Lesson 30)**

coefficient The factor in a term that is a number. **(Lesson 21)**

Example: In $3x$, 3 is the coefficient.

compatible numbers Number that are easy to compute with mentally. **(Lesson 8)**

complementary angles Two angles whose measures have a sum of 90°. **(Lesson 26)**

compound event More than one event in a probability experiment. **(Lesson 31)**

congruent Having the same size and shape as another figure. **(Lesson 25)**

convex polygon A polygon where the segment connecting any two points in the interior of the polygon is in the interior of the polygon. **(Lesson 27)**

corresponding angles Two angles formed by a transversal crossing two lines that are in corresponding positions. **(Lesson 26)**

cross products A cross product of two fractions is the product of the numerator of one fraction with the denominator of the other fraction. **(Lesson 22)**

cube A solid figure with 6 square faces. **(Lesson 24)**

cubic unit The volume of a cube, one of whose sides is 1 unit of length. **(Lesson 24)**

cup (c) A customary unit of capacity; 1 cup = 8 fluid ounces **(Lesson 23)**

degree (°) A unit used to measure angles. **(Lesson 26)**

difference The answer to a subtraction problem. **(Lesson 1)**

distributive property of multiplication To multiply a sum by a number, you can multiply each addend by the number and add the products. **(Lesson 2)**

dividend A number to be divided. **(Lesson 3)**

divisor The number by which the dividend is divided. **(Lesson 3)**

edge The line segment formed where two faces of a solid figure meet. **(Lesson 25)**

equally likely An event that is as likely to happen as to not happen. **(Lesson 30)**

equation A number sentence that shows that two quantities are equal. **(Lesson 17, 20)**

equilateral triangle A triangle with 3 sides the same length. **(Lesson 27)**

equivalent ratios Ratios that are represented by equivalent fractions. **(Lesson 22)**

estimate To find an answer that is close to the exact answer. **(Lesson 8)**

experimental probability Measures the probability of what has already happened. **(Lesson 30)**

expression A group of numbers and symbols that shows a mathematical quantity. **(Lesson 17)**

exterior angle An angle formed between one side of a polygon and the extension of an adjacent side. **(Lesson 27)**

face A flat side of a solid figure. **(Lesson 24)**

factors Numbers that are multiplied to give a product. **(Lesson 2)**

favorable outcomes The desired outcomes of a probability experiment. **(Lesson 30)**

fluid ounce (fl oz) A customary unit of capacity; 8 fluid ounces = 1 cup **(Lesson 23)**

foot (ft) A customary unit of length; 1 foot = 12 inches **(Lesson 23)**

function A relationship in which one quantity depends on another quantity. **(Lesson 19)**

Fundamental Counting Principle The number of outcomes for a probability experiment with two or more stages is the product of the number of outcomes at each stage. **(Lesson 31)**

gallon (gal) A customary unit of capacity; 1 gallon = 4 quarts **(Lesson 23)**

gram (g) A metric unit of mass; 1 gram = 1,000 milligrams **(Lesson 23)**

image The figure formed by a transformation. **(Lesson 29)**

impossible An event that cannot happen. **(Lesson 30)**

improper fraction A fraction that has a numerator that is greater than or equal to the denominator. **(Lesson 6)**

inch A customary unit of length; 12 inches = 1 foot **(Lesson 23)**

integer Any of the positive and negative whole numbers and 0. **(Lesson 14)**

intersecting lines Lines that meet or cross each other. **(Lesson 26)**

inverse operations Operations that are opposites, such as addition and subtraction, and multiplication and division. **(Lesson 20)**

isosceles triangle A triangle with at least two equal sides. **(Lesson 27)**

kilogram (kg) A metric unit of mass; 1 kilogram = 1,000 grams **(Lesson 23)**

kilometer (km) A metric unit of length; 1 kilometer = 1,000 meters **(Lesson 23)**

least common denominator (LCD) The least common multiple of 2 or more denominators. **(Lesson 4)**

least common multiple (LCM) The least whole number greater than 0 that is a multiple of each of two or more numbers. **(Lesson 4)**

like terms Terms that contain the same variables, with corresponding variables raised to the same power. **(Lesson 17)**

line A straight path that goes in two directions without end. **(Lesson 26)**

line segment A part of a line with two endpoints. **(Lesson 26)**

liter (L) A metric unit of capacity; 1 liter = 1,000 milliliters **(Lesson 23)**

meter (m) A metric unit of length; 1 meter = 100 centimeters **(Lesson 23)**

metric ton (t) A unit of mass equal to 1,000 kilograms. **(Lesson 23)**

mile (mi) A customary unit of length; 1 mile = 5,280 feet **(Lesson 23)**

milligram (mg) A metric unit of mass; 1,000 milligrams = 1 gram **(Lesson 23)**

milliliter (mL) A metric unit of metric capacity; 1,000 milliliters = 1 liter **(Lesson 23)**

millimeter (mm) A metric unit of length; 10 millimeters = 1 centimeter **(Lesson 23)**

minuend The number from which the subtrahend is subtracted. **(Lesson 1)**

mixed number A number that has a whole-number part and a fraction part. **(Lesson 4)**

net A two-dimensional pattern that can be folded to form a solid figure. **(Lesson 25)**

obtuse angle An angle with a measure greater than 90° and less than 180°. **(Lesson 26)**

obtuse triangle A triangle with one obtuse angle. **(Lesson 26)**

order of operations The agreed-upon sequence for conducting operations. **(Lesson 17)**

ordered pair A pair of numbers that gives the location of a point on a graph. **(Lesson 18)**

origin The point of a coordinate grid where the *x*-axis and *y*-axis meet, known as (0, 0). **(Lesson 18)**

ounce (oz) A customary unit of weight; 16 ounces = 1 pound **(Lesson 23)**

parallel lines Lines or line segments that stay the same distance apart from each other without ever crossing. **(Lesson 26)**

percent Per hundred. **(Lesson 11)**

perpendicular lines Lines or line segments that intersect at a right angle. **(Lesson 26)**

pint (pt) A customary unit of capacity; 1 pint = 2 cups (Lesson 23)

polygon A closed 2-dimensional figure with straight sides. (Lesson 27)

possible outcomes Any of the results that could happen in an experiment. (Lesson 30)

pound (lb) A customary unit of weight; 1 pound = 16 ounces (Lesson 23)

pre-image A figure before it is transformed. (Lesson 29)

probability The chance that an event will occur. (Lesson 30)

product The answer in a multiplication problem. (Lesson 2)

proportion An equation stating that two ratios are equivalent. (Lesson 22)

quart (qt) A customary unit of capacity; 1 quart = 2 pints (Lesson 23)

quotient The answer in a division problem. (Lesson 3)

rate A ratio that compares measurements or amounts. (Lesson 22)

ratio A comparison of two quantities. (Lesson 22)

rational number A number that can be written as a fraction with an integer in the numerator and a positive integer in the denominator. (Lesson 12)

ray A part of a line with one endpoint and which goes forever in one direction. (Lesson 26)

reciprocal The reciprocal of a number is a number such that the product of the number and its reciprocal is 1. (Lesson 7)

rectangular prism A solid figure with 6 faces, 12 edges, and 8 vertices. (Lesson 24)

reflection A transformation of a figure across a line producing a mirror image. (Lesson 29)

regroup A way to rename a number. (Lesson 1)

remainder A number less than the divisor that remains after the division is completed. (Lesson 3)

remote interior angle An interior angle of a triangle that is not adjacent to a given exterior angle. (Lesson 27)

right angle An angle that measures 90°. (Lesson 26)

right triangle A triangle with one right angle. (Lesson 27)

rotation A transformation that turns a figure around a point. (Lesson 29)

round To find the value of a number based on a given place value. (Lesson 8)

scalene triangle A triangle that does not have any equal sides or angles. (Lesson 27)

side One of the line segments in a polygon. (Lesson 24, 27)

solid figure Any figure that has depth. (Lesson 24)

square unit The area of a square, any one of whose sides is the given unit of length. (Lesson 23)

straight angle An angle with a measure of 180°. (Lesson 26)

subtrahend The number that is subtracted from the minuend. (Lesson 1)

sum The answer to an addition problem. (Lesson 1)

supplementary angles Two angles whose measures total 180°. (Lesson 26)

surface area The total area of all the faces of a solid figure. (Lesson 24)

theoretical probability The probability of an event occurring determined by mathematical reasoning. (Lesson 30)

ton (T) A customary unit of weight; 1 ton = 2,000 pounds (Lesson 23)

transformation The movement of a figure. (Lesson 29)

translation A transformation that moves a figure along a line. (Lesson 29)

transversal A line that intersects two other lines. (Lesson 26)

tree diagram A diagram with branches that represents the possible outcomes of a probability experiment. (Lesson 31)

trial One of the times that a probability experiment is performed. (Lesson 30)

triangle A polygon with 3 sides and 3 angles. (Lesson 27)

unit fraction A fraction with a numerator of 1. (Lesson 7)

unit price The cost of a single item or cost per unit of measurement. (Lesson 22)

unit rate A rate in which the second measurement or amount is 1 unit. (Lesson 22)

variable A symbol used to represent a number of group of numbers. (Lesson 17)

vertex The point where the rays meet in an angle or two line segments meet in a polygon. (Lesson 26)

vertical angles Two nonadjacent angles formed by intersecting lines. (Lesson 26)

volume The amount of space that a solid figure encloses. (Lesson 24)

***x*-axis** The horizontal axis of a graph. (Lesson 18)

yard (yd) A customary unit of length; 1 yard = 3 feet (Lesson 23)

***y*-axis** The vertical axis of a graph. (Lesson 18)

MEAP
Grade 6
Mathematics Tool

Protractor

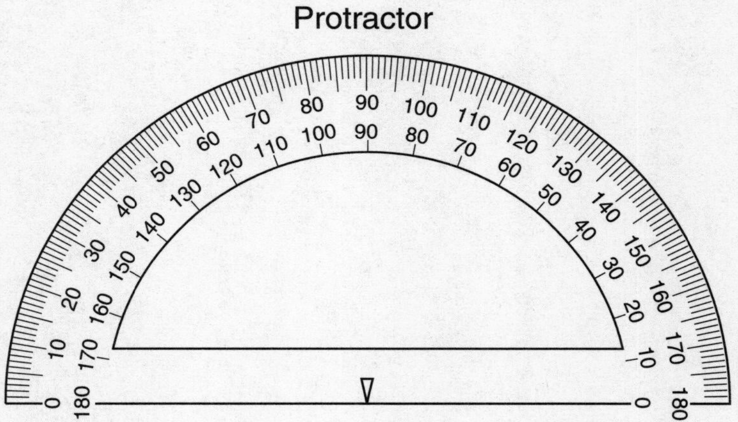

Pretest Answer Sheet

Fill in the circle for the correct answer choice.

Part 1

1. Ⓐ Ⓑ Ⓒ Ⓓ
2. Ⓐ Ⓑ Ⓒ Ⓓ
3. Ⓐ Ⓑ Ⓒ Ⓓ
4. Ⓐ Ⓑ Ⓒ Ⓓ
5. Ⓐ Ⓑ Ⓒ Ⓓ
6. Ⓐ Ⓑ Ⓒ Ⓓ

Part 2

7. Ⓐ Ⓑ Ⓒ Ⓓ
8. Ⓐ Ⓑ Ⓒ Ⓓ
9. Ⓐ Ⓑ Ⓒ Ⓓ
10. Ⓐ Ⓑ Ⓒ Ⓓ
11. Ⓐ Ⓑ Ⓒ Ⓓ
12. Ⓐ Ⓑ Ⓒ Ⓓ
13. Ⓐ Ⓑ Ⓒ Ⓓ
14. Ⓐ Ⓑ Ⓒ Ⓓ
15. Ⓐ Ⓑ Ⓒ Ⓓ
16. Ⓐ Ⓑ Ⓒ Ⓓ
17. Ⓐ Ⓑ Ⓒ Ⓓ
18. Ⓐ Ⓑ Ⓒ Ⓓ
19. Ⓐ Ⓑ Ⓒ Ⓓ
20. Ⓐ Ⓑ Ⓒ Ⓓ
21. Ⓐ Ⓑ Ⓒ Ⓓ
22. Ⓐ Ⓑ Ⓒ Ⓓ
23. Ⓐ Ⓑ Ⓒ Ⓓ
24. Ⓐ Ⓑ Ⓒ Ⓓ
25. Ⓐ Ⓑ Ⓒ Ⓓ

Part 3

26. Ⓐ Ⓑ Ⓒ Ⓓ
27. Ⓐ Ⓑ Ⓒ Ⓓ
28. Ⓐ Ⓑ Ⓒ Ⓓ
29. Ⓐ Ⓑ Ⓒ Ⓓ
30. Ⓐ Ⓑ Ⓒ Ⓓ
31. Ⓐ Ⓑ Ⓒ Ⓓ
32. Ⓐ Ⓑ Ⓒ Ⓓ
33. Ⓐ Ⓑ Ⓒ Ⓓ
34. Ⓐ Ⓑ Ⓒ Ⓓ
35. Ⓐ Ⓑ Ⓒ Ⓓ
36. Ⓐ Ⓑ Ⓒ Ⓓ
37. Ⓐ Ⓑ Ⓒ Ⓓ
38. Ⓐ Ⓑ Ⓒ Ⓓ
39. Ⓐ Ⓑ Ⓒ Ⓓ
40. Ⓐ Ⓑ Ⓒ Ⓓ
41. Ⓐ Ⓑ Ⓒ Ⓓ
42. Ⓐ Ⓑ Ⓒ Ⓓ
43. Ⓐ Ⓑ Ⓒ Ⓓ

Part 4

44. Ⓐ Ⓑ Ⓒ Ⓓ
45. Ⓐ Ⓑ Ⓒ Ⓓ
46. Ⓐ Ⓑ Ⓒ Ⓓ
47. Ⓐ Ⓑ Ⓒ Ⓓ
48. Ⓐ Ⓑ Ⓒ Ⓓ
49. Ⓐ Ⓑ Ⓒ Ⓓ
50. Ⓐ Ⓑ Ⓒ Ⓓ
51. Ⓐ Ⓑ Ⓒ Ⓓ
52. Ⓐ Ⓑ Ⓒ Ⓓ
53. Ⓐ Ⓑ Ⓒ Ⓓ
54. Ⓐ Ⓑ Ⓒ Ⓓ
55. Ⓐ Ⓑ Ⓒ Ⓓ
56. Ⓐ Ⓑ Ⓒ Ⓓ
57. Ⓐ Ⓑ Ⓒ Ⓓ
58. Ⓐ Ⓑ Ⓒ Ⓓ
59. Ⓐ Ⓑ Ⓒ Ⓓ
60. Ⓐ Ⓑ Ⓒ Ⓓ
61. Ⓐ Ⓑ Ⓒ Ⓓ
62. Ⓐ Ⓑ Ⓒ Ⓓ
63. Ⓐ Ⓑ Ⓒ Ⓓ
64. Ⓐ Ⓑ Ⓒ Ⓓ
65. Ⓐ Ⓑ Ⓒ Ⓓ
66. Ⓐ Ⓑ Ⓒ Ⓓ
67. Ⓐ Ⓑ Ⓒ Ⓓ
68. Ⓐ Ⓑ Ⓒ Ⓓ
69. Ⓐ Ⓑ Ⓒ Ⓓ
70. Ⓐ Ⓑ Ⓒ Ⓓ
71. Ⓐ Ⓑ Ⓒ Ⓓ
72. Ⓐ Ⓑ Ⓒ Ⓓ
73. Ⓐ Ⓑ Ⓒ Ⓓ
74. Ⓐ Ⓑ Ⓒ Ⓓ
75. Ⓐ Ⓑ Ⓒ Ⓓ
76. Ⓐ Ⓑ Ⓒ Ⓓ
77. Ⓐ Ⓑ Ⓒ Ⓓ
78. Ⓐ Ⓑ Ⓒ Ⓓ
79. Ⓐ Ⓑ Ⓒ Ⓓ

Posttest Answer Sheet

Fill in the circle for the correct answer choice.

Part 1

1. Ⓐ Ⓑ Ⓒ Ⓓ
2. Ⓐ Ⓑ Ⓒ Ⓓ
3. Ⓐ Ⓑ Ⓒ Ⓓ
4. Ⓐ Ⓑ Ⓒ Ⓓ
5. Ⓐ Ⓑ Ⓒ Ⓓ
6. Ⓐ Ⓑ Ⓒ Ⓓ

Part 2

7. Ⓐ Ⓑ Ⓒ Ⓓ
8. Ⓐ Ⓑ Ⓒ Ⓓ
9. Ⓐ Ⓑ Ⓒ Ⓓ
10. Ⓐ Ⓑ Ⓒ Ⓓ
11. Ⓐ Ⓑ Ⓒ Ⓓ
12. Ⓐ Ⓑ Ⓒ Ⓓ
13. Ⓐ Ⓑ Ⓒ Ⓓ
14. Ⓐ Ⓑ Ⓒ Ⓓ
15. Ⓐ Ⓑ Ⓒ Ⓓ
16. Ⓐ Ⓑ Ⓒ Ⓓ
17. Ⓐ Ⓑ Ⓒ Ⓓ
18. Ⓐ Ⓑ Ⓒ Ⓓ
19. Ⓐ Ⓑ Ⓒ Ⓓ
20. Ⓐ Ⓑ Ⓒ Ⓓ
21. Ⓐ Ⓑ Ⓒ Ⓓ
22. Ⓐ Ⓑ Ⓒ Ⓓ
23. Ⓐ Ⓑ Ⓒ Ⓓ
24. Ⓐ Ⓑ Ⓒ Ⓓ
25. Ⓐ Ⓑ Ⓒ Ⓓ

Part 3

26. Ⓐ Ⓑ Ⓒ Ⓓ
27. Ⓐ Ⓑ Ⓒ Ⓓ
28. Ⓐ Ⓑ Ⓒ Ⓓ
29. Ⓐ Ⓑ Ⓒ Ⓓ
30. Ⓐ Ⓑ Ⓒ Ⓓ
31. Ⓐ Ⓑ Ⓒ Ⓓ
32. Ⓐ Ⓑ Ⓒ Ⓓ
33. Ⓐ Ⓑ Ⓒ Ⓓ
34. Ⓐ Ⓑ Ⓒ Ⓓ
35. Ⓐ Ⓑ Ⓒ Ⓓ
36. Ⓐ Ⓑ Ⓒ Ⓓ
37. Ⓐ Ⓑ Ⓒ Ⓓ
38. Ⓐ Ⓑ Ⓒ Ⓓ
39. Ⓐ Ⓑ Ⓒ Ⓓ
40. Ⓐ Ⓑ Ⓒ Ⓓ
41. Ⓐ Ⓑ Ⓒ Ⓓ
42. Ⓐ Ⓑ Ⓒ Ⓓ
43. Ⓐ Ⓑ Ⓒ Ⓓ

Part 4

44. Ⓐ Ⓑ Ⓒ Ⓓ
45. Ⓐ Ⓑ Ⓒ Ⓓ
46. Ⓐ Ⓑ Ⓒ Ⓓ
47. Ⓐ Ⓑ Ⓒ Ⓓ
48. Ⓐ Ⓑ Ⓒ Ⓓ
49. Ⓐ Ⓑ Ⓒ Ⓓ
50. Ⓐ Ⓑ Ⓒ Ⓓ
51. Ⓐ Ⓑ Ⓒ Ⓓ
52. Ⓐ Ⓑ Ⓒ Ⓓ
53. Ⓐ Ⓑ Ⓒ Ⓓ
54. Ⓐ Ⓑ Ⓒ Ⓓ
55. Ⓐ Ⓑ Ⓒ Ⓓ
56. Ⓐ Ⓑ Ⓒ Ⓓ
57. Ⓐ Ⓑ Ⓒ Ⓓ
58. Ⓐ Ⓑ Ⓒ Ⓓ
59. Ⓐ Ⓑ Ⓒ Ⓓ
60. Ⓐ Ⓑ Ⓒ Ⓓ
61. Ⓐ Ⓑ Ⓒ Ⓓ
62. Ⓐ Ⓑ Ⓒ Ⓓ
63. Ⓐ Ⓑ Ⓒ Ⓓ
64. Ⓐ Ⓑ Ⓒ Ⓓ
65. Ⓐ Ⓑ Ⓒ Ⓓ
66. Ⓐ Ⓑ Ⓒ Ⓓ
67. Ⓐ Ⓑ Ⓒ Ⓓ
68. Ⓐ Ⓑ Ⓒ Ⓓ
69. Ⓐ Ⓑ Ⓒ Ⓓ
70. Ⓐ Ⓑ Ⓒ Ⓓ
71. Ⓐ Ⓑ Ⓒ Ⓓ
72. Ⓐ Ⓑ Ⓒ Ⓓ
73. Ⓐ Ⓑ Ⓒ Ⓓ
74. Ⓐ Ⓑ Ⓒ Ⓓ
75. Ⓐ Ⓑ Ⓒ Ⓓ
76. Ⓐ Ⓑ Ⓒ Ⓓ
77. Ⓐ Ⓑ Ⓒ Ⓓ
78. Ⓐ Ⓑ Ⓒ Ⓓ
79. Ⓐ Ⓑ Ⓒ Ⓓ